BTRIPP BOOKS

BOOK REVIEWS FROM

2015

BY
BRENDAN TRIPP

These reviews originally appeared on the
"BTRIPP'S BOOKS" book review blog:
http://btripp-books.livejournal.com/

Copyright © 2016 by Brendan Tripp

ISBN 978-1-57353-415-4

An Eschaton Book

Front cover photo courtesy Kenn W. Kiser via morguefile.com.
Back cover photo courtesy Sebastian Santana via morguefile.com.

PREFACE

From 1993 through 2004, I ran the *first* manifestation of Eschaton Books (now in its third revival). Initially started as a vehicle to publish my poetry, it soon became evident that the market for poetry is vanishingly small, and in 1994 we "pivoted" into being a metaphysical press.

During this time, I was largely a one-man shop, doing everything from editorial to shipping, which was a huge time commitment, and I typically worked 14 hour days, 7 days a week to keep things moving. I bring up all this here because, despite having been a life-long avid reader, during this period I had precious little time for reading, and what reading I *did* get done was largely reviewing book submissions. However, I never stopped *buying* books, which began to stack up in prodigious "to be read" piles.

When Eschaton went out of business (in a not unusual *denouement* for a small press – we had a distributor who ended up never paying us, while selling through all our stock) in 2004, I found myself with a lot of reading to catch up on, and a need to keep my writing chops sharp. So, I began to pen little reviews of what I was reading through, and post those on the web.

As the years went by, this became "a thing" that I was doing, and, for a while, I was targeting a fairly aggressive goal of getting at least 72 non-fiction books read per year. By 2015, this had resulted in my having read and reviewed 700 books over that 12-year span.

In recent years (since the upswing in print-on-demand publishing), I have had *numerous* acquaintances suggest that I put out my reviews as books. I was, at first, rather hesitant on the concept (as, after all, the material was free to read on the web), but I eventually figured that if various people thought it was a good idea, I might as well give it a shot.

While I could have started at the beginning, with the reviews from 2004, I decided that those were less representtative of the whole, so opted to begin with the most recent ones. While having fewer reviews than most years (I pulled back from the 72-book target the past three years), these at least are "fresher", with the commentary (and purchasing suggestions) more up-to-date.

A note on my review "style": I do not write classic reviews, but more a telling of my personal interaction with a particular book. This means that I talk about where and how I got the book, how it relates to other things I've read, what sort of reactions it triggered in me (and why), and how one can get a copy if it sounds appealing. Needless to say, if the reader is devoted to standard book reviewing styles, this might be an irritation ... however, it does make these reviews somewhat idiosyncratic to *me*, resulting in a collection that is something of a "my encounters with books" sort of deal, which will, hopefully, be appealing to many.

- Brendan Tripp

CONTENTS

v - Preface

vii - Contents

1 - Saturday, January 3, 2015
Wish I'd gotten more out of this ...
Do More, Spend Less: The New Secrets of Living the Good Life for Less
by Brad Wilson

4 - Sunday, January 4, 2015
Being Authentic ...
Will the Real You Please Stand Up: Show Up, Be Authentic, and Prosper in Social Media
by Kim Garst

8 - Saturday, January 17, 2015
Advertising philosophy, amusingly packaged ...
The Wizard of Ads: Turning Words into Magic and Dreamers into Millionaires
by Roy H. Williams

11 - Sunday, January 18, 2015
Much more under the hood ...
Secret Formulas of the Wizard of Ads: Turning Paupers into Princes and Lead into Gold
by Roy H. Williams

15 - Saturday, January 24, 2015
More Wizardry ...
Magical Worlds of the Wizard of Ads: Tools and Techniques for Profitable Persuasion
by Roy H. Williams

18 - Friday, January 30, 2015
Wish there was more ...
The Fran Lebowitz Reader
by Fran Lebowitz

22 - Saturday, January 31, 2015

A remarkable history of modern science ...
Conquering the Electron: The Geniuses, Visionaries, Egomaniacs, and Scoundrels Who Built Our Electronic Age
by Derek Cheung & Eric Brach

26 - Saturday, March 7, 2015

What you talking about?
Age of Conversation 3: It's Time to Get Busy!
by Drew McLellan & Gavin Heaton

31 - Sunday, March 8, 2015

Towards a "Protopia" ...
The Moral Arc: How Science and Reason Lead Humanity toward Truth, Justice, and Freedom
by Michael Shermer

37 - Sunday, March 22, 2015

An "exponential entrepreneur's" manual for "going big" ...
**Bold:
How to Go Big, Create Wealth and Impact the World**
by Peter Diamandis

41 - Friday, March 27, 2015

The only thing we have to sphere is sphere itself?
Manifesto for the Noosphere: The Next Stage in the Evolution of Human Consciousness
by José Argüelles

45 - Saturday, April 4, 2015

A look under the rocks ...
**Trust Me, I'm Lying:
Confessions of a Media Manipulator**
by Ryan Holiday

50 - Sunday, April 5, 2015

A brilliant look at a vile subject ...
**Mugged:
Racial Demagoguery from the Seventies to Obama**
by Ann Coulter

53 - Tuesday, April 21, 2015

Meet Harry Wormwood, SEO expert ...
**Win the Game of Googleopoly:
Unlocking the Secret Strategy of Search Engines**
by Sean V. Bradley

57 - Wednesday, April 22, 2015

Wagering with Pascal?
A God That Could Be Real:
Spirituality, Science, and the Future of Our Planet
by Nancy Ellen Abrams

61 - Monday, April 27, 2015

Not just one story ...
A Death on Diamond Mountain: A True Story of
Obsession, Madness, and the Path to Enlightenment
by Scott Carney

64 - Tuesday, April 28, 2015

That's the way you do it ...
Everybody Writes: Your Go-To Guide
to Creating Ridiculously Good Content
by Ann Handley

67 - Saturday, May 2, 2015

An unexpected seeker's memoir ...
Waking Up: A Guide to Spirituality Without Religion
by Sam Harris

72 - Sunday, May 10, 2015

Maybe with a different sub-title ...
The Art of Work: A Proven Path to Discovering
What You Were Meant to Do
by Jeff Goins

76 - Monday, May 11, 2015

How to become a "Thought Leader" ...
Stand Out: How to Find Your Breakthrough Idea and
Build a Following Around It
by Dorie Clark

80 - Saturday, May 23, 2015

Fascinating stuff ...
Mind Wars:
Brain Science and the Military in the 21st Century
by Jonathan D. Moreno

85 - Sunday, May 24, 2015

One a week?
Headstrong:
52 Women Who Changed Science – and the World
by Rachel Swaby

88 - Saturday, May 30, 2015

The sign points, the road falters ...
**The Divine Spark: A Graham Hancock Reader:
Psychedelics, Consciousness,
and the Birth of Civilization**
by Graham Hancock

91 - Sunday, May 31, 2015

Struggling with Science ...
**The Only Woman in the Room:
Why Science Is Still a Boys' Club**
by Eileen Pollack

94 - Sunday, June 7, 2015

Good News For "Type-A" Types ...
**The Upside of Stress: Why Stress Is Good for You,
and How to Get Good at It**
by Kelly McGonigal

99 - Thursday, June 18, 2015

For those about to Tweet ...
**Twitter Power 3.0:
How to Dominate Your Market One Tweet at a Time**
by Joel Comm & Dave Taylor

102 - Friday, July 17, 2015

Another job search book ...
**Highly Effective Networking:
Meet the Right People and Get a Great Job**
by Orville Pierson

106 - Saturday, July 18, 2015

"No fun, no sin, no you, no wonder it's dark ..."
The Picture of Dorian Gray
by Oscar Wilde

110 - Sunday, July 19, 2015

Walking out of the jungle ...
**One Spirit Medicine:
Ancient Ways to Ultimate Wellness**
by Alberto Villoldo

117 - Friday, July 31, 2015

An interesting journey ...
ALL THINGS GO: How I Became A Shaman
by Eric Durchholz

121 - Saturday, August 1, 2015

Claiming Your Personal Power ...
**Motivation Manifesto:
9 Declarations to Claim Your Personal Power**
by Brendon Burchard

124 - Sunday, August 2, 2015

Introducing "Quantum Biology" ...
**Life on the Edge:
The Coming of Age of Quantum Biology**
by Johnjoe McFadden & Jim Al-Khalili

128 - Tuesday, August 11, 2015

A love letter to an abiding urbs ...
Naples Declared: A Walk Around the Bay
by Benjamin Taylor

131 - Sunday, August 16, 2015

From an impressive leader ...
**Our Last Best Chance:
The Pursuit of Peace in a Time of Peril**
by King Abdullah II of Jordan

134 - Tuesday, August 18, 2015

When everything becomes nearly free ...
**The Zero Marginal Cost Society: The Internet of Things,
the Collaborative Commons, and the Eclipse of Capitalism**
by Jeremy Rifkin

139 - Thursday, August 20, 2015

Some things are older than you may suspect ...
**Forgotten Civilization:
The Role of Solar Outbursts in Our Past and Future**
by Robert M. Schoch

145 - Tuesday, September 1, 2015

How to freelance ... starting TODAY!
**Real Skills, Real Income: A Proven Marketing System
to Land Well-Paid Freelance and Consulting Work in 30
Days or Less**
by Diana Schneidman

150 - Wednesday, September 2, 2015

The why behind those rose colored glasses ...
**The Optimism Bias:
A Tour of the Irrationally Positive Brain**
by Tali Sharot

155 - Thursday, September 3, 2015

No, that's not a Harry Potter character ...
**Godless Grace: How Nonbelievers Are Making the
World Safer, Richer and Kinder**
by David Orenstein, Ph.D. & Linda Ford Blaikie, LC.S.W.

159 - Friday, September 4, 2015

So, that's how you get to be all those things ...
**The Power of Relentless:
7 Secrets to Achieving Mega-Success, Financial
Freedom, and the Life of Your Dreams**
by Wayne Allyn Root

164 - Saturday, September 5, 2015

"Change" as an euphemism ...
**Spreading the Wealth: How Obama is Robbing
the Suburbs to Pay for the Cities**
by Stanley Kurtz

169 - Sunday, September 6, 2015

"How soft your fields so green can whisper tales of gore ..."
The Legend of Sigurd and Gudrún
by J.R.R. Tolkien

175 - Monday, September 7, 2015

Woke up in a Soho doorway, a policeman knew my name ...
**Dataclysm: Love, Sex, Race, and Identity – What Our
Online Lives Tell Us about Our Offline Selves**
by Christian Rudder

180 - Saturday, September 19, 2015

Nice work if you can find it, I guess ...
**The Happiness Project: Or, Why I Spent a Year Trying
to Sing in the Morning, Clean My Closets, Fight Right,
Read Aristotle, and Generally Have More Fun**
by Gretchen Rubin

184 - Sunday, September 20, 2015
This is why Jefferson wrote of separation ...
A Simple Government: Twelve Things We Really Need from Washington (and a Trillion That We Don't!)
by Mike Huckabee

187 - Thursday, October 1, 2015
Let the buyer beware ...
Now, Discover Your Strengths
by Marcus Buckingham & Donald O. Clifton

190 - Friday, October 2, 2015
Falling asleep in the sun ...
Harness the Sun: America's Quest for a Solar-Powered Future
by Philip Warburg

192 - Sunday, October 11, 2015
Debates on freedom ...
Free for All: Defending Liberty in America Today
by Wendy Kaminer

196 - Monday, October 12, 2015
To sleep, perchance to dream ...
Questions & Answers About Sleep Apnea
by Sudhansu Chokroverty

198 - Tuesday, October 13, 2015
O Divine Poesy ...
The War of Art: Break Through the Blocks and Win Your Inner Creative Battles
by Steven Pressfield

201 - Friday, November 6, 2015
I did not need to know ANY of this ...
Public Apology: In Which a Man Grapples With a Lifetime of Regret, One Incident at a Time
by Dave Bry

203 - Saturday, November 7, 2015
Evolving the city ...
Start-Up City: Inspiring Private and Public Entrepreneurship, Getting Projects Done, and Having Fun
by Gabe Klein

206 - Sunday, November 8, 2015

America's traffic, cars, and roads ... and some things both mysterious and not ...

Street Smart: The Rise of Cities and the Fall of Cars
by Samuel I. Schwartz

210 - Saturday, November 14, 2015

Have you ever wondered ...

What If . . .: A Lifetime of Questions, Speculations, Reasonable Guesses, and a Few Things I Know for Sure
by Shirley McLaine

213 - Sunday, November 15, 2015

What we are becoming ...

Our Grandchildren Redesigned: Life in the Bioengineered Society of the Near Future
by Michael Bess

220 - Saturday, November 21, 2015

A really good autobiographical book ...

An Improvised Life: a Memoir
by Alan Arkin

224 - Sunday, November 22, 2015

Building wealth, starting from zero ...

Flipping Burgers to Flipping Millions: A Guide to Financial Freedom Whether You Have Your Dream Job, Own Your Own Business, or Just Started Your First Job
by Bernard Kelly

229 - Tuesday, December 1, 2015

Freak Think ...

Think Like a Freak: The Authors of Freakonomics Offer to Retrain Your Brain
by Steven D. Levitt & Stephen J. Dubner

234 - Wednesday, December 2, 2015

Around and around and around we go ...

The Upward Spiral: Using Neuroscience to Reverse the Course of Depression, One Small Change at a Time
by Dr. Alex Korb

240 - Wednesday, December 16, 2015

Once upon a time, in a corporation not so far away ...
Leadership and Self-Deception: Getting Out of the Box
by The Arbinger Institute

243 - Thursday, December 17, 2015

Exponential endeavors ...
The Compound Effect:
Jumpstart Your Income, Your Life, Your Success
by Darren Hardy

247 - Monday, December 28, 2015

As Seen On TV ...
Where Mercy Is Shown, Mercy Is Given
by Duane "Dog" Chapman

249 - Tuesday, December 29, 2015

When is enlightenment not enlightenment?
Siddhartha
by Hermann Hesse

253 - Wednesday, December 30, 2015

They don't make leaders like this anymore ...
Meditations
by Marcus Aurelius

256 - Thursday, December 31, 2015

More like "when stuff went wrong" with America ...
Seven Events That Made America America: And Proved
That the Founding Fathers Were Right All Along
by Larry Schweikart

263 - **QR Code Links**

281 - **Contents - Alphabetical By Author**

285 - **Contents - Alphabetical By Title**

Saturday, January 3, 2015[1]

Wish I'd gotten more out of this ...

A couple of months back I attended the UnCubed[2] event here ... this was my third or fourth UnCubed, and each has been different. They're typically 1/3 job fair, 1/3 conference, and 1/3 networking ... with an optional (paid) track of workshops. Frankly, generally speaking, the target audience for these is much younger than me and a whole lot more technical ... even though that brief writer gig I had out in the suburbs in 2013 came from a discussion with an exhibitor at a previous one – so my finding something at these *is* possible. This past one, not so much (although they did have a strange revolving – different categories getting in at different times - lounge for those with more than 5 years experience).

However, one of the exhibitors was Brad's Deals[3], and they were handing out copies of founder Brad Wilson's Do More, Spend Less: The New Secrets of Living the Good Life for Less[4] to those who seemed interested. I let on as how I did these reviews, and told them I'd throw it into my to-be-read pile.

Now, I'd not been familiar with the Brad's Deals site (I actually hadn't even *looked* at it until starting this review), so I didn't have any particular expectation of what the book would be when starting into it ... other than being 5½ years out of work and *hoping* that it was going to provide me with some actionable suggestions for "living the good life for less". I am also "allergic" to all things financial (down to managing check books and credit cards – thank goodness The Wife is into all that sort of stuff!), and a LOT of this book is targeted to people who like nothing more than to set up spreadsheets comparing fractions of percents of difference between various sources of home loans, car loans, credit cards, etc., so what might have excited the right sort of reader in many cases simply *horrified* me. In fact, there were chunks of this, where Wilson is going through detailed minutia of international airline frequent flier programs, or comparing credit card offers, that I was literally mentally saying "BLAH, BLAH, BLAH" while flipping the pages until he got to stuff that I could connect with. I am a fairly diligent reader, and it stood out to me that I really couldn't recall another book that I *so* "disconnected" with in various parts!

Again, this is likely do to my being phobic around several areas covered here, and not a particular fault of the book ... although there was a sense that sections of this were coming from an "enthusiastic hobbyist" standpoint, and held the same "fascination" (or lack thereof) that somebody going on about the details of various Pokemon cards sets, or different gauge model railroad systems, or wine collectors' tasting notes, would have for somebody with scant interest in that niche.

The book is also very close to being an autobiography ... Wilson gets into a lot of detail on how these various "secrets" work, but it's generally in the context of how he worked a particular deal ... frequently featuring vehicles that are no longer available. Additionally, from my perspective, it works a very fine line between "these are great ways to save money" and "these are effective ways to game the system" ... and I kept wondering when he was "going to get caught" doing a lot of these.

He starts off talking about how he was able to do these fantastic, 5-figure vacations with his new wife ... some of the approaches are basic, but most require jumping through a lot of hoops, some requiring the short-term expenditure of fairly significant funds. One approach he used to build up free nights at a major international hotel chain was to book nights at their lowest-level motel brand (which still counted to "nights stayed" in the chain's program), swing by the hotel, use the automated kiosk to check in, and then simply drive back home. Because he was going to be using those nights (in a stay 2, get 1 deal) in a $1,000+/night hotel, his expenditure of under $50 for each night in the cheap hotel was an investment he was happy to make (although, coming to this in a "flat broke" state, that sounds like a LOT of money to put in play). He claims that his eventual "$54,000" trip (with these hotel credits and a bunch of airline miles) cost him $20 (for a dessert), at no point does he account for the expenditures made to get those hotel nights.

Speaking of airline miles, he also details a "system" (I think it's closer to a "scam") where he took advantage of one airline's counting all miles accrued as equivalent to flight miles – and giving miles for every dollar spent on their affiliated credit card – and a promotion that the U.S. Mint was running when it was trying to get people to use the Presidential Dollar coins (where you could order a 250-count box of the coins, for face value, with free shipping). The goal here was to get both him and his wife up to the top "lifetime" status in this airline's frequent flier program – which required 1 million miles racked up in a calendar year. To achieve this, he ordered *more than **three million** $1 coins* over the course of several months, running the charges through his (no doubt multiple) credit cards that generated the mileage credits, and turning around and depositing the coins as they came in at his bank to pay off those accounts. I don't know about you, but the idea of trying to charge that much through a credit card is a terrifying concept, even if at each point the money was just "out there" until the next coin delivery (he even got a UPS store box half a block from his bank to make schlepping the 60lb loads of coins easier to deposit).

His "travel" schemes take up the first half of the book, with the rest being dedicated to "shopping" (where he describes getting kicked off of eBay for listing CDs and DVDs from Amazon Canada – at a time when the exchange rate was very skewed – and simply ordering the items with Canadian dollars for delivery to the customer, and making a chunk of money in the process), and "personal finance" (including how to game the car-buying and mortgage processes). In that section Wilson writes about signing up for numerous credit cards (he did as many as 17 in one day) for sign-up bonuses (no mention about paying the annual fees), and how to manipulate your credit score.

Again, I'd rather have dental surgery than a friendly sit-down with an accountant, so most of the "tricky" stuff the author outlines here made me extremely nervous reading it ... but if you're the type who switched accounts or services all the time to gain a percentage here or a percentage there, you might find all this a lot of fun. You probably need to have a fairly substantial bankroll, however, because a lot of what he talks you through here takes cash (or credit) outlays of various degrees of significance, and all I could think of is how *screwed* you could be if everything didn't work just *perfectly* (and having a sense that Wilson was *lucky* in a lot of his machinations).

If you're looking for a way to save some money here and there, Do More, Spend Less[5] is probably not the book for you (I guess BradsDeals.com would be a suggestion), but if you're looking to totally turn you life over to spreadsheets and reading the fine print in every mailing you get to eventually be able to take fifty-thousand dollar vacations "for nothing", this is the book for you. As noted, there is massive detail as to "how to do it" in the various sections here … but it made my head swim and wonder at what point the gendarmes arrive to stick you in a cell until the Forensic Accountants have picked their way through your finances!

Notes:

1. http://btripp-books.livejournal.com/162544.html
2. http://chicago.uncubed.com/
3. http://www.bradsdeals.com/
4. http://amzn.to/155E4e7
5. http://amzn.to/155E4e7

Sunday, January 4, 2015[1]

Being Authentic ...

I've known Kim Garst[2] through various social media channels for a while, starting, if my recall is correct, with my early days over on Empire Avenue. She's since been a familiar presence over on Facebook, and I'm signed up to get her frequent newsletter updates. She recently reached out to her audience to create a pre-sell surge on her new book ... which is coming out from something of a "hybrid" publisher, Morgan James[3], who touts their model as being the "Entrepreneurial Publisher™" which appears to manifest as a mix of traditional gate-keeper, print-on-demand (they work with Ingram's "Lightning Source") service, and vanity (or, in their terms "collaborative") press. I point this out because a) I'm something of a publishing industry geek, and I'm fascinated by the evolution of these models, and b) I'm seeing Garst implementing things like "Thunderclap" (a crowd-sourced promo platform[4]) to push the book ... which is not something I've encountered with folks working with "traditional" publishers. Frankly, when I reached out to Morgan James to request a review copy, I wasn't particularly expecting a response ... but I was very pleased to have heard right back asking for my mailing address ... so there's enough of a "traditional publisher" backbone to their model to support classic promotional practices.

Anyway, Kim Garst's Will the Real You Please Stand Up: Show Up, Be Authentic, and Prosper in Social Media[5] comes out in a couple of weeks, is focused on that issue of "being authentic" in social media marketing, and is primarily addressed at the business community ... although the messages here are applicable to anybody looking for exposure in social media. The book kicks off with a cautionary tale ... of how Quaker Oats lost *$1.4 billion* between its purchase of, and eventual divesting of, the Snapple brand. In this case, it was a mega-corp taking over a small, quirky, company with a dedicated fan base, and turning it into just another shelf slotting data entry. Needless to say, in that process the brand lost its *authenticity*, ceased to appeal to its fans, and got no traction with the new MBA-fueled marketing campaign. She follows this by setting out some basic points about the issue:

> ... Consumers are tired of being overpromised and underdelivered, and in a marketplace rich with alternatives, they are increasingly able to find companies whose authenticity is refreshing and real.
>
> ...
>
> ... One of the key hallmarks of sincerity in a company is a commitment to integrity in all actions associated with the brand's story, marketing, and promotion, as well as every other decision made in the operations and support services performed in the name of the brand.
>
> ...

> ... Customers who have had the pleasant experience of receiving sincerity from a brand are more likely to be repeat customers as a result. Given the cost of developing new leads versus that of retaining existing customers, this can be a huge for a brand's profitability.

Garst uses the image of the trust involved in the small town/neighborhood business of previous generations, where the people were known, and there was a relationship established that stood as the keystone for commerce ... and while it's obviously a different time with different elements, she suggests using social media as a tool to reach out to one's audience in a way that can emulate that sort of interaction. One interesting approach she touches on is "history and heritage", and cites the Oreo vs. Hydrox cookie brand battle where the perception never synched with the reality (Hydrox was the original, Oreo the later knock-off, both were products of large baking companies, etc.) and despite taste-test superiority, Hydrox was seen as the "off brand", and eventually went out of production ... in *"failing to leverage that brand history and tell the authentic story of the brand"* it missed its best opportunity. This is echoed in the New Coke fiasco ... where to appeal to the biases of upper management, Coke nearly destroyed over a century of consumer good will.

The idea of "passion" is the driving element in "authenticity", but it can be a difficult thing to implement in a big company. The founder might have genuine passion for the organization, as key others may, but spreading that across the entire enterprise can be a challenge. Garst presents these steps to bring passion to bear:

> 1 - Express your passion.
> 2 - Participate in the passion of others.
> 3 - Leverage the passion of your social advocates.
> 4 - Inspire your employees with your passion.
> 5 - Tie your passion to business-related outcomes.

In each chapter, there are a lot of "do this" sorts of lists like the above, plus a "conclusion" section which wraps up the concepts covered in it. Again, this is primarily addressed to marketing people who might not have a solid grasp on social media, so a significant amount of the message here is "old news" to those who have been involved in social for a while, but the pacing is set to bring along those who need to be tutored in the social approach. Here's a list of points, for example, Garst gives for "starting the conversation":

> - Don't be a know-it-all.
> - Provide true value.
> - Ask questions.
> - Reach out to others.
> - Express your passion.

She follows this with a concise, but reasonably comprehensive, look at what to do if things "go wrong", and how to structure responsibility levels, so when things go bad you can react as quickly as possible (and "quickly" in the social media sphere tend to run to less than an hour rather than after 3 meetings of the Board with the Legal team).

There are chapters on building and interacting with communities (with examples from Ford, Comic-Com, Harley-Davidson, and the Komen Foundation), and on the concept of "virality" ... I was disappointed with one piece of this, however, *especially* for a book slated for a 2015 release (rather than a few years back), where she suggests that Facebook is likely to provide "viral" spread with people averaging 400 connections ... her figures assume total reach to *all* one's connections (and to those connections' connections, etc.), when the reality (for nearly a year now) is that if you don't *pay* Facebook, you're unlikely to reach even 10% of those following you (and in many cases, as low as 3%), so rather than there being "64 million possible connections" (FREE!) three levels down, you really can only rely on (if not shoveling lucre to Zuckerberg & Co.) a couple of thousand impressions! Aside from this inexplicable reality gap, Garst outlines the upside, downside, benefits and risks of working towards "viral content", and how difficult is it to hit just the right tone to "catch the wave" (to mix my metaphors) of public attention ... she notes: *"In fact, in some cases, the very act of trying to make something go viral can have just the opposite effect ... there is always the potential for it to generate a significant amount of negative buzz for your brand."*

Returning to the theme of "authenticity" she notes that there are cases when attempts to be authentic backfire: *"... by openly expressing an opinion on something, you could face criticism from those who don't share your opinion. Also, since words can mean different things to different people, or can be misconstrued, it is possible to offend entire {groups} without intending to do so."* She counters this with a chapter on brands that are "dominating" social media, with Starbucks, American Airlines, Coca-Cola, Red Bull, and Disney providing in-depth examples of (admittedly large) companies that have found the right voice for their markets.

Garst closes out the book with a look at "how to get yourself heard", even if you don't have the resources of the big corporations. She suggests that *"being authentic is an alignment of what you do with why and how you do it"* (which is certainly a template applicable to any size organization), and spends the rest of the chapter summarizing the main points of the text.

As I mentioned, Will the Real You Please Stand Up[6] is due for release in a couple of weeks, and is presently available for pre-order from the on-line big boys at about a 25% discount. While there is little "new" in the book, it is certainly a useful look at social media marketing through the specific filter of *authenticity*, and it provides quite a lot of actionable material for those who have either not ventured into the social sphere as yet, or have not been successful in their previous attempts.

Notes:

1. http://btripp-books.livejournal.com/162696.html
2. http://kimgarst.com/
3. http://www.morganjamespublishing.com/

4. https://www.thunderclap.it/projects/20046-the-beyou-share-the-word-team
5. http://amzn.to/1AoQky8
6. http://amzn.to/1AoQky8

Saturday, January 17, 2015[1]

Advertising philosophy, amusingly packaged ...

A couple of months back, I was attending an entrepreneurial conference down in Chicago's Loop, and on one of the panels, one of the speakers was effusive in recommending the "Wizard of Ads" books by Roy H. Williams. I'd never heard of the guy, but figured I'd check him out. Turns out that he'd dropped out of college following his second day there, and has been making his way through the world by asking *"What makes people do the things they do?"*, and building up what sounds like quite a substantial marketing practice based on the fruits of that analysis.

It turns out that there's a *trilogy* of "Wizard of Ads" books, and I ended up getting all three and reading them in sequence. I was toying with "batching" them and doing one review covering all three, but I figured that wouldn't be fair to either the books or you readers, so a lot of the "over-all" stuff is going to be dispensed with here, and the following two reviews will simply assume you've read this one. The first thing you'll notice about these three books is that they're not your standard business books, being designed to "look and feel" like well-worn leather bound volumes, sporting deckled edges, cream paper, and design elements both drawn from medieval "hand-illuminated" texts and, well, frankly, scrapbooks.

The first of these, 1998's <u>The Wizard of Ads: Turning Words into Magic and Dreamers into Millionaires</u>[2] starts with a somewhat edgy assertion – the "9 Secret Words": *The risk of insult is the price of clarity."* which is pretty gutsy for most marketers ... and he follows that with:

> *If in your advertising you are willing to speak the simple, essential truth as plainly as you are able, and if you are willing to support what you say with illustration and example, meet me in the backyard ... we'll take over the world.*

While the book is sub-divided into fairly "business book"-like sections: "Turning Words into Magic", "Turning Strangers into Customers", and "Turning Dreams into Realities", things proceed in a rather unique manner. There are 100 "chapters" here, running just 1-3 pages, and most embellished by some graphic – from a charred twenty dollar bill, to vintage ads, to framed quotes ... needless to say, this is not a "dense" reading experience, but a series of "business parables" which illustrate particular points. These aren't all just "stories", as a number of them veer off into brain science, like:

> *Planting a reticular activator in the mind of a customer is the Mount Everest of ad writers. The reticular activator is a mental trigger in your*

> *unconscious that directs your attention and causes you to notice and remember things you never intentionally committed to memory.*

An example he gives is an exercise where you do a series of math problems, all of which end up as 14, and then you're asked to name a vegetable ... odds are you'll say "carrot" because the repeated impressions of the term "14-karat" for gold have anchored that combination in your brain (Williams also notes here that audio input is stronger than visual).

One thing he does (across all three books) is start off stories like he's talking about some guy down the block who's doing this or that, like "his friend" Al who said *"we do things, but we do not know why we do them"* which Williams projects to people not being able to be "fully trusted" when they tell you what they want ... the person looking for car wax doesn't really *want* the wax, they want a shiny car, the business owner who asks for advertising, really is looking for *more customers*, etc. Eventually he gets around to noting that his buddy "Al" is more famous for saying $E=MC^2$ ... and you find out that he's talking about an observation by Albert Einstein (who he doesn't know). There are many bits like this where the story plays out and has the "punchline" of having the tale being about a familiarly famous person.

There are lots and lots of little bits of what is no doubt hard-earned wisdom in here, like how certain locations can boost business far more than others (one that was 33% more expensive than a client's old space ended up bringing in as much business in 3 months as the old one saw in 12), and almost *nagging* on some points. One phrase that he highly recommends is "which means ...", because all marketers are way too close to their products and tend to assume that there are "self evident" aspects that anybody would know about them ... and typically they *don't* ... so when you say something even vaguely technical about your product or industry, it's wise to follow up with a plain-talk re-framing about what that means. There are also "old saws" thrown in, like *" The man who sells to the classes / will live with the masses. / Sell to the masses / and you'll live with the classes."*, with the further note that "people who make a living by serving the rich are called *butlers*"!

Aside from the "punch line" stories, there are some other straight-forward historical pieces here, like the one about how Sears got started with a mis-directed shipment of pocket watches ... the addressee hadn't ordered them, but rather than send the case back, railway agent Sears bought them himself and started what was to become a huge retail empire. In the words of Johnny Carson: *"I did not know that!"* despite having lived in Sears' hometown for most of my life.

I'm skipping over a lot of the specific "philosophy" here, not so much as to leave you itching to get to the details, as that a lot of this is presented in ways that don't conveniently translate to bullet lists ... things like "The Seven Laws of the Advertising Universe", which is brilliant, but not easily distilled to something scaled to this review. However, The Wizard of Ads[3] is a very enjoyable and informative read, and I'd guess that nearly anybody would find something of interest in here, although it is, obviously, targeted to the marketer.

Perhaps a testament to its on-going utility is that it's still in print (even in this fancy design), and at a very reasonable cost via the on-line big boys (I don't know if, after 17 years, this has a lot of penetration into the brick-and-mortar stores). Of course, I ended up getting *my* copy via the new/used vendors, and you can presently get a "very good" used copy of this for a penny (plus the $3.99 shipping), so you don't have much of an excuse of passing it by.

Notes:

1. http://btripp-books.livejournal.com/162817.html
2. http://amzn.to/1ya3amF
3. http://amzn.to/1ya3amF

Sunday, January 18, 2015[1]

Much more under the hood ...

OK, so I'm going to work on the assumption that you are reading this review in sequence, or at least in context of my previous and following reviews of the three books in Roy H. Williams' "Wizard of Ads" trilogy. If you've not read the review yet of the first book, you might want to go there[2].first, as I'm leaving a good deal of my typical "how I got to this book" stuff un-repeated here. This volume, Secret Formulas of the Wizard of Ads: Turning Paupers into Princes and Lead into Gold[3], from 1999, is both very similar to, and significantly different than its predecessor. Like that volume, this strives to give the impression of being an ancient tome (now with metallic accents on the cover), now with more "margin notes" "penciled in", but it seems to me that Williams has rolled up his sleeves and opted to dig more into the work here than the story telling of the earlier book.

This also comes in 100 short chapters, but this time broken out over *six* sections: "Philosophy of Advertising", "Room with a View", "Side Door into the Mind", "Turning Lead into Gold" (with "pencil" and "advertising" written in where you'd expect them), "Doing the Hard Thing", and "How, Then, Should We Live?".

When I was first contemplating what I'd do for these reviews, I thought I had a killer hook, as these three books from Mr. Williams reminded me quite a bit of the various books coming out from Seth Godin, and I figured, with these coming out in 1998, 1998, and 2001, that they would have certainly predated Godin. However, when I checked, I was surprised to see that Godin had two of his books out *prior* to these, and this particular volume shared a release year with Godin's landmark *Permission Marketing*. So, I lost that story angle, but suffice it to say that there are certain similarities between the two writers' approaches to "marketing wisdom", just Williams said his piece in three books, while Godin's releases have gone on and on.

As I mentioned ... this book seems more "in the trenches" ... an early stop discusses "branding", but puts it in the context of Ivan Pavlov's work with dogs:

> ... There are three keys to implanting an associative memory into the mind of your customer. The first key is consistency. Pavlov never offered food without ringing the bell, and he never rang the bell without offering food. The second key is frequency, meaning that Pavlov did it day after day after day.
>
> ... The third key anchoring, is the tricky one. When an associative memory is being implanted, the new and unknown element (the bell) has to be associated with a memory that's already anchored to the dog's love for the taste of meat. If the dog did not love meat, the frequent and consistent ringing of the bell would have produced no response other

than to irritate the dog.

Obviously, one needs to *know* what moves your customers if you're wanting your business/product/service to get associated with that pre-existing positive attitude.

The second section of the book, "Room with a View" is specifically looking at the brain ... ranging from one-liners like *"In your advertising, don't speak to the world outside your customers, speak to the world inside their minds."* to relatively detailed looks at specific brain functions. In one chapter Williams goes on a tour of the various areas of brain activity, with special focus on "Wernicke's area" and "Broca's area" ... the former being "king of nouns", bringing up what things are called, and the latter being "the center of action words". The author states:

> *The objective of advertising is to influence the prefrontal cortex – the seat of emotion, planning and judgement, located just across the motor association cortex, right behind your forehead. And the shortest leap to it is from Broca's area.*

He goes on to assert:

> *Describe what you want the listener to see, and she will see it. Cause her to imagine taking the action you'd like her to take, and you've brought her much closer to taking the action. The secret of persuasion lies in our skillful use of action words. The magic of advertising is in the verbs.*

Another fascinating bit here, that I probably had encountered in some previous material, but really didn't "know" it, is the concept of "the magic square", where in a 3x3 grid, a box drawn around the intersection of the upper and right lines within the whole image will be the place of greatest attention ... this is constantly used from classic art to modern graphics ... so it's a handy thing to have at least mentally filed!

In the third section, "Side Door into the Mind", Williams gets into some "Jedi mind tricks" that could be useful ... for instance: *"People tend to follow through with what they have heard themselves say they would do."*, so getting people to voice your intents for you (in a chant or rhyme, for instance), they're a lot more likely to move forward with the action. Also, if you can speak to a "deeply felt need", you can pretty much claim anything, as the emotion attached to the need will over-ride any intellectual disbelief of the claim. In this section, he also gets into "The Six Tugs-of-War" (which are very similar to the "7 Laws" in the previous book, but not identical), with a chapter each on:

- *Intellect vs. Emotion*
- *Time vs. Money*
- *Opportunity vs. Security*
- *Style vs. Substance*

- *Pain vs. Gain*
- *Sight vs. Sound*

These have some interesting research associated with them, as well as some applied tactics for making the best of each of those dualities. He also discusses different media and how effective they are on other levels, and then returns to the "sleep as eraser" idea requiring extensive repetitive exposure: *"The goal of a long-term (branding) campaign is to expose the listener to the identical ad approximately three times within each seven night's sleep, fifty-two weeks a year. ... You must have sufficient repetition (and patience) to overcome the cleansing effects of sleep."* Frankly, Williams' books are the *only* place I've encountered this sleep model, so I don't know if it's a research-based "common knowledge" that I've missed (having been on the PR side of things) or if this is just something spun out of his own experience.

There is so much good stuff in here that I could go on and on ... but I'm going to try to wrap this up. A few more choice bits: *"The key attribute of print media is accuracy. The power of the spoken word is persuasion"*.... writing in the present tense helps to put readers "into the scene" ... *"While the journalist seeks to inform us and the creative writer entertains, it is the poet who changes how we see the world."* (in the context of "using unpredictable words in unusual combinations").

He does go on a bit with, perhaps, *too* much nitty-gritty when he delves deeply into calculating ad budgets, and especially the arcana of radio (and to some extent, TV) buys. Interesting, perhaps ... TMI, possibly ... although there is this question: Which is better – a schedule that reaches 100% of the city and persuades them 10% of the way, or a schedule that reaches 10% of the city and persuades them 100% of the way? (it's the same money, just one plan works and the other doesn't).

The last two sections of the book sort of lost me ... the "Hard Things" section is about specific "running a business" kinds of things that didn't much resonate with me, and the final section, while engaging was a bit unfocused (I'm still not sure why that piece on him wanting to do a movie about Oscar Wilde is in there), and there was a regrettable sense that he'd used up the "good stuff" in the previous ¾ of the book, and was looking for stuff to "fill" to get to 100 pieces. However, that could just be me.

Other than this mild caveat, I found Secret Formulas of the Wizard of Ads[4] a really remarkable book, and is one of those *extremely rare* books that I anticipate re-reading in anticipation of getting more quality info from it in a second go-around. This is also still available (even in hardcover), so should be obtainable through whatever sales channel you're inclined to use. Like its predecessor, it is also available from the online new/used guys for a mere penny ... so, again, you have no excuse for not grabbing a copy!

Notes:

1. http://btripp-books.livejournal.com/163210.html
2. http://btripp-books.livejournal.com/162817.html
3. http://amzn.to/1ISYZzg
4. http://amzn.to/1ISYZzg

Saturday, January 24, 2015[1]

More Wizardry ...

OK, so this is the third of three reviews covering the three books of the "Wizard of Ads" trilogy by Roy H. Williams, and you probably should consider reading the two previous ones before launching into this. Like its predecessors, Magical Worlds of the Wizard of Ads: Tools and Techniques for Profitable Persuasion[2] is designed to look like a leather-bound "ancient tome", with similar interior styling, although this time featuring yellow (gold?) accents on the interior pages. As were the previous two volumes, this is comprised of 100 short chapters, this time collected into four sections: "Architecture of the Mind", "Tools for Profitable Persuasion", "Charting Your Destiny & Dreams", and "Wizards at Large".

Once again, Williams has a lot of material for what these days would likely be called "brain hacking" ... elements of perception and mental processing that can be channeled to particular persuasive ends. One early point he makes in this is *"Lyrics are absorbed and processed almost exclusively in the 'nonverbal' right hemisphere."*, implying that putting messages into songs can "sneak them past the Inner Critic" (of the left hemisphere). A lot of this first section looks at right/left brain issues, and how different types of impressions are experienced and integrated in perception. It also is less targeted to actual marketing messaging, and much more "theoretical" than the material in the previous books (for instance particle/wave duality ... hard to turn that into a product pitch!). There is a wealth of *interesting* stuff, however, such a the 4 kinds of thought, 3 kinds of people (verbal, analytical, abstract, and symbolic, and artists, businesspeople, and scientists) ... which is immediately followed by a chapter analyzing some James Taylor lyrics.

Williams again revisits the "sleep" model of his previous books, only now noting that sleep tends to clear *electrical* short-term "working" memory, which is contrasted with "procedural" memory – the sort of thing like having learned how to ride a bike or type, which he suggests is primarily stored chemically. He also comes back to "Broca's area", which he here describes as a "tollbooth" ... if what is coming in to the brain is "predictable", it will be shunted off as being of "low importance", leading to it not getting much attention. So, playing with language, and surprising those parts of the brain, are key to getting messages in.

One thing presented here I found fascinating is the author's debunking of the visual/auditory/kinesthetic model so popular with network marketers and other salesmen whose approach requires building rapport with their targets ... he quotes *"This is a groundless theory based on zero medical research."* ... so much for "cold reading" prospects for see/hear/feel verbs. Another very similar "myth" is also addressed here: the saw that "93 percent of all human communication is nonverbal", which turns out to have been a generalization from a very specific study (of "the resolution of inconsistent messages") which got picked up and spread by the self-help seminar crowd. On a less contentious footing, he closes out the "mind" section with a look at the Myers-Briggs type of personality sorting, which he seems to approve of, but (oddly) doesn't even make a stab at relating to marketing.

Of course, "Tools for Profitable Persuasion" flips over to nearly *all* business. He talks of "business morphine" - approaches that *work*, but are addictive and progressively less effective over time ... these are great in the short-term, but damage the business long-term. He counters this will a look at a study in customer loyalty, there being 3 types of customers: nonswitchable – those that will not be convinced to change, switchable – those who, with the right messaging, can change brands, and price-switchable – those who will constantly switch, looking for a cheaper option. The latter are the prime audience of "business morphine".

This section gets a bit complicated with theories ... like his "gravity well" (much like a "sales funnel") of increasing interaction with a brand, "share of voice", "impact quotient", "share of mind", "personal experience factor", "share of market", "market potential", and the "advertising performance equation" ... all of which are inter-related: (SoV x IQ) = SoMi, (SoMi x PEF) = SoMa, (SoMa x MPo) = Sales Volume, or SoV x IQ x PEF x MPo = Sales Volume (yeah, I "glazed over" early on in this too). He spins out of this into a piece about statistics and how TV bundles up bad slots and tries to sell you less effective packages ... which I guess would be useful to some.

Fortunately, the rest of the "tools" section gets back to more generally applicable stuff, from how to facilitate brainstorming sessions that will involve both introverts and extroverts, the New Coke fiasco as a study in what we say vs. what we do, etc. He then moves into a series of chapters where he turns various figures into verbs – Robert Frost into "frosting", Dr. Seuss into "seussing", and "being Monet" - all in the interest of "sneaking past the security guard" by getting into the right brain with messages that will then slip into the left using tools like "humor", "mental participation", and "subliminal associations" where a slight change in otherwise synonymous words can create big changes in people's perception and behaviors. He discusses how "numbered lists" ("7 habits", etc. ad nauseum) appeal to the brain, and eventually works his way around to "chaotic systems".

The third section, "Charting Your Destiny & Dreams", involves quite a lot of "navel gazing", about one's purpose, one's goals, one's dreams, and how you go about trying to define and/or reach these. He notes that the universe is *"built on mutually exclusive truths"*, such as the admirability of *"reaching for the stars" and "being content the way you are"*, which Williams links thusly:

> *Being content and reaching for the stars both require an absence of fear. The fear of being average robs you of contentment. The fear of failure robs you of the joy of your dreams.*

He also asks whether you'd prefer to spend a week with noted investor *Warren* Buffet, or Margaritaville's *Jimmy* Buffet.

There is a lot of reminiscing into the author's past here, some random notes, and bits and pieces that one might find useful, aside from amusing.

One of these is pointing out how both pessimists and optimists tend to make the reflections on events, positive or negative, Persona, Permanent, and Pervasive ... as in "it's about me", "it's not going to change", and "it's universal" ... an interesting way to break down those sorts of thought patterns. Another piece here has a heading which is wise all by itself: *"Experience must first be a verb."* ... which he backs up with a quote from Oscar Wilde.

The final section, "Wizards at Large", primarily looks at historical figures that Wiliams holds up as examples of his "Wizardry". Many of these are of the "punch line" variety I've mentioned previously (he doesn't tell you who he's talking about until the very end), but others are more general descriptions. These range from Geoffrey of Monmouth, to Baron Rothschild, Coco Chanel, Mark Twain, Andrew Jackson, Lewis Carrol, etc., plus Ben Franklin advising Thomas Jefferson on editing, *and* the origin of the Tuxedo. Not a whole lot of "actionable" stuff in here, but interesting tales in the category that Arsenio Hall calls "things that make you go *hmmmmmm*".

Magical Worlds of the Wizard of Ads[3] is still available, at least through the on-line big boys, and you can land a used copy of the paperback edition for under a buck (plus shipping). This (like its predecessors) was and interesting read, but seemed to be a lot more oriented toward "folk wisdom" (or what its author had picked up over his career).

Notes:

1. http://btripp-books.livejournal.com/163514.html
2. http://amzn.to/1z5jXKc
3. http://amzn.to/1z5jXKc

Friday, January 30, 2015[1]

Wish there was more ...

In a recent blog post elsewhere[2], I was looking to accurately source a quote, so did a little legwork on Fran Lebowitz ... a humorist whose *bon mots* I have been happy to regurgitate for many years ... and found this book (which I promptly ordered from new/used vendors over on Amazon).

As noted, I knew *of* Lebowitz for quite a long time, but really didn't know much in terms of the details[3] of her career until looking into this book. She actually started out with Andy Warhol, doing pieces for *Interview*, and later moved on to being a columnist for *Mademoiselle* ... however, her actual written output appears to be *limited*, and most of which seems to be within the covers of The Fran Lebowitz Reader[4], which features both her earlier collections, 1974's *Metropolitan Life*, and 1981's *Social Studies*.

Frankly, I found this quite disappointing, as I had envisioned some vast trove of witty material lurking out there, just off my radar, which I could delve into ... but, no ... this appears to be pretty much what there is. I (like others) had thought of Lebowitz as a latter-day Dorothy Parker, but, although she holds her own quip-for-quip with her great predecessor, the material she's generated has thus far been fairly thin (this 2-in-1 volume is 333 pages). Of course, this is not counting her unfinished work ... she's been playing off her long-unfinished *Exterior Signs of Wealth* for decades (in a 1994 interview she was noted to have recently "broken through" a 10-year bout of writers block, and elsewhere was quoted as saying the book ... *still* unfinished ... would be out by the turn of the millennium), and supposedly has another book, *Progress* (which was first excepted from a decade ago), that supposedly has a release date for later this year.

It seems that Ms. Lebowitz maintains her Manhattan lifestyle primarily on the public speaking circuit (although she has had a recurring role as a judge in the *Law & Order* TV shows, and has appeared in a couple of movies – recently in *The Wolf of Wall Street*), which, I assume, allows her to be witty and noticed without having to *actually write*. Which brings me to my first clip from the *Metropolitan Life* side of the book, in the initial chapter, *My Day: An Introduction of Sorts*, which is set up with times, activities, and commentaries, winding up with:

> 2:05 A.M. – *I enter my apartment and prepare to work. In deference to the slight chill I don two sweaters and an extra pair of socks. I pour myself a club soda and move the lamp next to the desk. ... I pick up my pen and stare at the paper. I light a cigarette. I stare at the paper. I write "My Day: An Introduction of Sorts." Good. Lean yet cadenced. I consider my day. I become unaccountably depressed. I doodle in the margin. ... I look longingly at my sofa, not unmindful of that fact that*

> it converts cleverly into a bed. I light a cigarette. I stare at the paper.
>
> 4:50 A.M. – The sofa wins. Another victory for furniture.

I've deleted a couple of sentences there, which gave some specifics of how she was distracting herself, but felt, for illustration purposes here it stood better without them. The whole 2.5-page chapter is, by these last two entries, evidently the introduction that she was needing to write, which eventually loses to the sofa. I literally "LOL'd" when it hit that last line (made more poignant that her family's business for generations had been in the furniture trade).

The two component books here have somewhat different tones, largely expressed in length, with the latter book having some substantially longer bits, but also in "social context", 1974 and 1981 being variant ages of the New York scene (which reminds me of the note in the front matter of the book which says *"Fran Lebowitz still lives in New York City, as she does not believe that she would be allowed to live anywhere else."*). Both books are divided into "thematic" sections, with *Metropolitan Life* featuring Manners, Science, Arts, and Letters; and *Social Studies* offering People, Things, Places, and Ideas. One thing to note here is that much of the activities described in the text are somewhat dated ... the latter volume came out in the year that New York's notorious/celebrated Studio 54 *closed*, and the IBM PC first appeared ... and the former came out in that post-hippy era (I think there needs to be a label for the early 70's, like how Punk was followed by New Wave in the popular imagining, there should be something to tag the "post-hippy" years – which were freaky enough on their own) of 1974 ... neither of these time frames being particularly relevant to "millennials" and their generational neighbors.

Speaking of dated ... the following quote comes from a section condemning pocket calculators ... and, kids, there *was* a time when these did not exist, only coming to market in the early '70s ... so these would have been the equivalent of the iPads of the day:

> *The rigors of learning how to do long division have been a traditional part of childhood, just like learning to smoke. In fact, as far as I am concerned, the two go hand-in-hand. Any child who cannot do long division by himself does not deserve to smoke. I am really quite a nice girl and very fond of children but I do have my standards. I have never taught a child to smoke before he has first taken a piece of paper and a pencil and demonstrated to my satisfaction that he can correctly divide 163 by 12.*

Oh, yes ... among other anachronisms here, Ms. Lebowitz is a very *enthusiastic* smoker, which (even evidenced by the bits in this review) constantly surfaces in her (less enthusiastically pursued?) writing.

In the chapter "No News Is Preferable", she goes on quite a run about the news industry, from its ancient Greek antecedents (including killing the bearer of bad news – *that* would create quite a churn in front of the network cameras!) to the very early days of cable TV. She notes that many people like the news, and *"consider it to be important, informative, and even entertaining"*, and details each of these elements – of which the "informative" struck me as particularly wry:

> Informative
>> Strictly speaking, the news is informative insofar as it does indeed provide information. Therefore the questions one must ask here are:
>> 1. Do I want this information?
>> 2. Do I need this information?
>> 3. What do they expect me to do about it?
>
> Answer to Question Number One
>> No. If a genetically handicapped Scientologist attempts to take the life of the vice-president of the 4H Clubs of Texas with a crossbow and somebody knows about it, I would prefer that he kept it to himself.
>
> Answer to Question Number Two
>> No. If three unemployed psychopathic blacksmiths have stolen the daughter of the inventor of lead paint and are threatening to read to her aloud from Fear of Flying until everybody in Marin County is given a horse, I fail to see how knowing this will help me to find a large but inexpensive apartment in a better neighborhood.
>
> Answer to Question Number Three
>> I can not possibly imagine.

Needless to say, some things never change, with the banality of the News being one of them. This brings me back to bemoaning that there is not *more* by Fran Lebowitz out there ... if anything, the world has gotten more twisted in the decades of her "writers block", and I, for one, would welcome having had her impressions of that downward spiral accessible.

The Fran Lebowitz Reader[5] is still in print (with a different cover than pictured here – the used copy I got was from when they were pushing the Public Speaking[6] documentary that Martin Scorsese did about her a few years back), and the on-line big boys have it currently at 27% off of cover price ... however, "very good" copies can be had from the new/used vendors for as little as a penny (plus shipping). As discussed above, I was happy to have "gotten caught up" with Ms. Lebowitz with this combination volume, but am sorely disappointed that there's not more stuff from here out there.

* a 1994 piece[7] by Bob Morris in *The New York Times*, in which were such gems as *"The words are in the cigarettes."* and *She says the only thing she likes less than writing is*

exercising, which she does because her doctor says it's the only way she can keep smoking and not aggravate her bronchitis. "It's the only time I wish I was writing, because at least you can sit down." plus this barb: *"I don't like avocados. They're the mayonnaise of vegetables."*

Notes:

1. http://btripp-books.livejournal.com/163700.html
2. http://www.chicagonow.com/green-tech-chicago/2014/10/perfect-day/
3. http://en.wikipedia.org/wiki/Fran_Lebowitz
4. http://amzn.to/1JBLFhf
5. http://amzn.to/1JBLFhf
6. http://en.wikipedia.org/wiki/Public_Speaking_%28film%29
7. http://www.nytimes.com/1994/08/10/garden/at-lunch-with-fran-lebowitz-words-are-easy-books-are-not.html

Saturday, January 31, 2015[1]

A remarkable history of modern science ...

It's a vanishingly rare occurrence that I give a "star rating" over on LibraryThing.com, in fact I have rated exactly *six* books out of the 2,186 books I have cataloged over there, all of which got 5 stars "in the heat of the moment" of enthusiasm I had for a particular book. This is the sixth of those.

Frankly, this is somewhat surprising as the book came into my hands as a Library Thing Early Reviewer program "win", and, more often than not, LTER books tend towards the "meh" rather than the "wow". However, Conquering the Electron: The Geniuses, Visionaries, Egomaniacs, and Scoundrels Who Built Our Electronic Age[2] by Derek Cheung and Eric Brach is definitely on the "wow" side of the spectrum, being one of the best "history of science" books I've encountered.

One of the notable things about this was that it was *first published in Chinese* in Taiwan in 2011, with the English translation coming out in late 2014. I don't know how many books make *that* transition, but I'm guessing it's only a few ... although with growing globalization, that may not be the case for long. Given this reality, it is *especially* admirable how seamlessly the book in hand reads ... it's not only informative, but is beautifully executed, a feat that I can only imagine being "Herculean" in moving the material between such divergent languages.

The book is structured in three parts, with 20 chapters between them, and nearly 100 sections on specific subjects (from 3 to 11 sections in the various chapters). While I realize this is seen as something of "a crutch" for writing a review, I think it might be useful to give an over-view of the book by listing the parts and chapters here:

> Part I: Age of Electromagnetism
>   1 - The Knowledge Foundation
>   2 - The Telegraph
>   3 - The Telephone
>   4 - Wireless Telegraphy
>   5 - Lighting and Electrification
> Part II: Age of Vacuum Electronics
>   6 - Current Flow in a Vaccum
>   7 - Controlling the Flow of Electrons
>   8 - Radio
>   9 - Television
>   10 - Radar
>   11 - Computer
> Part III: Age of Solid-State Electronics
>   12 - The Semiconductor

> 13 - The Birth of the Transistor
> 14 - Launching the Electronics Industry
> 15 - The Dawn of Silicon Valley
> 16 - The Integrated Circuit and the Chip
> 17 - Chip Technology Blossoms
> 18 - Evolution of the Electronics Industry
> 19 - LEDs, Fiber Optics, and Liquid Crystal Displays
> 20 - The Information Age and Beyond

As you might imagine, if there are only a handful of individuals profiled in each of those sections (and there are often quite a few), that is a *vast* number of stories … which means that I'm only going to touch on the broad strokes here.

The book starts with a description of the modern smart phone, and pretty much frames the whole as an investigation of "how did we get here?". The first discoveries go back thousands of years, to ancient Greeks finding that rubbing a cloth on a chunk of amber ("elektron") produced what we know as static electricity, and how, some centuries later, another Greek (from Magnesia in Thessaly) discovered a stone which attracted other stones including iron, being thus known as a "magnet". At the same time, similar discoveries were being made in China, producing working compasses. Despite the early awareness of these phenomena, the West had study in them smothered by the Church for over a thousand years, and it only began to flower in the Renaissance … a key figure establishing "the scientific method" was Queen Elizabeth I's Royal Physician, William Gilbert, who in 1600 published extensive research (such as it was at the time) on electricity and magnetism.

Over the next 200 years discovery led to discovery, and advance to advance, with many "familiar names" from the measurement of electrical and magnetic scales and phenomena, including Coulomb, Galvani, Volta, and even Franklin (who didn't, as far as I know, end up lending his name to a gauge, but being on the hundred dollar bill has got to be *some* consolation). In 1800, Volta demonstrated what was to come to be known as the "Voltaic pile" battery. Volta was also one of the key individuals behind the expansion of the knowledge, as he made all his information public, retiring into a cushy position in Napoleon's government … at numerous points in the over-all arc of the story here there are similar "open source" diffusions that boosted the development of new technologies. In Volta's case, within *two years* of his releasing his research there were commercially available batteries based on his initial design.

From that point on, a lot of names roll through the book, Humphry Davy, Hans Oersted, André-Marie Ampère, Michael Faraday, James Clerk Maxwell, Heinrich Hertz, bringing the basic science story up to the late 1800's. At this point the tale shifts to the telegraph, and the first of several "competing technology" stories, this one with Samuel F.B. Morse and Englishman William Cooke. These competitions were not strictly on the systems' technological merits, as the political sphere came in, along with issues of economics. Another notable science name comes into the mix with telegraphs, when the competition was laying cables across the Atlantic ... Professor William Thompson (Lord Kelvin) was instrumental in the successful cable installation, which went live in 1865. At the same time, another familiar name (for the company that's still thriving) was developing telegraph systems in Germany, and eventually Russia ... Werner von Siemens.

There are stories of intellectual property fights, outright corruption in government, and massive egos going head-to-head here, with the likes of Edison popping up in the telegraph arc. However, things really got ugly when the telephone came around ... Elisha Gray and Gardiner Green Hubbard are names not so well known, vs. that of Alexander Graham Bell, but it was Hubbard that pushed Bell to assemble a patent application, which he then *bribed* clerks at the patent office to register a few hours earlier than that of Gray's ... giving Bell precedence, despite his filing being only vague material on the concepts, while Gray's was a substantial work from the Western Union company. Hubbard additionally pushed Bell's patent through the system, getting it approved in a matter of weeks (as opposed to many months or even *years*), and arranging for Bell to have (totally illegal) access to Gray's filing ... aspects of which were immediately incorporated into Bell's demonstration units. So, when you hear of "Bell System", it probably should have been Western Union, with Gray being the poster boy for the telephone!

Wireless telegraphy brings us to Marconi, but that's a prelude to the Radio story. The next big element here is electrical lighting, which, of course, brings in Thomas Edison, with General Electric, and Nikola Tesla, with George Westinghouse, and the great AC/DC battle. Which brings the story up to about 1900.

At this point we hit a phase where the names and stories don't have the recognition factor that their "mythologized" predecessors have, so I'm going to gloss over a lot. However, the book has *fascinating* details of who did what with particular technologies, and how the advancements proceeded. Cathode ray tubes led to x-rays, which led to discoveries about how electrons behaved, leading to the vacuum diode, and the development of the triode, when then led to the basics of radio, TV, and radar ... and eventually to the computer. "Computers" had been around in various forms for centuries (arguably an abacus or slide-rule is a mechanical computer), but starting with the ENIAC this moved to all-electronic systems (if based on highly unreliable tube technology – as many as 18,000 tubes that regularly needed to be replaced). The ENIAC project at Iowa State was, however, another one of those key points,

> *Since {John} Atanasoff was the inventor of the computer but neither he nor Iowa State College had ever followed through in applying for a patent, the courts ruled that the patent rights would be assigned to the public domain. This ruling allowed any individuals or companies to develop computer products without having to worry about basic patent infringement, clearing the path for the rapid growth of the computer industry.*

This, along with the massive cold-war investment that the military was making in basic research, set up the eventual explosion of computer technology.

A similar pattern played out in the early days of "Silicon Valley". Again, there are *many* names involved, both individuals and companies, as chip technologies grew ... but one, William Shockley, seems to be the reason that "Silicon Valley" happened where it did. He had been a major figure at Bell Labs, but had been frustrated by not getting significant paydays for the patents he produced for the company, and opted to eventually (after a brief stint as a professor at CalTech) to form his own company, which he did in his home town of Palo Alto. He tapped a pool of brilliant students in the area, and founded Shockley Semiconductor Laboratory. Unfortunately, although a top-notch engineer, Shockley was an abysmal businessman, and eventually a team of eight key engineers sought to leave the company en mass ... finally entering into a deal with the New York based Fairchild Camera and Instrument company to found Fairchild Semiconductors. After some time, key players began to leave Fairchild to set up their own companies and *"... Fairchild management chose not to litigate against any of these corporate offspring, and this turning of a blind eye served as tacit encouragement for people to go off on their own. ... Maybe it was just that they appreciated the fact that {their previous employers} had never tried to sue them, and they collegially paid this genteel treatment forward."* ... thereby setting the pattern for much of the growth in the industry.

Anyway, Conquering the Electron[3] continues through the development of ever more sophisticated chips and displays, walks through the rise of Asian manufacturing concerns and how they integrated with the growing computer field, and eventually ends up at the now fairly ubiquitous smart phone. All in all, it is a *remarkable* read.

The (English version) of the book just came out last October, so it should still be around in the brick-and-mortar book vendors who have books on science, and the on-line big boys have it at around ¼ off of cover. This is one of my favorite reads of late, and would recommend it to anybody with an interest in Science, history, business, computing, or biography. It's a really impressive book!

Notes:

1. http://btripp-books.livejournal.com/163981.html
2. http://amzn.to/1EG2hTW
3. http://amzn.to/1EG2hTW

Saturday, March 7, 2015[1]

What you talking about?

A number of years ago, I was very pleased to have been queried about writing "a chapter" for a collection of essays that was being pulled together: Age of Conversation 3: It's Time to Get Busy![2] from the team of Drew McLellan and Gavin Heaton (who served as editors for this). As one might guess, this was the third in a series, but it, unfortunately appears to have been the *final* edition, as there was one a year from 2008-2010, but nothing since (and the URL for the series having been hijacked, or so Firefox seems to think, throwing up those warning screens when I've tried to go there of late). There is a "Note from the Editors" up front that indicated that they assembled this as a bit of an afterthought (they felt there was still "something missing" from the previous two), but it seems to me that it might have been a concept that could have had a bit more staying power.

It actually took me a very long time to connect with a copy of this ... contributors didn't get anything for participating, and the cost on the book took a *long* time to drop anywhere significantly lower than its cover price. I had initially figured that this had come out via some print-on-demand press (notorious for not having much leeway for discounts – and no truckloads of cases to dump on the secondary market), but it appears that it came from one of those odd hybrids – a "media communications" firm (PR/Social) that has an integrated publishing arm. Frankly the model isn't a bad one ... they're selling "building a market" for the title even before it comes out, which is a very sensible approach. Anyway, I stuck this on my Amazon wishlist and kept checking until somebody in the new/used vendor offered a copy at what I was willing to pay to get the minor ego boost of seeing my sterling verbiage on a single page of a $19.95 sub-200-page book. It not only took a few years for a copy to rattle through that way, it also sat around for quite a while, as my main interest in having it was my piece, and the other 180-or-so writers', not so much.

It was one of those "almost OOPS" things that got me to read this, as it had somehow *not* come off my Amazon wishlist when I ordered it, and I'd forgotten I had a copy when I came close to ordering it *again*. Fortunately, I had a "*wait a minute ... didn't I see that over in that stack of books over in that other room?*" moment of clarity before pulling the trigger on getting another copy. As an aside ... it's one of the downsides of my LibraryThing.com[3] usage strategy of *not* logging in books that I've not as yet actually *read* - as I will, on rare occasion, not recall having bought something that's whiling away in some to-be-read book stack, and get an extraneous copy. Having discovered that I did, indeed, have Age of Conversation 3[4], I opted to give it a boost to the front of the reading line.

Now, in this series, the editors sought to get a rather wide range of material, including voices from all over the globe. As you might suspect, this resulted in a somewhat uneven mix. It's been a while, but I seem to recall that they gave us a target word count (I could have probably gone about 30% longer given the way it lays out on the page, but I think I wrote it to right at the suggested length), and asked us to pick a general topic from a list of several. I don't know if these were specifically those of the section headings, but these, under (I suppose) the general rubric of the sub-title of "It's Time to Get Busy!", are as follows:

> At the Coalface
> Identities, Friends and Trusted Strangers
> Conversational Branding
> Measurement
> Corporate Conversations
> In the Boardroom
> Innovation and Execution
> Influence
> Getting to Work
> Pitching Social Media

My piece, entitled "Who Are You?" appears in the second section, and dealt with on-line identities, informed by my long involvement on BBSs, IRC, AOL Chat Rooms, the LiveJournal heyday (where I had a good half-dozen "sock puppet" accounts with their own personalities for saying the nasty stuff), and on into the much more transparent on-line identities demanded by the big dog platforms of social at present.

While I've not counted, I seem to recall reading somewhere that there are 180 pieces arrayed within those 10 topics ... so there's a lot of "stuff" here, and no real "theme" aside from the general thrusts of the sections. I ended up dropping in little book markers as I read this, so I'm going to give you something of a "random sampling" of things that snagged my attention as I was going through the book.

The first tag that I have in here is also in the "Identities" section, in a piece by Emily Reed entitled "Interesting Is the New Bland" ... where she looks at the balance of TMI and blandness, framed in the context of a trip through Europe with a new boyfriend – when she learned that his *parents* were going to be reading the intended-to-be "tell all" blog she'd envisioned ... *"I made the mistake that many brands make – I went generic; I went boring."* She further sorts out the approaches of "writing" vs. "dinner party chat", one being fearless, the other, more restrained.

> *But the bloggers and Twitterers and brands that I love do push the comfort zone. They say things that are surprising and controversial and personal. They apply the basics of good writing to the genre.*
>
> *So I'm forever bouncing in my mind between asking myself, "is this good, interesting writing?" and "Would I be embarrassed if my clients or in-laws were reading this in front of me right now?" If the answer is "yes" to the first question, I move to the second. If the answer to the second is "yes," I hit the "save as draft" button and wait a day. Ninety*

> percent of the time, I've gotten over myself enough to remember that, as long as I remember the public-ness, being part of the conversation is also about entertaining my fellow dinner guests."

The next bit that caught my attention was "The Dual Life of the Flaneur" by (oddly enough) one of the series' editors, Gavin Heaton. I found it very interesting that he didn't name-check Nassim Nicholas Taleb in this, as it's been in <u>Taleb's writing</u>[5] that I, and many others, first encountered the concept of the <u>Flâneur</u>[6], although he does quote Baudelaire, so perhaps he's sourcing the concept closer to the root. I found the following notable in Heaton's piece:

> The transition we have seen over the last decade on the web, from static or even database driven content to social, pluralistic, real time conversations is marked not by its wavelength but by its amplitude. The digital flaneur is not interested in the spread of ideas but in their relevance. She seeks not the voices of many but the conversations of the passionate. This journey carries its destination in the heart of its interactions not in its logical end point.

Another piece (in the "Measurement" section) that I found fascinating was by New Zealander Phil Osborne, whose "The DANGER of Measurement" looks at "metricfication", "efficiencies", the turn-offs of the "managed relationships" inherent in CRM systems, etc. He wanders between examples of business procedures and his worries, and I'm going to be cherry-picking a bit in the following to focus on his main point:

> ... the existence of metrics does not change the basis of my concern. If the purpose of measuring is ultimately control, then there is a significant consequence that must be considered before adopting any metric (or measurement program). ... [are we] seeking to manage conversations and social interaction? The fate of that has been revealed already (<u>Cluetrain Manifesto</u> anyone?). Be afraid, because I for one worry that metricfication, as currently practiced, has a limited place in a post industrial economy in which the hegemony of production is being supplanted by collaboration, co-creation and customer centricity. ... Social media can easily go the same way as CRM. Be careful what you wish for.

The next is a very short piece, in the "Innovation and Execution" section, by Mark McGuinness, set up almost like a prose poem, called "New Media, Same Difference" ... rather than re-type the whole thing here, I'm snagging 3 lines:

> There has never been such a wealth of new creations – and never such a volume of crap.

> ...
> As always, the one who succeed will be the ones who resolve this creative tension.
> The ones making the remarkable things, not churning out "content".

This certainly echoes the words of Godin, Brogan, and Stratten ... where it's not about the tools, but about producing the remarkable.

Finally, from the "Influence" section, there is "The Influence of Not Being Influenced" by Amy Jussel, where she (from a non-profit's perspective), states:

> With an increasingly exhausted public struggling to sift "what is real" in everything from reality shows to product placement (savvy consumers know buzz can be bought, viral can be "seeded" and vested interests can permeate citizen journalism as well as mainstream media) the open ended question we're all trying to grapple with is, "How do you monetize influence in a trust-based economy?"
>
> I won't use the hackneyed "a" word (authenticity) or even "b" words (brand-building) even though both are essential in earning trust via reputation. I'm going to hang my hat on the "c" words of creating credibility through content while curating a conversation that adds value to the readers without the perception of asking for something in return.
>
> ...
>
> Influence is not a commodity to be brokered, but rather an intimacy to be earned.

Again, there are a lot of voices in Age of Conversation 3[7], addressing a lot of topics. Some parts are fascinating, some parts are pretty dull, but if the above sounds of interest, you might consider picking up a copy. This is available via the on-line big boys for full retail (making me suspect that its publisher is basically a print-on-demand service), but copies have started to filter down into the used channel ... at about a third of cover. And, hey, you never get tired of reading *my* stuff, and there's some different type of my scribblings in there!

Notes:

1. http://btripp-books.livejournal.com/164100.html
2. http://amzn.to/1xQkWIj
3. http://btripp-books.com/
4. http://amzn.to/1xQkWIj
5. http://btripp-books.livejournal.com/141931.html
6. https://en.wikipedia.org/wiki/Flâneur

7. http://amzn.to/1xQkWIj

Sunday, March 8, 2015[1]

Towards a "Protopia" ...

I know that I frequently grumble about the quality of books coming out from the LibaryThing.com "Early Reviewers" program, but this was another really great one, expansive (it's about 500 pages), strenuously researched (there are over 50 pages of small-type notes at the end), and seemingly effortlessly describing an eventually-inspiring story arc across a dozen main subjects. Author Michael Shermer is a founder of *Skeptic* magazine, a regular columnist for *Scientific American*, and has a dozen other science books on his resume. The Moral Arc: How Science and Reason Lead Humanity toward Truth, Justice, and Freedom[2], while grounded in science, is more a book on history and philosophy, asking the "why" questions on top of a basis of "how" analysis. What's the book about? Well, the subtitle pretty much sketches the intent, but I found this snippet from the Prologue a good window on the whole:

> ... we are living in the most moral period in our species' history
>
> ...
>
> For tens of millennia moral *regress* best described our species, and hundreds of millions of people suffered as a result. But then something happened half a millennium ago. The Scientific Revolution led to the Age of Reason and the Enlightenment, and that changed everything. As a result, we ought to understand what happened, how and why these changes reversed our species' historical trend downward, and that we can do more to elevate humanity, extend the arc, and bend it ever upward.

Because there is *so much* in here, I'm going to fall back on the crutch of replicating the ToC below ... as this will give you the general outline of the book, making it easier for me to touch on highpoints without necessarily having to backfill in all the context ...

> Part I: The Moral Arc Explained
> 1. Toward a Science of Morality
> 2. The Morality of War, Terror, and Deterrence
> 3. Why Science and Reason Are the Drivers of Moral Progress
> 4. Why Religion Is Not the Source of Moral Progress
>
> Part II: The Moral Arc Applied
> 5. Slavery and a Moral Science of Freedom Rights
> 6. A Moral Science of Women's Rights

> 7. A Moral Science of Gay Rights
> 8. A Moral Science of Animal Rights
>
> Part III: The Moral Arc Amended
> 9. Moral Regress and Pathways to Evil
> 10. Moral Freedom and Responsibility
> 11. Moral Justice: Retribution and Restoration
> 12. Protopia: The Future of Moral Progress

Early on here Shermer establishes some baselines, citing research on other social apes, and young children of various ages ... discussing *"our multifaceted moral nature that evolved to solve several problems at once in our ancestral environment – be nice to those who help us and our kin and kind, punish those who hurt"*, and detailing experiments that suggest:

> ... the moral sense of right (...) and wrong (...) emerges as early as three to ten months of age – far too early to attribute to learning and culture. Young children who are exposed in a laboratory to an adult experiencing pain ... typically respond by soothing the injured party. Toddlers who see adults struggling to open a door ... or to pick up an out-of-reach object, will spontaneously help without any prompting from the adults in question.

An interesting point connected to some of this research is how much the child learns in the womb – studies with newborns show pronounced preferences not only for their mothers' voices, but in general for the *language* spoken by their parents.

In the chapter dealing with issues of War, etc., there is a 10-point (several page) section called a "Path to Nuclear Zero", which includes this interesting bit on the concept of taboo:

> The psychology behind the taboo against chemical and biological weapons transfers readily to that of nuclear weapons. Deadly heat and radiation – like poison gas and lethal diseases – are invisible killers that are indiscriminate in the carnage they wreak. ... the revulsion people feel towards nuclear weapons may be linked in the brain to the emotion of disgust that psychologists have identified as being associated with invisible disease contagions, toxic poisons, and revolting materials ... that carry them – reactions that evolved to direct organisms away from these substances for survival reasons.

Of course, it is one thing to negotiate with Russia or China, and a completely different thing to be faced with non-rational states or movements who may obtain nuclear weapons. MAD – Mutual Assured Destruction – worked for decades (thankfully), but it *"does not make nuclear war impossible, but simply renders it irrational" ...*

> *But if your religion has convinced you that you're not really going to die, and that the next life is spectacularly better than this life, and that you'll be a hero among those you've left behind – it changes the calculation."*

Again, the challenge in giving a perspective on the book is that there is SO much stuff in there ... I'm skipping over a lot of fundamental material, and trying to point to things that seemed highlights to me. Here's a key bit from the early parts of the Science chapter:

> *From an intellectual history perspective, I have described this shift [the move to a "Science of Man"] as the "battle of the books" - the book of authority vs. the book of nature. The <u>book of authority</u> – whether it was the Bible or Aristotle in the Western world – is grounded in the cognitive process called <u>deduction</u>, or making specific claims from generalized principles ... by contrast, the <u>book of nature</u> is grounded in <u>induction</u>, or the cognitive process of drawing generalized principles from specific facts ...*

Fast-forward to the American revolution, and you have these *scientific* approaches applied to matters of state:

> *Many of the founding fathers were, in fact, scientists who deliberately adapted the method of data gathering, hypothesis testing, and theory formulation to their nation building. Their understanding of the provisional nature of findings led them to develop a social system in which doubt and dispute were the centerpieces of a functional polity. Jefferson, Franklin, Paine, and the others thought of social governance as a <u>problem to be solved</u> rather than as power to be grabbed. They thought of democracy in the same way that they thought of science – as a method, not an ideology.*

The benefits of the scientific approach should be obvious, but here's a great quote for our current world situation:

> *The hypothesis that reason-based Enlightenment thinking leads to moral progress is one that can be tested through historical comparison and by examining what happens to countries that hold anti-Enlightenment values. Countries that quash free inquiry, distrust reason, and practice pseudoscience, such as Revolutionary France, Nazi Germany, Stalinist Russia, Maoist China, and, more recently, fundamentalist Islamic states, stagnate, regress, and often collapse. Theists and postmodernist critics of science and reason often label the dis-*

> astrous Soviet and Nazi utopias as "scientific", but their science was a thin patina covering a deep layer of counter-Enlightenment, pastoral, paradisiacal fantasies of racial ideology grounded in ethnicity and geography ...

Of course, even in modern democracies, there are deep divides, and Shermer details several takes on this:

> The left-right divide also depends heavily on the vision of human nature that you hold – as either <u>constrained</u> (right-wing) or <u>unconstrained</u> (left-wing) ... or as <u>utopian</u> (left-wing) or <u>tragic</u> (right-wing) ... Left-wingers lean towards believing that human nature is largely unconstrained by biology, and thus utopian-like social engineering schemes to overcome poverty, unemployment, and other social ills are appealing in their logic and feasibility. Right-wingers lean toward believing that human nature is largely constrained by biology and thus social, political, and economic policies must necessarily be limited in their scope and ambition.

In the "Religion" chapter there's an interesting "Deconstructing the Decalogue" section, where the author picks apart the Ten Commandments, on the basis that *"they were written by and for people whose culture and customs were so different from ours as to make them either irrelevant to modern peoples or immoral were they to be obeyed."* ... such as #2 inspiring acts of cultural savagery by the Taliban (as noted here), or more recently by the thugs of ISIL. From an Enlightenment perspective, most of the Commandments are pretty monstrous, and Shermer suggests a "Provisional Rational Decalogue", based on generally-aspired to principles of the civilized world.

The middle section, on specific rights movements is interesting, full of fascinating research, but not full of particularly quote-worthy bits. The chapter on Animal rights stands out, however, in that it raises the subject to nearly the same plane as dealing with slavery, women, and gays. Much of that chapter is both grim and difficult ... as we, as a species, are deeply "speciesist" and have millennia of cultural acclimation to eating, wearing, and working animals. However, the research outlined in this chapter makes one pause about how animals, especially "higher" animals, are treated worldwide. The author cites a striking piece of legislation in India which suggests that dolphins should be considered "nonhuman *persons*" – a classification change that could make radical shifts in our species' view of others.

This leads (somewhat unsubtly) to the chapter on "Evil", which starts out looking at the infamous Milgram experiments (and similar studies on obedience, including ones the author developed for a reality TV show), and then a deep look into the Nazis, from Eichmann on down ... delving into very disturbing psychological territory ... the process is sketched out as:

> ... these factors are interactive and autocatalytic – that is, they feed on one another: <u>dehumanization</u> produces <u>deindividuation</u>, which then leads to <u>com-

pliance under the influence of <u>obedience to authority</u>, and in time that morphs into <u>conformity</u> to new group norms, and <u>identification</u> with the group, which leads to the actual performance of evil acts. No one of these components inexorably leads to evil acts, but together they form the machinery of evil that arises under certain social conditions.

The final chapter has an odd theme – "Protopia" – which the author notes "A better descriptor than <u>utopia</u> for what we ought to strive for is <u>protopia</u> – a place where progress is steadfast and measured ... the general principle is relatively simple: try to make the world a slightly better place tomorrow than yesterday." One of the things that's covered here is the idea of a return to "city-states" as the main level of governmental organization ... where Mayors would be the big dogs, and things would be run, not by *bureaucracies* but by (another odd word – this one from Alvin Toffler) "*adhocracies*" – organizations "*premised on innovation and real-time problem solving in response to dynamic and ever-changing environments that require unique solutions to new problems ... decentralized and highly organic, horizontal instead of hierarchical in nature, and ... engages in creative effort to find a novel solution ...*". An example given is that NASA in the 1960's was an adhocracy, but by the 1990's, it had become just another bureaucracy.

In this section there is a lot of name dropping of people on the cutting edge of pretty much everything, and how these innovators' projects may play out. One piece of information that I found amusing was the "data curve" that most people are at least generally familiar with:

> ... from the earliest stirrings of civilization 10,000 years ago to the year 2003, all of humankind created a grand total of about 5 exabytes of digital information [1 exabyte = 1 billion gigabytes] ... from 2003 through 2010 humans created 5 exabytes of digital information <u>every 2 days</u>. By 2013 we were producing 5 exabytes <u>every 10 minutes</u>. ... Make all that digital knowledge available to every person on the planet instantly through the Internet, and ideally all citizens of the world can become citizen-scientists capable of reasoning their way to solving personal, social, and moral problems.

<u>The Moral Arc</u>[3] just came out in January, so it should be available at surviving brick-and-mortar book vendors who carry science books, but the on-line big boys have it for about a quarter off the cover price. This is *not* an "easy" read, as there's a lot of material here (some of it quite challenging), but it is a *fascinating* read, and is ultimately hopeful on a lot of levels ... worth the time to work your way through it.

Notes:

http://btripp-books.livejournal.com/164622.html

http://amzn.to/1uyGVSw
http://amzn.to/1uyGVSw

Sunday, March 22, 2015

An "exponential entrepreneur's" manual for "going big" ...

As long-term readers might recall, I was (am) a great fan of Peter Diamandis' previous book Abundance, which is a remarkable rallying cry for a positive futurism, featuring a lot of "gee wiz!" technologies that are supposedly just around the corner. When I requested a review copy of his new book from the good folks over at Simon & Schuster, I was sort of anticipating (and/or hoping for) an *Abundance II*, but this is focused in a different direction. Bold: How to Go Big, Create Wealth and Impact the World is a more "grounded" book, being (as one might get from the subtitle) a bit of a "how to" based both in trends the author has identified and his own experiences.

Bold is structured in 3 sections, "Bold Technology", "Bold Mindset", and "The Bold Crowd", and much of it is predicated on the concept of exponential growth and becoming an "exponential entrepreneur". In fact, it starts with one of the sadder stories of recent corporate evolution/devolution, that of Kodak. While Kodak invented the digital camera, in 1976 (with the digital info for the images being saved on cassette – with a capacity of 30 images, deliberately set in the middle of the range of their film products at 24 and 36) there was no place in the corporate culture for it, which asked things like *Why would anybody want to look at pictures on an electronic screen?*. Diamandis notes that 20 years later, in 1996, Kodak was all but a monopoly, with 90% of the market and worth 28 billion dollars, yet in another decade they were no longer profitable and by 2012 they were in Chapter 11. Interestingly, it was also in 2012 that Instagram released its Android app, went from 30 to 80 million users in little over a month, and were bought by Facebook.

> *Welcome to the New Kodak Moment – the moment when an exponential force puts a linear company out of business. As we shall see over and over again, these New Kodak Moments are not aberrations. Rather they are the inevitable result of the six Ds of exponential growth. And for those linear-thinking executives trying to hang on to their jobs, this leads us to the three final Ds: distraught, depressed, and departed. But for exponential entrepreneurs, these New Kodak Moments are rife with possibility.*

OK, so you're wondering what those "six Ds" he mentions are ...

1. Digitalization
2. Deception
3. Disruption
4. Demonetization
5. Dematerialization
6. Democratization

Now, the first of these is pretty self-explanatory, something that had been only physical, becomes digital ... the second, however, is less obvious: this "deception" phase is when exponential growth goes unnoticed because *"the doubling of small numbers are so minuscule they are often mistaken for ... linear growth"*. In the case of Kodak's digital camera with an initial resolution of only 0.01 megapixels, going to 0.02 then to 0.04 and to 0.08 all still look an awful lot like "zero", but if their growth continues, it's not long before the technology has made a *"billionfold improvement"*, at which point "disruption" of the industry in question is almost certainly under way. There's an interesting chart in here which plots "all photos" against "analog photos", and, naturally enough, the curves match from 1826 to about 1990, and there's only a little separation around 2000, with 86 billion photos being taken, however, at that point the "all" curve surges, and the "analog" curve tanks, with 380 billion photos taken in 2011, with only one or two billion of those being analog.

I well recall the days when, if I was going on vacation, I'd have to pre-plan to get enough film to shoot when I was off climbing Mayan ruins, etc. ... what was a *major* expense back in the day (between buying the film and then having it developed), today would involve picking up a few tiny chips that would hold hundreds, if not thousands, times the images I used to budget for. This is the "demonetization" phase of the exponential model, where things which once had a physical presence and were reasonably expensive, now were nearly, if not actually, free. The entertainment and publishing industries have certainly faced this

Another chart illustrates the "dematerialization" phase, which suggests that a modern smart phone encompasses a dozen technologies which used to require a separate device ... which all would have totaled somewhere around $900,000.00 if bought when introduced. Needless to say, this "when introduced" figure seriously inflates the costs, as a GPS system, when introduced in 1982, cost $119,900.00, which is then interpreted to $279,366.00 in "2011 dollars" (making up nearly a third of the total), when a free-standing GPS system could be had currently for under a hundred bucks ... but the general point is that the smart phone "has in it" a digital watch, a video camera, an encyclopedia, etc., none of which one would "need" to physically have anymore.

The final D, "democratization" addresses the drive to ubiquity of technology such as smart phones ... while high-end phones can be pricey, there are also "name" units (like some of Microsoft's new Lumina models) which have *list prices* as low as seventy bucks ... this means that soon everybody can have the technology.

So much for the *first chapter*. Diamandis goes on to look at the "hype cycle", how 3D printing is effecting numerous industries, how communicating sensors are reaching into everything, and how the connectivity of the Internet is exploding in both access (with major players competing to develop global free service) and bandwidth/speed (a replacement for 4G is being phased in that is 6-7x the current standard). He projects that in a few years (2020) a chip that runs your cellphone and can perform a billion calculations per second will cost about a penny – leading to what he calls "infinite computing". He quotes Rackspace's Graham Weston saying: *"Today the computation speed that somebody in the middle of Mumbai has access to outstrips what the entire US government had during the sixties and seventies."*, and entrepreneurs don't even need to have the infrastructure, as the computing resources can be used "as needed" from cloud providers. He covers Artificial Intelligence and the strides being made there, as well as related developments in Robotics, and "Genomics and Synthetic Biology".

The second section is a whirlwind of examples of "doing" on a developmental level, from Lockheed's "Skunk Works" – and Kelly Johnson's "fourteen rules for going skunk" – to permutations on that across various other industries and contexts. An interesting example provided is that of Google's "moonshot factory", GoogleX, which sets audacious goals, and churns through concepts, letting most of them fail. There is also a list of "eight innovation principles":

1. Focus on the User.
2. Share Everything.
3. Look for Ideas Everywhere.
4. Think Big but Start Small.
5. Never Fail to Fail.
6. Spark with Imagination, Fuel with Data
7. Be a Platform.
8. Have a Mission That Matters.

Diamandis then takes an extensive look at the concept of "flow" (as popularized by Mihaly Csikszentmihalyi[4]) which is framed as *"an optimal state of consciousness where we feel our best and perform our best ...when we become so focused on the task at hand that everything else falls away"* here, and goes point-for-point through "flow's 17 triggers" (more than I can summarize).

Next is "going big", introducing the concept of "the line of super-credibility", and many examples from the author's own projects ... including a list of his 28 "laws". The last chapter in the second section is "Billionaire Wisdom", and looks at the careers of four top-tier innovators: Elon Musk, Richard Branson, Jeff Bezos, and Larry Page (all of whom the author has worked with in various contexts). One thing I found fascinating here was that Musk had built a multi-billion dollar business, lost it all, and built back into the ranks of billionaires … and he's only just in his 40's!

This brings us to the third section, and second half, of the book, "The Bold Crowd". As engaging as the first half was, I suspect that this part is what is going to sell most copies of Bold, as it's an in-depth and reasonably step-by-step look at Crowdsourcing, Crowdfunding, and Building Communities, followed with a specific look at Incentive Competitions – a specialty of Diamandis, whose X Prize challenges have become legendary (interestingly, this sort of thing has a long history, Lindberg crossed the Atlantic to win the Orteig Prize, and as early as 1714 innovations were being seeded this way, with the British Parliament establishing the Longitude Prize for the first person to measure longitude at sea). This section is so dense, so full of details and "how to" info, that I can't begin to cherry-pick meaningful bits to put in here. Suffice it to say, it's a concise "course" on how to achieve remarkable goals using a whole brand-new infrastructure of platforms and systems that are currently available, and no doubt well worth the cover price of the book to those who are looking to make moves in those realms (I'm handing my copy of this over in the next couple of days to an associate who's about to launch a crowdfunding effort!).

Bold[5] is brand-new, just being out a month as I'm writing this, so it should be pretty easy to find in the ever-dwindling brick-and-mortar book world … the on-line guys, of course, have it, and are currently knocking off about a quarter of the cover price. While based on the sort of futurism that was so enticing in *Abundance*, this is its own critter, with a couple of sections of context, and then the pay-off of the "manual" … if you have interests in any of the stuff noted above, you'll want to get a copy.

Notes:

http://btripp-books.livejournal.com/165005.html

http://btripp-books.livejournal.com/128282.html

http://amzn.to/1JWXqV5

http://btripp-books.livejournal.com/25086.html

http://amzn.to/1JWXqV5

Friday, March 27, 2015[1]

The only thing we have to sphere is sphere itself?

One of the fathers of the whole "2012" thing, José Argüelles, has been on my radar for a long time, but I wonder how much he's known by the "general public". I recently picked up a copy of his Manifesto for the Noosphere: The Next Stage in the Evolution of Human Consciousness[2] which came out in September 2011, six months posthumously (and a year prior to the 12/21/2012 "end date"). I am sure I would have *loved* this back in the 1980's when his *The Mayan Factor* and *Earth Ascending* came out (heck, he was instrumental in popularizing the "Harmonic Convergence" in 1987, which found me down at Tulum in the Yucatan with a merry band of shamans and Zen practitioners) ... however, at this point it's almost embarrassing, and one is tempted to feel that it was a blessing for him to die prior to all his predictions falling flat.

It was Argüelles' work that inspired Terrance McKenna to develop his "Timewave Zero" stuff (after coupling the Mayan calendar round to the progressions of the I Ching), which is a very deep rabbit-hole, probably best appreciated by those experimenting with DMT.

This book is not significantly more grounded than that, although it has some very interesting info on calendar systems in general ... albeit with Argüelles blaming the ills of the modern world in no small part to the (admittedly) unnatural restrictions of the Gregorian calendar and our time cycles (the "unconscious timing frequency" of 12:60 versus the "universal synchronization" frequency of 13:20).

So, what *is* this "Noosphere"? (BTW, it's pronounced[3] pretty close to "*Noah's Fear*")

> Just as the biosphere is the unified field of life and its support systems ... so the noosphere is the unified field of the mind, the psychic reflection of the biosphere."

and, further ...

> The conscious activation of the Noosphere is the next stage in the evolution of life on Earth, bringing with it a truly planetary consciousness. This transition to the Noosphere is the most significant change since the appearance of abundant complex life on Earth at the end of the Precambrian period some five hundred million years ago.

Argüelles was obsessed with Pacal Votan, the Mayan ruler whose (now famous) tomb was discovered buried deep within the Pyramid of Inscriptions at Palenque. By his calculations, the tomb was opened (in 1952) exactly 1,260 years (oh, that dang 12:60 ratio) after the burial. I'm not particularly good at "following along" with these sorts of numerical coincidents and so he largely lost me at this point as far as that goes. The book also features diagrams of systems involving the Earth, overlaying "mystical" realities on physical realities and positing assorted levels such as the Noosphere – Circulating Thought Belt, and the Theosphere – Primal Self-Existing God Source ... "your mileage may vary" on these sorts of things, but I have a hard time taking them seriously, as they're filled with so much "wishful thinking" elements and so little solid establishing factors.

One thing he discusses here that I found notable, however, was the "Cybersphere" and the "Technosphere", which reminded me very much of *other* theories, such as that of "The Singularity" (which I suspect is a lot more reality-based than Argüelles'). It would be ironic if he had gotten *that* part right (if in dismissing it as a transitory stage).

> *By the end of 2010, some 5.2 billion mobile phones were in operation. Probably no other technology in human history has attracted the attention of the individual human being, nor transformed so immediately the nature of his/her self-perception. The mobile phone personalizes the present moment into a synchronistic medium of instantaneous ego gratification. ... Through this technology and its attendant social networks, each person finds his or her individual world compressed into an electronic instrument the size of the palm of the hand. This is the technological analogy or precursor of the noospheric concept of psychic compression and interiorization. ... This new threshold of technological innovations also desensitizes and abstracts the individual from the surrounding world. It is the supreme "subjectivization of consciousness", where each being becomes surrounded in his/her own electro-ego bubble, virtually unaware of the world around them, much less the plain fact that the biosphere is necessary to sustain them.*

He goes on quite a bit on how the Noosphere is an "ego-free state" (full of flowers, rainbows, and unicorn farts ... or similar) so the Technosphere/Cybersphere is something to be quickly dashed through.

Interestingly, the Noosphere concept is *taken seriously* in a number of settings ... the Russians, it appear, consider it *science* and have conferences and institutions devoted to its "study" ... apparently based on the writings of Soviet geochemist Vladimir I Vernadsky. The concept (and name) itself comes from Jesuit writer Pierre Teilhard de Chardin, whose works on the subject were suppressed by the Church until after his death in 1955, and was continued by Vernadsky and what Argüelles describes as "little-known" philosophers Edouard Le Roy and Oliver Reiser. Reiser's synthesis of these concepts supposedly even influenced Carl Jung and Buckminster Fuller (although I have a sneaking suspicion that the author was largely "name checking" Fuller to point out that he had had a few phone conversations with the famed thinker), and on to the likes of Lovelock and Sheldrake.

If you're looking for *real* "woo-woo", here are how he defines "The Four Types or Stages of Cosmic Civilization":

> I. Planetary-cosmic – Psycho-technical unification
>
> II. Helio-cosmic (stellar) - "New Solar Age"
>
>> {featuring the "Emergence of <u>Homo noosphericus</u> as a biosolar telepathic being ("biosolar" refers to a biological being that is consciously activated by higher solar frequencies).}
>
> III. Galacto-cosmic – omnigalactic Supermind
>
> IV. Omnicosmic – metagalactic

Needless to say, the *evidence* for any of this is slim to delusional, and largely comprised of intricate diagrams whose "proof" appears to be slapping on labels such as "Projecting Lens of the Boundless Universal Self" or "Holographic Perceptions" at various points.

Argüelles also puts a lot of faith into "Synchronized Communities", where *"synchronized telepathic meditations based on the 13-moon calendar and the synchronic codes of the Laws of Time"* (coordinated, I'm assuming, by the Western 12:60 clock) are supposed to "manifest a true living harmonic rainbow message" and untie "the six astral knots".

Now, I'm probably a bit more cynical about this stuff than most would be ... as back in the 80's I was chasing after it, from the aforementioned Harmonic Convergence, to the StarLink event in 1988 (organized by "angel walk-ins", and held in the Los Angeles Coliseum - which seats over 90k, but drew less than 2,000), and the likewise ill-fated "World Unity Festival" in 1994. The things the author is hitching his wagon to here are in the same vein, based on a few dozen (hundred?) hippie wannabes looking to transform the world with (synchronized) happy thoughts. As noted, it was probably for the best that he died before the (hard-and-fast) timeline for his vision slipped away with nothing of note coming from it.

Anyway, Manifesto for the Noosphere is still in print, and can be had at the on-line big boys for under ten bucks, but I just noticed that a .pdf version of it is available out there as well (from various sources, the reliability of which I can't vouch for). There is a certain type that will *love* this book (me, 25 years ago, for instance), and other types who would throw it across the room after a few pages as "delusional twaddle" ... I'll leave it up to your self-analysis where you fall on that spectrum. At least it's out there for free if you do want to check it out.

Notes:

http://btripp-books.livejournal.com/165201.html

http://amzn.to/1C9zeKl

http://wordsmith.org/words/noosphere.mp3

http://amzn.to/1C9zeKl

Saturday, April 4, 2015[1]

A look under the rocks ...

This is a scary book. Even more so than a "horror" title, as it's delving into corners of reality where the public narrative gets warped, and how easily said narrative is manipulated. Ryan Holiday's Trust Me, I'm Lying: Confessions of a Media Manipulator[2] came to my reading pile through a somewhat convoluted path ... it had initially been brought to my attention at a Social Media Club of Chicago event where Gini Dietrich, principal of the Arment Dietrich agency (and author, previously reviewed here[3] and here[4]), used it as a key point of a presentation ... highly recommending it, in fact. This became odd when I got into the book, as she had apparently written a blog post *slamming* it, and earned herself a footnote in this paperback edition for her claiming the book was *"hurting an entire industry"*. Of course, she was addressing a room full of marketers, and maybe she felt this was important information for us to get.

Frankly, this book brings to mind the famed (and variously re-formulated and mis-attributed) quote about "laws and sausage" ... in that the less you know of their making the more you like/trust them. The author here was a hot-shot edgy marketer who figured out ways to totally "play" the media, and especially the "blogosphere". Holiday worked the trenches ... buying billboards, only to later deface them, with the interest of creating a story of how much people hated his client and/or product – in order to create buzz and seed subsequent coverage. More centrally, he discovered that he could feed stories into "low level" blogs that were frequently picked up by "higher level" blogs, which were eventually picked up by substantial news vehicles ... none of which would ever vet the information being fed them! And, bizarrely, it wasn't just "manipulators" like himself that were creating false stories, even major outlets like *Politico* would create stories from *nothing*, assigning resources to cover non-existent campaigns only so they could generate endless fabrications, all simply to generate clicks and ad revenue.

> *The economics of the Internet created a twisted set of incentives that make traffic more important – and more profitable – than the truth. With the mass media – and today, mass culture – relying on the web for the next big thing, it is a set of incentives with massive implications. ... Blogs need traffic, being first drives traffic, and so entire stories are created out of whole cloth to make that happen.*

Call me naïve, but I always wondered why so many things I'd click on in Facebook ended up in total-waste-of-time sites/stories which not only didn't provide the info that I was looking for when I clicked, but spread the info that *was* there over page after page after page ... it was those clicks and page views that were the point ... the story was only a lure to get my mouse involved. Doh!

As scary as the revelations of how little quality control there is out there are, what's really scary here is that this book is a virtual *manual* for "how to manipulate the system". Holiday walks the reader through project after project where his efforts (and sometimes a small amount of cash) managed to create stories about stuff that was purely the fruit of his imagination … but were getting exposure in the highest tiers of the media pyramid. This starts at the level of small "hyperlocal" web sites (this is where he targeted the aforementioned billboard vandalism) … he notes:

> *What's important is that the site is small and understaffed. This makes it possible to sell them a story that is only loosely connected to their core message but really sets you up to transition to the next level.*

The next level is what he calls "the legacy media", the web components of major media, the newspapers, the TV stations, the major magazines.

> *Legacy media outlets are critical turning points in building up momentum. The reality is that the bloggers at Forbes.com or the <u>Chicago Tribune</u> do not operate on the same editorial guidelines as their print counterparts. However, their final output can be made to look like they carry the same weight.*

He gives an example of getting a useable quote out of a site like Wired.com which you could then re-purpose for what looks like a major endorsement on your product packaging, appearing as if you'd scored a cover story in the magazine. But these vehicles, too, are simply stepping stones:

> *The sites that have already taken your bait are now on your side. They desperately want their articles to get as much traffic as possible, and being linked to or mentioned on national sites is how they do that. These sites will take care of submitting your articles to news aggregator sites like Digg, because making the front page will drive tens of thousands of visitors to their article. Mass media reporters monitor aggregators for story ideas, and often cover what is trending there … In today's world even these guys have to think like bloggers – they need to get as many pageviews as possible. … You just want to make sure that such reporters notice the story's gaining traction. Take the outlet where you'd ultimately like to receive coverage and observe it for patterns. You'll notice that they tend to get their story ideas from the same second-level sites, and by tailoring the story to those smaller sites (or site), it sets you up to be noticed by the larger one.*

Even more surprising, he notes that sometimes you just have to target smaller groups, if they're being read by the "right people":

> *Katie Couric claims she gets many story ideas from*

> her Twitter followers, which means that getting a few tweets out of the seven hundred or so people she follows is all it takes to get a shot at the nightly network news.

The bulk of the first half of the book is Holiday going through 9 specific "tactics" in substantial detail. Here's how he sums up the "help pay their bills" (tactic #1) chapter:

> In the pay-per-pageview model, every post is a conflict of interest. It's why I've never bought influence directly. <u>I've never had to.</u> Bloggers have a direct incentive to write bigger, to write simpler, to write more controversially or, conversely, more favorably, to write without having to do any work, to write more often than is warranted. Their paycheck depends on it. It's no wonder they are vicious, irresponsible, inaccurate, and dishonest. ... They call it a "digital sweatshop" for good reason.

In the "give them what spreads" chapter (tactic #3), he has seemingly contradictory advice, on one hand:

> ... "if something is a total bummer, people don't share it". And since people wouldn't share it, blogs won't publish it.

Yet, on the other hand:

> According to {a Wharton School} study, "the most powerful predictor of virality is how much anger an article evokes" ... The most powerful predictor of what spreads online is anger.

He notes that *positive* stories are also good, but the strength of *feeling* that they spur is the key indicator (although these need to be things that people want to *share*, sadness, for instance, doesn't get much traction). Of course, this means that "rational" materials don't stand much of a chance of going viral.

> Navigating this quandary forces marketers and publishers to conspire to distort this information into something that will register on the emotional spectrum of the audience. To turn it into something that spreads and to drive clicks. ... The press is in the evil position of needing to go negative and play tricks with your psyche in order to drive you to share their material on-line ... the kind of stuff that will make you hit "share this". They push your buttons so you'll press theirs.

He goes into some detail about why it's sometimes frustratingly difficult to get to the point of being able to comment on some blogs ... "The site

> doesn't care about your opinion; it cares that, by eliciting it, they score free pageviews."

> > A click is a click and a pageview is a pageview. A blogger doesn't care how they get it. Their bosses don't care. They just want it.

Trust Me, I'm Lying[5] is split into two "books", the first being "Feeding The Monster – How Blogs Work", and the second "The Monster Attacks – What Blogs Mean". All of the above is from the first part, where Holiday goes into the nitty gritty of the blogosphere, but the second evolves from his "repentance" (to a certain extent), when he began to see how dangerous and out-of-control the system has become. The final twelve chapters are a point-by-point listing of bad situations brought on by the sort of manipulations detailed in the first twelve chapters, with subjects such as the "Illusion of Sourcing", "Facing the Online Shakedown", "The Myth of Corrections", and "The Dark Side of Snark". The details in there are more grim (though less quote-worthy), with a lot of *"mea culpa"* tinged commentary ... here are a couple of bits from the "Cheering On Our Own Deception" chapter:

> > Nobody online wants to point out how fake and insidious {this} is because it's too lucrative.
> >
> > ...
> >
> > I never got over the shock of discovering that it was basically impossible to burn a blog. No matter how many times I've been caught leaking bad info, spinning, spamming, manufacturing news – it never changed anything. The same bloggers continued to cover my stories and bit when I created news. They don't mind being deceived, not at all.

The book ends strong, with a chapter on "How To Read A Blog" which starts with a long lists of "translations" such as:

> > When you see a blog begin with "According to a tipster ..." know that the tipster was someone like me tricking the blogger into writing what I wanted.
> >
> > When you see "We're hearing reports" know that reports could mean anything from random mentions on Twitter to message board posts, or worse.
> >
> > When you see "leaked" or "official documents" know that the leak really meant someone just e-mailed a blogger, and that the documents are almost certainly not official and are usually fake or fabricated for the purpose of making desired information public.

This is then followed by a "Conclusion" where Holiday takes a look at what can be (or is being) done to counter the chaos of what passes for news, and delves both into philosophy and naming names of both the good and bad actors in the game. An addition to the current edition of the book are two appendixes, one with a few case studies that analyze in detail specific campaigns, and another that's a collection of several articles that he wrote for *The New York Observer* likewise picking apart various elements of the business.

Trust Me, I'm Lying[6] is not a *pleasant* read … in many ways it's the equivalent of moving a rotting log to suddenly be face-to-face with an entire environment of vermin that have been contentedly operating just out of sight. However, it is, by the same token, a *revealing* look at the news infrastructure that has devolved to the point of being cynically driven by rumor, lies, and slander. I actually paid "full price" (the on-line big boys have it at about 35% off of cover) for this as an add-on to another order, but you could maybe get it for half that if going through the new/used vendors. While a difficult read (due to content, not the writing), this is likely more "for anybody" than most business books, since everybody is subject to the "poisoning the well" across the information infrastructure of the internet, and so might find it interesting to see how the lies we're being constantly fed are generated.

Notes:

1. http://btripp-books.livejournal.com/165464.html
2. http://amzn.to/1AwHvoS
3. http://btripp-books.livejournal.com/155380.html
4. http://btripp-books.livejournal.com/149388.html
5. http://amzn.to/1AwHvoS
6. http://amzn.to/1AwHvoS

Sunday, April 5, 2015[1]

A brilliant look at a vile subject ...

This was one of those remarkable Dollar Store finds ... it's always a pleasure to run across a book, that had better-than-even odds of being something that I would have *bought* on its own merits, sitting there on the shelf with all those other one-buck books. Of course, long-time readers of this space will know that I'm a big fan of Ann Coulter (minus, of course, when she's under the sway of her "imaginary friend" problem), and Mugged: Racial Demagoguery from the Seventies to Obama[2] is pretty much her at her best. It's also a relatively recent release, coming out in 2012, in time for the re-election campaign of the subtitularly-mentioned POTUS.

Now, my liberal-leaning readers can (and probably should) **just stop reading NOW**. Ms. Coulter and I are in fairly solid agreement with our distaste (to use the mildest word for it) for the Left/Progressive agenda, and the *maddening* hegemony it holds over the realms of media, entertainment, and education ... and it is this nauseating political stance (and the institutions that propagate it) that is really the subject here. Of course, those on the Left will say this book is R – A – C – I – S – T and anti-black, but if you were to actually *read* it (I know, a hard concept for Liberals, who prefer to hold their opinions in spite of any contravening facts), it becomes VERY clear that the "villains" in the tale are the knee-jerk Leftist press, and the vile pandering politicians for whom "victim culture" is a key to imposing "progressive" programs which serve nobody but the politicians and related power brokers.

As I was reading this, it became evident to me that this was yet another "book I wish they'd teach in the schools" (obviously, a ludicrous concept given how unyielding a death-grip the Left has on the "education industry" in this country) because this is an intense light being shone on the lies, deceit, falsehoods and brainwashing that passes for news and civics these days.

Frankly, Ann could have issued an update to this any time in the recent past, as the media (and the insufferable current administration) has *repeatedly* fanned the flames of racial conflict, inflating minor issues into national "outrages" to suit their nefarious ends, and this book is chock full of *similar* stories to those in recent headlines.

As regular readers of my reviews may recall, I have a "system" of tearing off little bits of paper (typically register receipts) to mark places to come back to in a book, either for things to quote in these reviews, or (generally in the business books) things to look into and/or follow up on. I think I usually have only 4-6 of these in any given book, but Mugged[3] has well over a dozen ... and this in a book that I'm not running off to check mentioned web resources from. Here, I've primarily flagged *"you go girl!"* passages where I felt that Ms. Coulter had either scored a serious "debate point" or exhibited that delightful snark which endears her to me and her other fans ... such as:

> *The North's zero-tolerance policy for a backward culture forced the white trash out of both the Irish*

> and southern rednecks, leaving just enough of them in their natural state to populate modern reality shows and the Kennedy family.

Of course, Ann's snark is based in a deep resentment of the insanity that the Left has imposed on America ...

> Next, liberal judges and academics decided it was a bad idea to punish criminals. Instead, they suggested we try to <u>understand</u> the criminal, persuade him that the system is fair and give him 157 second chances.
>
> ...
>
> Between 1960 and 1973, the number of FBI index crimes – which are serious offenses such as murder, rape, robbery, arson, assault, kidnapping, and burglary – nearly tripled from 2,019,600 offenses a year to 5,891,924. Hundreds of thousands of Americans had to die, be raped, or have their property destroy or stolen because liberals had some neat new ideas about crime.

Of course, the Left doesn't care, because any failing in their policies get blamed on "racism", and phony stories are fed to the press, who like packs of wild dogs are salivating to sink their teeth into a nice juicy "controversy", no matter how thin the data is to support it. A substantial part of the book is in-depth looks at story after story after story that the media and politicians blew up ... and then never mentioned again when their lies became evident enough to be inconvenient for continued spewing (much like the "hands up, don't shoot" meme out of Ferguson, MO, which ended up being a *total fabrication*, yet was echoed on major talk shows, university events, and *even on the steps of the Capitol*). While leftist rags like The New York Times will shift stories from A-1 to somewhere back with the lost pet ads, Coulter digs through the research materials (she's a big fan of Lexis/Nexis) and shows how, time after time, the fake outrage gets covered *everywhere* but the facts (inevitably disproving the media story) get swept under the rug ... hundreds of media outlets spewing the lies, but only a small handful eventually following up with the real story, usually long after the fact and with no fanfare.

> When it comes to claims of racism, empirical evidence is irrelevant. It's not the number of racist Web sites {most of which "didn't even have enough visitors to register on Web site trackers"} that's important, but their mythopoetic resonance with the master political narrative of the day. If blacks murder more whites than whites murder blacks, it doesn't matter because that's not the story. As racism becomes less of a factor in American life than agoraphobia, the media work overtime to find illustrations – true or not – of their larger thesis.

Again, Ann looks in detail how bogus story after bogus story was spun out as real, only helping the hard-core Left. I can not imagine a person of good character who could read this book and not be *enraged* at the press and the "progressive" political machine they support … but I know they're out there … it's pretty clear if you look at the Amazon reviews for Mugged[4], as for a book that's running 2/3rds to 3/4ths 5-star reviews (depending on edition), there are those 1-star reviews where Leftists heads are exploding in rants about "racism".

Another very interesting part of the book is where it traces the "co-opting" of the anti-slavery movement, and the changing electoral maps. The Republican party was the party opposing slavery and the oppression of blacks, right up into the 1960's, and the *Democrats* were the party clinging to "Jim Crow" and similar tactics … yet if you ask the average person today which way that played out, they'd probably have the Leftist through-the-looking-glass inversion as their view of it.

In closing, here's another telling quote (in a section looking how the "progressives" will attribute *anything* said by a conservative as "racist", but will give a pass to even the most *blatantly* racist speech – a lot of Joe Biden whoppers cited – if said by one of their camp):

> As French philosopher Jean-François Revel said of the left, while most regimes are judged on their records, only communism is judged only by its promises. Similarly, modern liberals are judged on their motives; conservatives are judged on what liberals claim we really meant.

I wish more people would read this book, as it is a wake-up call on how *vile*, conniving, duplicitous, and untrustworthy the mass of the Mainstream Media and their political co-conspirators are, *especially* when dealing with questions of race. I'm surprised that, having gotten to the dollar store shelves, this hardcover (which appears to be out of print at this point, in favor of the subsequent paperback) isn't going for less in the new/used channels, although deals on the paperback can be had. I hope you'll make the effort to get this, because it's important to understand how *twisted* the "progressive"/Left/Liberal narrative is!

Notes:

1. http://btripp-books.livejournal.com/165714.html
2-4. http://amzn.to/1AhasHK

Tuesday, April 21, 2015[1]

Meet Harry Wormwood, SEO expert ...

This is another of those books that was made available to me by the good folks at Wiley ... one of the best sources of books on marketing, social media, etc. A few months back, my contact there sent out a list of new books coming out and this was on that, and I figured it would be an interesting read, as I'm such a dinosaur when it comes to SEO and stuff like that.

As regular readers of this space will no doubt recall, I ran my own publishing house for a decade, starting back in the 90's, so I have a rather hands-on perspective on the book biz, and "author wrangling". I bring this up because this was one of those cases where a more assertive editorial hand would have improved the book. I can't recall another book which so clearly brought up the classic quote (generally attributed to Vince Lombardi): *"act like you've been there before"* ... in the original context, telling players not to overly celebrate reaching the end zone, but in this case something like "don't be so impressed with yourself just because you've got a book out"!

While the "peacocking" tones down as Win the Game of Googleopoly: Unlocking the Secret Strategy of Search Engines[2] progresses, in the early parts Sean V. Bradley sounds like Steve Martin's character in "The Jerk" being so impressed that his name is in the phone book ... with his repeatedly pointing out belonging to some speaking organization, and now being published (hey, once in the introduction would have covered it - *really*). Between that and the endless mentions of his hot model wife[3], it's *real* easy to dislike the author from the get-go here.

He's also a car salesman ... he dropped out of college and ended up selling cars, and because of his youth, got assigned to doing the dealership's web sales ... in which he excelled. However, it's hard for the image of the "ethically challenged" car salesman (think Danny Devito's role of Harry Wormwood in *Matilda*) to *not* hover over this book, because *everything* that Bradley advocates comes from a "cash first" profit-driven standpoint ... plus almost all of his examples involve car-sales sites, which is his area of expertise.

Frankly, I'm not sure that the majority of this book's material is particularly translatable to other industries ... I spent a lot of time turning his instructions around in my mind to see how they could be applied to organizations and projects that I've been involved in, and frequently couldn't trace out any direct parallels. On the other hand, every car dealership in the country should (and probably *does*) have a copy of the book by this point, as it's certainly a doctoral-level course in how to push car sales on the internet.

While the specifics are largely focused on how to move that SUV, the broad strokes on the search industry are fascinating. For instance, Google is so huge that its unique monthly visitors are just about equal to the next four (Bing, Yahoo!, Ask, and AOL) *combined*, and that's not counting that the #2 "search engine" in terms of traffic is Google's own YouTube! Google gets

1.1 billion unique visitors per month, which means that over 15% of all the people on the planet use Google at least once a month (and YouTube gets almost as many). Between Google and YouTube, they get over a hundred *billion* searches per month. The point that he's making here is that there really isn't any "plan B" ... you're either maximized for Google, or you're picking up the crumbs.

So, it's Google or nothing. The next thing he does is break down the Google page ... which I was not familiar with in this context. These sections are PPC (Pay Per Click ads), Organic Results, Local Search (G+ Business listings), News articles, and "Top 10 Results". He cites some really amazing (frightening?) statistics here ... for instance, only *5 percent* of searchers will go past the first page of Google results ... which he notes: *"If you are not on the first page, you are statistically invisible."* Another shocking figure is how low the click-through is on the PPC listings ... these are the money machine for Google (pulling in $55 billion in 2014!), but *only 6%* of searchers will click on the PPC listings. Frankly, I found this staggering, because I'd have doubted that (statistically) there were anywhere near enough people using the search engines who were *smart enough* to recognize an ad when they see it ... yet 94% of the folks being served PPC ads pass over them to get to the other listings on the page.

Needless to say, he uses this as an illustration of just how essential getting those high first-page listings are, since you can't even realistically *buy* your way into getting clicks.

This leads into some serious "how to do it" material on domain names, key words, geo-targeting, title tags, heading tags, etc. ... including his recommendations for software packages to walk you through the system. This section could be called "why I hate SEO", because (as a writer) it all comes out as such a mess of keywords and product mentions that there is no way to make it look like anything other than ... well, *a scam*. However, I guess the world is a LOT more interested in grabbing the dollars than making pretty prose, so I'm no doubt in a minority who think it's a horrible thing to do to words (a domain that he seriously holds out as *good* is the massively unwieldy cheapmanhattanplumber.com ... but he points out that "exact match domains" are efficient if the words that folks are searching on are in the damn URL). He gets deep into keyword research (and tools for same), but notes that one has to be careful to not "keyword stuff" one's site because Google (thankfully) has gotten its programs smart enough to see that happening.

As the phrase goes: "It's all about the Benjamins" ... or at least in the author's world. Here's a quote, which, quite rationally, throws whatever ethical babies might have been in play out with the bathwater (when discussing SEO strategy for heading tags):

> *I am going to focus on what Google wants. As mentioned in Chapter 2, it's all about Google. No egos, no distractions, just focus on exactly will appease Google, and you will be successful.*

Now, to be perfectly honest, I bookmarked this section for my own edification, as I have never been fond of using "H tags" because in web1/web2 sites those headers just looked *ugly* and made pages both look bad, and like every other damn page on the web. However, these days with the ability to dictate the look with CSS, those tags are less gross, and the SEO use of them would, indeed, seem to be called for (if making the page *read* like they were written by an idiot savant).

He goes on into how to optimize graphics and videos (he's very big on videos – recommending car dealerships to do endless versions of these to grab the most search volume). His recommendations for SEO work on YouTube pages is very interesting, and is one of those things that should be useful across most industries … it's another piece from reading the book that I've already put into action on some YouTube channels I manage. Of course, he *also* goes on at length on car videos … how dealerships should do dozens of variations with names of local towns, or how x model is better than a half-dozen comparable competitors' models (and a version done for every town name in the region, etc., etc., etc.).

Social media is a blood sport in Bradley's world as well:

> *Every time you have one of your pages ranked for a search, it means another page (possibly a competitor) is ranked lower. You want your social profiles to rank for branded searches as well as unbranded searches. … The biggest mistake that so many businesses make is that they try to do too many social sites. … In fact, by focusing on the right ones, you'll be able to maintain the highest chance of dominating on search.*

In this context, "the right ones" start with G+, simply because it's Google … he also goes into depth on strategies for Facebook, Twitter, YouTube, Pinterest, LinkedIn, and Flickr … but some of the stuff he says is so "sleazy" - like if you don't have at least one "action per hour" to a post on Facebook, you should *delete* it and post something else hoping for engagements to trigger the algorithm to build visibility. He notes the elements that are judged by that algorithm to justify more views … which he notes only run 5-10% of your likes/friends (if that!) "organically".

One of the last things he deals with is responsive and mobile web designs. He *strongly* recommends against having a separate .mobi site, as it will cut your traffic in half, and totally mess with the way Google directs your traffic. Personally, one project I've been working on just switched from a basic HTML site with a WordPress blog attached to a Ning site because the new version has built-in responsive design (and Google is just now changing the rules to make this a big plus).

Anyway, verdict on Win the Game of Googleopoly[4] - some really good material, but in a generally insufferable format. I'm *sure* if you flushed your scruples down the toilet and let ~~Harry Wormwood~~ Sean V. Bradley, CSP (can't forget his speaking accreditation, can we?) train you to game Google, you'll vastly improve your SEO results (your soul, maybe not so much). It's been out since January, so should be in the brick-and-mortars, with the online vendors offering it at a slight discount. I'm glad I got the info that's in this book, but I can't say I enjoyed reading it!

Notes:
1. http://btripp-books.livejournal.com/165957.html
2. http://amzn.to/1LlaofV
3. https://www.google.com/search?q=karina+bradley
4. http://amzn.to/1LlaofV

Wednesday, April 22, 2015[1]

Wagering with Pascal?

I had really high hopes for this when I "won" it from the LibraryThing.com "Early Reviewer" program, as I was anticipating some nice logical presentation about a rational society's "God substitute" coming out of Science. Eh, not so much. Not that it doesn't have its moments, but Nancy Ellen Abrams' A God That Could Be Real: Spirituality, Science, and the Future of Our Planet[2] suffers from being something of a self-therapeutic exercise that bizarrely floats off into the sorts of mushy introspection that is typical of new-age writers and not what one would expect of "hard science" folks. I guess I got confused by her extensive referencing of her "famed astrophysicist" husband, Joel Primack, and how she starts off the book in nearly "full Dawkins" mode:

> *I have no interest in a God that has to be believed in. If I am going to have God in my life, it has to be a God that cannot help but exist, in the same way that matter and gravity and culture exist. We don't need to believe in these things; they just <u>exist</u>.*

However, her personal struggles with addiction (in her case, "food addiction") hang heavy over the book, as what ultimately drives her to seek out an otherwise unnecessary deity is the notorious "God stuff" of popular addiction management ... as without a God to release her responsibility to, she could not keep from over-eating, plain and simple, so "science be damned", there was going to BE a God in her universe. In retrospect, I suppose I am being harder on Abrams than I should, as it's her *husband* who's the scientist ... she has a philosophy degree from University of Chicago, and is a *lawyer* - so weaseling around the theistic 12-step doctrines to make them look less creepy is what's she's trained for. This doesn't make them any more palatable from where I'm sitting, however.

Needless to say, I would have found this a MUCH better book without those elements ... and maybe somebody without a "doughnut problem" is out there who will take the useful concepts of this and run with them, generating an actual "rational deity" that could, indeed, enhance "the Future of Our Planet" by freeing it from the bronze-age insanities of the big-ticket monotheisms. There is a core of logic here which could be built on ... hooked into the concept of "emergence". Noted cosmologist and science writer Paul Davies provided a Foreword to this (the other is by Archbishop Desmond Tutu, to throw an additional bone to the theists, I suppose) and in it he frames the idea in Abram's conceptualization:

> *The core of her bold challenge to the atheist position is that because emergent phenomena can be real in their own right, even if they depend on a lower-level substrate to instantiate them, a God that is the product of the human mind and human society can also be real. After all, life emerges from*

> and is dependent on, the chemical substrate of organic matter, and life is not only real but has its own (emergent) agenda consistent with, but transcending, the chemical substrate that hosts it. So too can it be for an emergent God. ... Her God is not even cosmic but planetary, being tied (until now at least) to our particular terrestrial species. ... For those steeped in traditional monotheism, a God that springs solely from the collective human intellect seems like heresy. But for those who reject the idea of God entirely as ridiculous and superfluous, an emergent God holds many attractions.

The first part of the book looks at the *evolution* of the idea of God, from the earliest flat-world-with-a-dome conceptions, through the great ancient polytheisms, into the Dark Ages, the Medieval period, and on into the Renaissance, when God and Nature began to diverge. Abrams argues that up till then, our vision of God moved in lockstep with our understanding of the cosmos, with God being the element that harmonized humanity with the cosmos *"as the culture best understands it"*. Living in an astrophysics/cosmology household, the author obviously has a better grasp on the "twenty-first-century scientific" understanding of the universe (with dark matter, dark energy, and other hard-to-get cosmic realities) than most, but it's her belief that we *need* to develop a concept of God that fits that universe.

> ...the idea of God has persisted through thousands of years and thousands of cultural changes neither because God is an independently existing being in control of the universe nor because it's a purely psychological need. God persists and always will because it's a <u>fundamental characteristic of the connection</u> between ourselves and the universe. That we're connected to the universe is inevitable and indisputable, but until we had a scientific understanding of the universe, we could not imagine <u>how</u>.

She argues that the disconnection of the idea of God from the realities of the cosmos is the seed of the present insanity of most religions ...

> In each subset of these belief systems, a somewhat different version of God's character and expectations of us is held not only to be true for the believers but to be <u>universally and eternally true</u>.

In the next section she picks apart those ossified version of deity in relation to our current understanding of the universe, and how various aspects of physics rule out most of the cherished "God stuff" that the believers (of assorted stripes) hold so intensely to. This is then followed by a section in which she starts to set up a justification of God, returning to the "emergence" theme. Looking at how the laws of thermodynamics were largely framed on emergent phenomena (entropy being an averaged factor of trillions of atoms – which at the time were purely theoretical), and how scaling is important to understand the whole. An example she gives is of an ant colony ... on the level of the individual ant, everything is a response to some chemical signal, but over the entire colony we perceive an intelligence expressing as a system. This is due to having a sufficiently higher level *consciousness* ... *"We humans are able to do this because our kind of intelligence discerns abstract patterns in social behavior and constructs theories."* She goes down a bit of a rabbit-hole here, looking at culturally inherited expectations and aspirations which shape how we see God, even to the point of suggesting that God is, from generation after generation of people working with the concept, hard-wired into our neurological make-up ... an idea that I might disparage if it wasn't for my study of shamanic expressions across cultures, where certain key elements appear in widely differing contexts, leading me to posit that there is, likewise, a *real* (and physically hard-wired) "otherworld" in which the shaman is able to operate.

On the subject of familiar belief systems, perhaps my favorite part of the book is how Abrams borrows the Nordic concept of *Midgard* (that's Earth to the Marvel Comics' Asgardians such as Thor), and blends this with the Uroboros – the snake eating its tail. On this "Cosmic Uroboros", there are three realms, the extremely small on the tail end, the extremely large on the head end, and "Midgard" in between ... that "Goldilocks" zone of "just right" sizes for us to be able to understand them without too much difficulty – from about the size of an ant to the size of the Sun. On the extremes are things as small as 10^{-25}cm and as large as 10^{25}cm, with the head/tail coming in at the GUT – grand unified theories – zone around $10^{+/-30}$cm ... creating a scale which essentially encompasses the entire of the universe. It's in Midgard, however, that we can have a meaningful God.

Abrams tries to fit a lot of traditional religious thinking into the following bits, including life after death (she has an interesting thing about being an *"honored ancestor"*, and how we should live our lives as *"our great-great-grandchildren's keeper"*). Unfortunately, she sort of lost me as she tried to sort things out ... for every reasonable suggestion that we (and any other similarly sentient alien life forms) are the universe's "brain" (by which it explores and understands itself), there were a handful of things that felt more like her working through a need for something to pray to. As Dennis Miller would have it, however, *your mileage may vary*.

A God That Could Be Real[3] is brand new (it just came out last month), so it's possibly in a book store near you, and the on-line big boys have it available for about a quarter off the cover price. I liked a lot about this book, but really resisted a similarly large amount of it. Again, I felt that had the author *not* been dealing with her addiction issues via 12-step theism-based approaches, and came to the subject from a more solidly science-based perspective without that other baggage, it would have been a far, far better book.

Notes:

1. http://btripp-books.livejournal.com/166350.html
2. http://amzn.to/1Eh1mqY
3. http://amzn.to/1Eh1mqY

Monday, April 27, 2015[1]

Not just one story ...

This is another book coming into my hands via the LibraryThing.com "Early Reviewers" program. Due to the number of Buddhist books in my collection, it was hardly surprising that the LTER "almighty algorithm" opted to hook me up with this, but I'm getting ahead of myself. I'm not sure exactly what I was expecting this to be when I clicked "request" on Scott Carney's A Death on Diamond Mountain: A True Story of Obsession, Madness, and the Path to Enlightenment[2], but I'm sure, in retrospect, that I'd have been off in my expectations. It's a very odd book ... not so much in its subject matter (although I'm sure many would find that odd enough), but how that's *structured*, and approached. From the title/subtitle, you might expect it to be a basic non-fiction tale of somebody who ended up dying on "Diamond Mountain", and it *is* that in the widest arc here, and that trajectory gives the book its basic skeletal outline, but that in and of itself would be fairly thin, as the implied protagonist is a fairly minor (although sufficiently connected to allow his tale to suffice for the "story") character in the over-all world of the book.

For regular readers of my reviews, the fact that I ended up without a single little bookmark[3] should give you pause. The lack of these meant that there were never any particular points in the narrative that I stopped to say "hey, that would be a good way to illustrate this aspect of the book", or to generally highlight something that I might want to eventually get back to. This also means that I'm "working without a net" in writing this, having to play off of raw recall, rather than having juicy quotes to fall back on (although I may end up pulling some stuff out of the book if it catches my eye tonight).

It might be useful to quote the book jacket's blurb about the author, as this leads well into the obvious question, "what's the book about?" ... *"Scott Carney is an investigative journalist who blends narrative nonfiction with ethnography."* ... roll that around in the folds of your grey matter for a bit. What you're imagining from that statement in terms of what the book's about is probably pretty close. It's got a journalistic narrative feel to most of it, and deep dives into ethnographic waters, albeit in terms of Buddhism and Cults and Megalomania, and assorted relatively damaged or delusional people.

While the "spine" of the story is how Ian Thorson ended up dead on that mountain, most of the "meat" of the book deals with Geshe Michael Roach, a Princeton grad who made his way to Tibet, and was able to study at the Sera Monastery, returning to the U.S., on the recommendation of the Dalai Lama, to work with a New Jersey based teacher, Khen Rinpoche Geshe Lobsang Tarchin. Working with this Lama, in 1976, he had a moment of enlightenment and based most of his subsequent career on that experience.

Now, Roach's background sounds very solid ... doing a *lot* of dharma work over a *lot* of years ... and his enlightenment experience sounds perfectly legit, but his "take" on the Gelugpa form of Tibetan Buddhism is idiosyncratic at best, and "heretical" (he was eventually in trouble with various more traditional elements) at worst. While, I am hardly an *expert* on the subject, I did spend a number of years studying (and, to be very clear, *not practicing* - mine is an "outsider's view" certainly) Tibetan Buddhism, including attending the Avalokitesvara initiation twice and the Kalachakra three times. Back then, I never heard of Roach nor encountered mention of his "personal deity form" of Vajrayogini, who is very similar to the Hindu goddess Kali in her descriptions. While my lack of experience with this is likely to have been from rarely having the opportunity to have complex iconographies of thangkas, etc., specifically explained to me, it is my impression that Geshe Roach had focused his practice (and subsequent teachings) on a particularly esoteric corner of the Tibetan Buddhist cosmos, and as his work developed, he moved farther and farther away from Gelugpa orthodoxy, and closer and closer to a classic American "Cult".

As I likewise spent a number of years in the orbit of one such cult in my youth, I have a pretty good radar for the sorts of things that come with that, and Carney's descriptions of Roach's organization certain have that vibe ... right down to running off to the desert to have an environment of isolation where the group's teachings and practices wouldn't have to run into the cognitive dissonances of friction with the "common world" – such as enveloped Roach's center in New York. However, Roach has so many things in the "plus column" (his work, at the behest of his teacher, as a diamond merchant in New York – in which he was remarkably successful, and helped fund numerous Buddhist outreaches and institutions – is a substantial one, plus the work he did to make a vast amount of Tibetan documents available via scanning and releasing on CD) that is impossible to write him off as an insignificant figure.

The book spends a lot of time backgrounding Buddhism, the various characters involved in the tale, and even the geography and history of key locations ... at times to the virtual abandonment of the narrative. Aside from Michael Roach and Ian Thorson, the other "key player" in the story is Christie McNally (later *Lama* Christie McNally), who started out as an eager follower of Roach, then became his lover (tantra partner), inspirational embodiment of Vajrayogini, main organizer, and eventual partner of Thorson. Each of these characters is essential to the story, but it is Ian Thorson whose life tracks the over-arching flow of the book. Thorson was a seeker, who was noted as having been suspected of being neurologically damaged, his manifestations of spiritual exuberance often appearing more "clinical" than "mystical". He had a similar passion of esoterica such as Vajrayogini, and a history of being willing to "go all in" for his metaphysical pursuits. His path leads him to latching onto Roach and his organization, and is in place when Roach and McNally eventually have a parting of the ways.

The main reason that Roach's group ran off to the desert was to have major multi-year retreats, and it was in a second of these that McNally and Thorson were evicted, and ended up sneaking back into the area (in a cave up on the mountain), to still carry out the retreat in the presence of the rest, if in secret. This is, essentially, what causes Thorson's eventual death, as the couple is living without any dependable food or water or fuel or pretty much other creature comforts, and Thorson ends up succumbing to the privations before McNally is able to summon any outside help (also not aided by their well-secluded cave location).

I'm giving short shrift to a lot here (perhaps McNally most of all), but it is a complicated story that keeps jumping into different contexts … from Thorson's family's attempts to have him "deprogrammed" at points, to the interesting conflicts between Roach's organization and the orthodoxy. There is one bit here which sort of frames the rest, at least at what was the arc of Roach's teaching:

> The Great Retreat broke the hierarchy between Roach and Tibetan authorities. Now that he was under the direct guidance of angels, there was no need to appeal to the Dalai Lama. With Lama Christie by his side, he promised they would breathe new life into Tibetan Buddhism. They would forge a faith that shucked off anachronistic Tibetan traditions and make their interpretation of ancient Buddhist wisdom relevant for modern-day America.

Thorson was pretty much just a damaged seeker caught up in that maelstrom, but it's a fascinating read.

Again, A Death on Diamond Mountain[4] is not the most *linear* of tales, but it is more informative than most narratives would be, largely from the journalistic chops of the author. This book, while basically a story (or, is that a history?), is hardly a "thriller", but more a telling set out on which to hang bits of research, creating a work with unexpected depth, if not a simple synopsis. This just came out a few weeks ago, so should be widely available in the brick-and-mortar book vendors, and the on-line big boys have it for the usual discount. While I found *writing about* the book very frustrating, reading it was a pleasure. Whether this was due to my familiarity with a lot of the component elements (leading to it being quite engaging for me), or not is something you may want to consider, but I liked it, and you might too.

Notes:

http://btripp-books.livejournal.com/166574.html

http://amzn.to/1bBMPiU

http://ic.pics.livejournal.com/btripp/2663/403387/403387_original.jpg

http://amzn.to/1bBMPiU

Tuesday, April 28, 2015[1]

That's the way you do it ...

I've met Ann Handley of MarketingProfs[2] a couple of times, and her new book was getting a lot of play over in the marketing discussions of Facebook, so I dropped a line to the good folks at Wiley to request a copy of Everybody Writes: Your Go-To Guide to Creating Ridiculously Good Content[3]. I was a bit hesitant about slogging into this, as, frankly, having been a professional writer of one kind or another for decades, I'm a bit resistant to having people tell me what I should be doing in what I've been doing for (in many cases) longer than they've been alive. Fortunately, Ms. Handley is not dictating from these pages like some schoolmarm with a Ruler of Pain at the ready (or the "style guide" equivalent), but as a fellow wordsmith bringing the consensus view of a lot of fellow marketing communicators on what works and what doesn't and how to get your verbiage closer to the former. The book also has a particularly comforting Epigraph: *Beware of advice – even this.* - Carl Sandburg

One thing I especially liked about the book is that it's presented in "bite-size chunks" ... with its ≈300 pages divided up into 74 chapters spanning five "parts", with a sixth part devoted to Content Tools. The other five are: Writing Rules: How To Write Better (And How To Hate Writing Less), Writing Rules: Grammar And Usage, Story Rules, Publishing Rules, and 13 Things That Marketers Write. There's a lot of humor in this (like the chapter heading "The More the Think, the Easier the Ink"), and a lot of context building (such as having Ben Franklin's personal daily schedule displayed in the "Writing Is a Habit, Not an Art" chapter).

Early on, Handley presents a 12-point "Writing GPS" ... a GPS because *"in writing you need a road map to get you to where you need to be"*. This serves as a framework for the first section of the book ("Writing Rules"), as the chapters that follow pretty much step through these in sequence:

1. Goal.
2. Reframe: put your reader into it.
3. Seek out the data and examples.
4. Organize.
5. Write to one person.
6. Produce The Ugly First Draft.
7. Walk away.
8. Rewrite.
9. Give it a great headline or title.
10. Have someone edit.
11. One final look for readability.
12. Publish, but not without answering one more reader question: what now?

This list, I think most writers will agree, is a pretty good approach to getting work done. One quirk in how things are handled here is that Handley refers to what I'm calling chapters as "rules" - even though these generally feel more along the line of how *Pirates of the Caribbean*'s Captain Hector Barbossa framed the Pirate's Code: *"more what you'd call "guidelines" than actual rules"*. Of course, not all of these are created equal, some chapters run to 8 pages or so, and some are a mere handful of lines.

So, the basics on Everybody Writes[4]: it's very useful, it's very entertaining, it's crammed full of good stuff, and if you're in Marketing Communications, you should definitely go grab a copy, because you'll be happy that you did. That being now out of the way, I'm going to indulge in cherry-picking some bits & pieces that I bookmarked while reading through it.

In the "Develop Pathological Empathy" section she notes:

> *... you have to meet people where they are, with an attitude of benevolence and largesse, to help them find answers to the problems that they have. All of your content – your product pages, your landing pages, your customer support text, your About Us pages, and so on "need to use language to support people's needs and goals".* {that quoted bit is from Facebook's Jonathon Coleman}

In the "Keep It Simple – but Not Simplistic" chapter she delves into her journalism school experience for some classics:

> *No one will ever complain that you've made things too simple to understand.*

and

> *Assume the reader knows nothing. But don't assume the reader is stupid.*

To which she adds:

> *Simplicity comes primarily from approaching any writing with empathy and a reader-centric point of view to begin with – that is, it's the result of writing with clarity and brevity, and in human language ...*

There's an interesting chapter on readability, which looks at the various scales and provides information on and links to resources for testing your text (including one that's built in to Microsoft Office that I'd been unaware of). I'd never really looked into this, personally, and was interested in the following ... a score of 90.0 to 100.0 would be understood by an average 11-year-old student, a score from 60.0 to 70.0 would be understood by 13-15 year-olds, and a score of 0.0 to 30.0 is best suited to college grads ... and she breaks out how an assortment of types of material fall on that scale.

Another suggestion I found on-target was for writing goals ... that one should *"make sure you measure your writing in output (words) rather than in effort expended (time)"*, which is coupled with a concept taken from boxing – one's "weight class" (an idea borrowed from Mitch Joel), where a novice writer might be only good for 50 words at a sitting, while a "heavyweight" can *"churn out 5,000 words ... before breakfast"*. The idea here is to know what your limits of quality composition are ... and to work to build up those "writing muscles", to 250 words, 500 words, 750 words, etc. Interestingly, I recent found a resource on-line for doing 750 words as an exercise (http://750words.com/[5]) ... Handley notes that 750 words is about 3 pages of text, so getting to the point where you can generate that without much strain is a fairly significant accomplishment.

There's a section on words one may be misusing or confusing ... but I'm hoping that most writers aren't having problems with those words ... the part, however, on "usage confusion" is very useful, with discussions of "fewer vs. less", "bring vs. take", "who vs. whom", "that vs. which vs. who", and several others that I'm *sure* even the most seasoned word mongers trip up on from time to time!

The book's full of anecdotes, quips, and borrowings from industry sources, and the fifth part is a platform-by-platform look at "writing for" Twitter, Facebook, Linkedin, email, hashtags, landing pages (and other web real estate), blog posts, annual reports, and how long everything from these to podcasts ought to be. There's also a look at infographics and resources for developing them.

As you can no doubt tell by this point, I'm a fan of Everybody Writes[6], and really have nothing negative to say about it. This came out last September, but I'm sure it has settled in to its long-term niche in the brick-and-mortar bookshop shelves, with the on-line sources having it at predictable discounts. Of course, it's targeted to Marketing Communications folks (like me), and might not be quite the awesome resource to playwrights, poets, and technical manual writers. However, if you want to improve your marketing writing, you'll want to add this to your stack of "books about writing" (oh, come on, you know you have one).

Notes:

1. http://btripp-books.livejournal.com/166844.html
2. http://www.marketingprofs.com/
3. http://amzn.to/1Gdmq6k
4. http://amzn.to/1Gdmq6k
5. http://750words.com/
6. http://amzn.to/1Gdmq6k

Saturday, May 2, 2015[1]

An unexpected seeker's memoir ...

I think it is *very* fortuitous that I hadn't read Sam Harris' Waking Up: A Guide to Spirituality Without Religion[2] prior to a book I reviewed a week or so back, as had Harris' book been "fresh in mind", the other would have suffered more in the reviewing. Just as I was hoping in my review of that other[3] book that there might be someone *"who will take the useful concepts of this and run with them"*, this comes close to providing the sort of narrative for a "rational religion" (or, as the sub-title would have it: *spirituality without religion*). However, upon further reflection, I believe that I found out about *this* book when doing some background research for the review of the other ... so there's a timeline involved.

Given that I've read and reviewed most of Harris' books, I ended up chastising myself that I hadn't recalled some of the notable bits of his biography. Admittedly, I read The End of Faith[4] and Letter to a Christian Nation[5] more than seven years ago, but I very clearly was commenting in my review of the former about the author's spirituality ... yet this was something that rather blind-sided me in the current book. Who would think that the clear-headed Atheist of "Letter" would have been a life-long seeker of things spiritual? But, there it is, the author is another inquisitive mind digging into psychology, brain science, and practicing Buddhism ... hardly what one would expect for somebody whose name rolls off the tongue with "Dawkins", etc. This is hardly a "Pilgrim's Progress" for the Atheist camp, but Harris does define it thusly:

> *This book is by turns a seeker's memoir, an introduction to the brain, a manual of contemplative instruction, and a philosophical unraveling of what most people consider to be the center of their inner lives: the feeling of self we call "I". I have not set out to describe all the traditional approaches to spirituality and to weigh their strengths and weaknesses. Rather, my goal is to pluck the diamond from the dunghill of esoteric religion. ... Just as a modern treatise on weaponry would omit the casting of spells and would very likely ignore the slingshot and the boomerang, I will focus on what I consider the most promising lines of spiritual inquiry.*

I'm sure that the author could have produced a tome many times this one's length had he indulged in a fine sorting of gems out of dung, but he does keep this moving along on a particular heading ... which can be reasonably triangulated with notes such as *"many of my fellow atheists consider all talk of spirituality to be a sign of mental illness, conscious imposture, or self-deception"* which is countered with *"millions of people have had experiences for which spiritual and mystical seem the only terms available"* ... i.e., there seems to be something happening out there (or, more to the point, *in here*), but the valuable bits are hard to isolate when encased in the deposits of bronze-age belief systems churned through millennia of power-hungry control freaks.

Waking Up[6] takes the reader through a journey across five specific sections, each covering several sub-topics ... the main chapters are "Spirituality", "The Mystery of Consciousness", "The Riddle of the Self", "Meditation", and "Gurus, Death, Drugs, and Other Puzzles". His first steps are to sort out the bits from the other bits of religion, and how these can't (or shouldn't be) seen as equivalent (please pardon the extensive quote, but I found his analogy quite on-target, along with its surrounding contextifying material):

> Devout Jews, Christians, and Muslims believe that theirs is the one true and complete revelation – because that is what their holy books say of themselves. Only secularists and New Age dabblers can mistake the modern tactic of "interfaith dialogue" for an underlying unity of all religions.
>
> I have long argued that confusion about the unity of religions is an artifact of language. Religion is a term like sports: Some sports are peaceful but spectacularly dangerous ("free solo" rock climbing); some are safer but synonymous with violence (mixed martial arts); and some entail little more risk than standing in the shower (bowling). To speak of sports as a generic activity makes it impossible to discuss what athletes actually do or the physical attributes required to do it. What do all sports have in common apart from breathing? Not much. The term religion is hardly more useful.
>
> The same could be said of spirituality. The esoteric doctrines found within every religious tradition are not all derived from the same insights. Nor are they equally empirical, logical, parsimonious, or wise. They don't always point to the same underlying reality – and when they do, they don't do it equally well. Nor are all these teachings equally suited for export beyond the cultures that first conceived them.

As opposed to some of his previous books, Harris doesn't spend a lot of time picking apart specific religions (although he does have a few zingers strewn throughout the text!), but he walks through the various chapters in a fairly logical (albeit, frequently from a Buddhist perspective) progression. The "Spirituality" chapter covers "The Search for Happiness", "Religion, East and West", "Mindfulness", "The Truth of Suffering", and "Enlightenment" ... an arc which is obviously *informed* by Buddhist thought, but the specifics are hardly doctrinal, with his looking at ancient Greek philosophy, the lens of Theosophy in popularizing Eastern thought, the mysticism indulged in by Newton, and the phenomenon of the Dalai Lama. At one point he is contrasting the east and west version of medicine and spirituality ...

with the West being clearly the place you want to find your medical care, but things are flipped around when it come to spiritual traditions:

> As manuals for contemplative understanding, the Bible and the Koran are worse than useless. Whatever wisdom can be found in their pages is never *best* found there, and it is subverted, time and again, by ancient savagery and superstition.

Much is made here of meditative states, and there's even a box with how-to instructions, with the Cliff's Notes versions on Suffering and Enlightenment, which gives an opportunity to criticize his stances, if one is coming from the hard-core Atheist camp.

The second chapter looks at Consciousness from both philosophical and medical standpoints ... asking questions about "transporter" tech (if the transportee has appeared at the destination before the de-materialization of the traveler at the source, is the subsequent removal *murder*?), with fascinating materials about patients whose *corpus callosum* is severed, rendering the two halves of the brain virtually independent, creating a situation where there is, for all intents and purposes, *two people* in the one body. Indeed, other studies show that the corpus callosum can't sufficiently transmit enough data to "synch" the two brain halves in even undamaged brains, leading to the assumption that there are *always* multiple "consciousnesses" operating (an example he gives in this section is when you can't remember a name that you *know* you know ... one part of the brain knows the name is known, but the operative part can't, for whatever reason, access that data point ... a frustration that I frequently have!).

In the third chapter, "The Riddle of the Self", where he contrasts what he calls *"the intrinsic selflessness of consciousness"* with the general feeling *"that our experience of the world refers back to a self ... a center of consciousness that exists somehow ... inside the head"* ... and tries to pick out what it is that we call "I". His aim here is to argue that *"the conventional sense of self in an illusion – and that spirituality largely consists in realizing this, moment to moment"* ... and he posits that *"the selflessness of consciousness is in plain view in every present moment – and yet, it remains difficult to see."*, which leads him to discuss (and instruct a self-guided demonstration) the "optic blind spot" as an example of a similar "not noticed" but clearly evident (once one finds a way to see it) reality. He goes quite a bit into the "Theory of Mind", and material related to that, from Jean-Paul Sartre to V.S. Ramachandran.

The chapter on Meditation is largely grounded in the author's own practice, and the studies he made with various teachers from a number of traditions. There is also a basis here in more brain biology, examples of perceptive quirks (negative space being "filled in" as an actual present element, etc.), some general philosophy, and even some art ... which leads to a sidebar called "look for your head".

The final chapter, "Gurus, Death, Drugs, and Other Puzzles" gets into the crunchy bits ... in talking Gurus, he notes how Alan Ginsberg was strident in his defense of some of the more extreme (and challenging to justify) actions of "crazy wisdom" Tibetan teacher Chögyam Trungpa (whose books

I've read, and who I had the chance to hear speak once ... an engagement he arrived at several hours late), he paints G.I. Gurdjieff as a "gifted charlatan" (despite the popularity with "smart successful devotees" in his lifetime, and the on-going influence of his writings), discusses Bhagwan Shree Rajneesh, and rattles off a string of others, ranging from Joseph Smith to L. Ron Hubbard, and even Charles Manson. He does almost a side-issue section on Near Death Experience reports, focusing largely on the Evangelical Christians who have grabbed on to the NDE stories as "proof" for their version of Heaven (frequently with details as ridiculous as Hubbard's DC-8 space planes) ... based on reports that *"seem especially vulnerable to self-deception, if not deliberate fraud."* This does allow Harris to transition to the drug discussion, as (in opposition to the insistence of the Evangelicals that these visions are unique and have no parallel in other contexts) they are almost exactly like DMT experiences, and he even throws in a *long* quote from psychedelic adventurer Terence McKenna to give a first-person narrative to the comparison. He discusses various psycho-active compounds, some from his own experiences, others from related literature, and looks at how various drugs interact with the brain's chemistry. One interesting bit goes back to Aldous Huxley, where it's suggested that the main function of the mind is to act as "reducing valve" to filter down what ends up actually being part of our awareness ... Harris argues against this on a number of functional and medical bases, but he gives the concept its due.

His conclusion wraps things up pretty well (given as open-ended a subject as this), with at least one good jab at religion: *"sins against reason and compassion do not represent the totality of religion, but they lie at its core"*, which sets up what could be viewed as a closing statement:

> *Spirituality remains the great hole in secularism, humanism, rationalism, atheism, and all the other defensive postures that reasonable men and women strike in the presence of unreasonable faith. ... Until we can talk about spirituality in rational terms – acknowledging the validity of self-transcendence – our world will remain shattered by dogmatism.*

Needless to say, I found Waking Up[7] both a surprising (the "seeker's journey" that I hadn't expected), and delightful read. While I'm certainly "in the choir" to which Harris is preaching, I'm also hoping that others will read this and (in the last words of the book) *"open your eyes and see"*. This just came out last fall, so should be out there in the surviving bookstores. I got mine through the new/used vendors ("like new" copies are going for about 1/5th of the cover price), and the main on-line guys have it at a substantial discount (oddly, this is only available in the US in hardcover, although there's an export paperback available via the used channels – at twice the price you could get the hardcover – go figure). I highly recommend this to anybody who has an open mind about what it means to be conscious.

Notes:

http://btripp-books.livejournal.com/167002.html

http://amzn.to/1PsH9Xh
http://btripp-books.livejournal.com/166350.html
http://btripp-books.livejournal.com/44948.html
http://btripp-books.livejournal.com/43169.html
http://amzn.to/1PsH9Xh
http://amzn.to/1PsH9Xh

Sunday, May 10, 2015[1]

Maybe with a different sub-title ...

I came to having Jeff Goins' The Art of Work: A Proven Path to Discovering What You Were Meant to Do[2] through a relatively unusual route ... author Chris Brogan[3] (he gets mad anymore if you call him "social media guru") - whose books you've seen covered in this space previously, put out an offer in one of his on-line vehicles about being able to get a copy of this for just covering shipping, and I figured if Chris was pushing it, it was probably something worthwhile. Which is making me somewhat uncomfortable, as I was expecting something more ... direct, perhaps ... for a book sub-titled *"A Proven Path to Discovering What You Were Meant to Do"*, and this is proving to be one of those occasional titles that *everybody else* loves (97% of the 217 Amazon reviews of this are 4 or 5 stars, with 86% at five), and I can't figure out *why*.

As regular readers of this space (and my personal blog in particular), will know, I have had a *long* bout with unemployment, and when I signed up to get The Art of Work[4], I assumed that it was a book-length permutation of one of those self-assessment things that would help guide me to some new unsuspected realization of what I was "meant to do" which would lead me into some vastly rewarding new career. Nope. In fact, while this *does* have some material along those lines, it's a whole five pages in an appendix at the back of the book.

Now, this is no doubt another example of "Brendan isn't like the other kids" ... I have never found parables and related teaching stories particularly convincing or moving ... with these sorts of things typically eliciting mental comments of "who cares?" and "why am I reading this?". I certainly appreciate that there is a whole genre for that sort of stuff ... and a wide audience that can't get enough of it. But that's not me. And, as you might suspect at this point ... *most* of this book is stories about people encountering some sort of adversity, and either finding some way of dealing with it, or finding a way out of it due to some external factor or *whatever* (did I mention the "who cares?" reaction?). As noted ... it may be too sweeping to say I *never* get anything out of these kind of stories, but it's pretty close ... and that's the core of this book. To me, this might as well be describing things the author is seeing in the clouds as a way to discuss electronic circuitry ... I want to hear about the circuitry ... and that's limited to that one appendix.

There *is* a "system" here, and it encompasses the over-all arc of the book ... as each chapter is set up to somehow "illustrate" the subject of one of these:

1. Awareness
2. Apprenticeship
3. Practice
4. Discovery
5. Profession

6. Mastery
7. Legacy

The first three of these are in a section called "Preparation", the next three in a section entitled "Action", and the last in its own section, "Completion", with an additional "Conclusion" section following. The book shifts in and out of narratives about the people featured in the various chapters, moving into "commentary" which *does* offer some concrete "action points", but it was hard (for me at least) to get much out of that. Here's an example out of the "Accidental Apprenticeships" chapter (which otherwise is dealing with a gal from Singapore who ended up with an older guy who, when she got pregnant, wanted her to have an abortion ... she didn't want to, and her family threw her out and blah, blah, blah, blah, blah, she encountered somebody who got her into being a "doula", and the next thing she's doing TED talks) about finding mentors:

> *How do you find these people? Where do they come from? It's hard to tell. Likely they'll surprise you, appearing seemingly out of nowhere at just the right time. The whole thing will look like an accident or a mystery but, of course, it is far from it. As Paulo Coelho writes, "When you want something, all the universe conspires in helping you to achieve it." There's some truth to that. Fortune favors the motivated. When a person is determined to not just succeed but to do work that matters, the world makes room for such ambition. You won't be able to predict how this apprenticeship unfolds, but you can be prepared for it when it comes.*

OK, how does one APPLY that? Again, this is about as "direct" as things get here ... how do I force the universe to send me a mentor to make everything head in the right direction? Clap my hands and say "I do believe!" until Tinkerbell appears with a magic wand?

Now, these chapters aren't *just* filled with wishful pablum, the Apprenticeship chapter does have some interesting historical material about how this worked in the age of guilds, etc., and more recently in the arts, and even including a story of how Steve Jobs passed off a program written by Wozniak as *his work* to fraudulently get an engineering job (that's some funky "apprenticeship"). The closing instructions for this chapter are:

> *These experiences are impossible to engineer but easy to recognize once you know what to look for. ... Sometimes the people who help us find our calling come from the least likely of places. It's our job to notice them.*

Yeah, but HOW? Do we wait forever until the "mentor" arrives? Waiting for pixie dust to fall on one's head does not sound like a *plan*, let alone a "proven path".

Jumping ahead to the "Discovery" step, in the chapter "Building Bridges":

this is about a couple who decided to pull up stakes in the U.S. and move to one of the poorest countries in Africa – Burundi – where they intended to grow coffee. The husband had a passion for coffee, and they pretty much just went to Africa to follow that ... it was a year and a half, in a backwards place where they didn't even speak the language (and they brought their kids), before they even started the business. Goins seems to think this was a *swell* plan, and notes:

> *{they} uprooted their family and moved to a remote part of the world because it was an opportunity to make a difference doing what they love. As it turns out, this is a great formula for moving in the direction of any calling: find what you love and what the world needs, then combine them.*

Personally, this sounds more like a recipe for a good way to end up either dead or impoverished and stranded in a festering hell-hole, but hey, *what do I know*?

Goins then goes into a discussion of "callings" and how the idea that "you just *know*" what you're supposed to be doing **isn't** true, and that most have to "take a leap" and go with it. Additionally, this chapter spends a lot of pages discussing a biblical parable (that of Samuel), an approach which rarely clarifies *any* point. Of course the difficulty here is "finding what you love" (or, at least it is for *me*), and then finding some way that this activity can be packaged in some manner that the world will not simply ignore it. In the case of this couple, they'd identified a neglected coffee industry (started by the Belgians in the 1930's) which produced a very high quality bean, and they figured they could make something of this. However, is this a "plan" for you? I suspect that the ability to find a personal passion and a niche that would support it is vanishingly rare ... and, of course, there's nothing here to get you from "I wish" to your goal.

I *really* wanted to like this book ... and, mind you, it's not an *unpleasant* read, just nothing that I could connect with. As noted up top, I had sincerely *hoped* that I would have found something useful for me here, but I'm obviously not the "parable and postulate" kind of guy. You, however, might find this sort of stuff *splendid* (acid test: do you think the proposition *"do what you love and the money will follow"* is a universal law or a Big Lie? ... if *that* resonates with you, you'll probably like this book, if you're like me, not so much).

The Art of Work[5] just came out in March, and as I mentioned, people are falling all over themselves praising it. The on-line vendors have it at nearly a third off of cover price at the moment, and it's reasonably value-priced going in. While I was *horribly* disappointed in it, I realize that I'm an "outlier" on the cynical/bitter end of things, and get nothing out of stories like the ones at the core of this ... but you might find them highly instructive.

Notes:

1. http://btripp-books.livejournal.com/167340.html

2. http://amzn.to/1CKnetr
3. http://chrisbrogan.com/
4. http://amzn.to/1CKnetr
5. http://amzn.to/1CKnetr

Monday, May 11, 2015[1]

How to become a "Thought Leader" ...

Speaking of books that took odd paths to get into my hands ... Tim McDonald, a buddy I've known from the Social Media Club of Chicago (who, ironically, is currently "taking time off from social media"), has a personal project he's working on called #365DaysOfGiving[2], where he (wait for it ...) *gives away* something every day for a year. This manifests variously, from postcards on his travels, to *very expensive* tickets for events, to framed graphics of his favorite sayings, to, well, books. He'd attended the book launch party for this, and was offering it on his list. As it turned out, I was one of a number of people who requested it, and he (randomly) sent it off to somebody else, but when I mentioned that I'd do a review of it, he was essentially wanting to "gift" that to *her*, and so (over my protestations – at this point I can pretty much hit up any publishing house for review copies of new books, and was certainly willing to do so in this case) he ordered me a copy from Amazon.

I figured that it would only be polite to bump this up to the top of my "to be read" pile when it came in, so I got Dorie Clark's Stand Out: How to Find Your Breakthrough Idea and Build a Following Around It[3] read over the past week. This book is, essentially, a how-to manual for becoming a "Thought Leader" ... and, as I've always somewhat aspired to this sort of role (albeit, hoping for "organic growth" to get me there), I was certainly interested in the topic.

Ms. Clark's bio is interesting ... from her site[4]: *"At age 14, Clark entered Mary Baldwin College's Program for the Exceptionally Gifted. At 18, she graduated Phi Beta Kappa from Smith College, and two years later received a Master of Theological Studies from Harvard Divinity School"* ... so she's smarter than either of us. Unfortunately, I suspect that her experiences give her a somewhat "unrealistic" view of what is generally possible for "most folks". While I mean this to be a *mild* caveat on the book, I did find myself reacting to a number of things in here with some incredulity as to their "general applicability".

As regular readers know, I fall back on this crutch *way* too often, but sometimes the best option for giving you the "broad strokes" of the book is to pass along the contents listing ... of course, for some books that would be pointless, but others, like this one, are *very* clear on how the info's set out ... so:

> Part 1 – Finding your Breakthrough Idea
> - The Big Idea
> - Develop Your Expert Niche
> - Provide New Research
> - Combine Ideas
> - Create a Framework

Part 2 – Building a Following Around Your Ideas
- Build Your Network
- Build Your Audience
- Build a Community

Part 3 – Making It Happen
- Putting Thought Leadership Into Practice

Now, I'm pretty sure that *most* of my issues with this come from my own personal situation … I'll have been stuck in my current job search for *six years* as of next week, so when Clark talks about "becoming a recognized expert *in your field*", I have to ask "and *what* field would that be?" … if I was in my 36th year in Public Relations, or 22nd year in Publishing, I'd have an answer for that (and I'd anticipate that I'd already *be* a "thought leader" in either by now), but *no*. While my situation is, quite likely, extreme … I'm guessing that *not* being on the cutting edge of one's field is a majority state – especially among Millennials, who are notorious for job/field hopping. While Clark insists: *"If you want to become recognized as the best in your industry, you'll have to fight for it, but the promise of this book is that your goal is possible"*, I can't help but see a parallel to Lake Wobegon's *"… and all the children are above average"* in the possibility of each and every reader becoming the "best" in their industry!

However, we're talking about *you*, not me … you're likely in "an industry", you've got some ideas, you want to be a "thought leader" … well, Stand Out[5] does systematically walk you through the steps. Interestingly, the book starts with a story of a gal who was in a VC firm, who did an analytic report on its performance … not even *looking* to be a "thought leader", she got to that by just sticking to her guns on the (very disturbing) report … she faced a lot of resistance on what she was researching, on releasing the results, and doing subsequent articles on it … and came out as a go-to voice on (the pitfalls) of venture capital. So this is possible even if you're not specifically *looking* for it.

There are many, many stories in here illustrating specific points, more than I could possibly name-check in this review … in fact, they're the saving grace of the book, as they show *how* many of the steps here (which, as noted, frequently sound on the surface pretty much only achievable by some tiny minority), have played out in people's lives on the way to their becoming a "thought leader". The other recurring element that is of *great* value in this are the "Ask yourself:" lists at the end of major sections. Starting with "The Big Idea" (once she gets out of the way that one need not be an Einstein, Gandhi, or Jung to come up with significant idea), there are subsections walking the reader through how to get to a "big idea" - "What Assumptions Are We Making?", "What's Next?" (trends), and "What Can You Draw On From Your Own Experience" - each of which focuses on the experience of particular individuals, and offers a list of questions to elicit what *you* may have to offer (such as: *"What experiences have you had that others in your field most likely have not? How does that difference shape your view of the industry?"*).

The next part, "Develop Your Expert Niche" addresses the questions of how to best stand out: *"Building a base of knowledge in a narrow subject area may seem like a career-limiting move, but sometimes it's the only way to get past the competition."*, noting Robert Scoble's recommendation (for tech blogging – but generalizable from there) of *"... choosing one segment to specialize in so that your coverage can be much deeper than that of even the better-funded players ... if you write exclusively about that subject you're going to rapidly outstrip {the other players} and become the definitive source on the subject"*. Clark suggests looking at what you're a "local expert" in, or what you are "passionate" about (even your long-time hobbies), as a way of narrowing down the niche. Once one finds that, it's time to look for ways to "distinguish yourself" in it ... even if by being *"not that"* of the expected traits (and example she gives is how Rachel Ray got hired by Food Network for *not* being a chef). Next there's "developing" your niche – digging deeper into the subjects, and "expanding" your niche – moving in to adjacent areas, or producing new channels of exposure.

Not being "in an industry", the next part was one I had issues with, as "Provide New Research" can be painfully broad if one is not starting from some settled place. However, the section walks you through some illuminating examples, and the "Ask Yourself:" questions, such as: *"Who are the usual information sources in your industry? Who else is knowledgeable but doesn't often get asked for their insights or opinions? How can you reach out to them?"*.

I felt one of the key parts of the book was the "Combine Ideas" chapter, as this is where the successful "mashups" come from. One of the examples Clark offers is how Steve Jobs' college class in calligraphy ended up spurring some of the typographical features of the Mac ... and refers to this ability as "Janusian thinking" (from the two-faced Roman god Janus). The focus here is how to take the things you may know from one area and bring them to bear in another ... with some very interesting examples. She states: *"If you want to develop breakthrough ideas, something outside the norm, you need to be willing to live outside the norm. At times, that can subject you to scorn ... even when you're not being attacked, you may be greeted with a subtler form of skepticism ..."* {people not seeing the potential in your ideas}.

The last part of the first section is "Create a Framework", which is set up in regards to Kübler-Ross' work on grief or Maslow's famed "needs" structure. Clark suggests: *"If you want to make a mark in your field, try to spell out the fundamental principles behind it. Surprisingly often, the central tenets of a field have never been consciously articulated."* ... and follows up with questions about what in your field are "mysterious", "secret", or "misunderstood". The more "systematized" you are able to make the material, the better it will be understood – and spread: *"Creating a framework means helping others think about a topic ..."*.

That, of course, brings us to the second part of the book - "Building a Following Around Your Ideas" - with individual chapters on building one's Network, Audience, and Community. This is very nitty-gritty, and familiar territory for those toiling in the social media trenches. She gives and extensive look at Seth Godin (obviously in the "Create a Tribe" sub-section) and how he's built himself up into a global phenomenon, and offers several other stories from varied settings. This part of the book, however, didn't lend itself as much to cherry-picking quotes, so I'm pretty much going to leave it at this.

The last part of the book (consisting of the one chapter "Putting Thought Leadership into Practice"), is for a fairly rarefied audience … those who have both come up with a breakthrough idea, and have built their "tribe". Needless to say, most people reading it won't be there. The subsections here are "Making Time For Reflection", "Making Time For Luck", "Making A Living", and "Making the Effort".

Despite all the aforementioned concerns about the "general applicability" of Stand Out[6] (and, I must admit, Ms. Clark *does* address a lot of my own personal issues up front in terms of how "a generalist" can find that one idea … although, she sort of stumbled into *hers*, as one 700-word blog post she'd done for the *Harvard Business Review* "took off" and gave her the platform to build all the rest on), it is quite an engaging read. Her combining direct discussion of the main points with examples of how this has played out in "real life" is quite effective, and, as noted, the questions for digging into one's own experiences are *awesome*.

While this book is probably best for those in a significant position in an identifiable "industry", it is a worthwhile read for anybody who has ever contemplated the possibility (dream?) of becoming a "thought leader". This is brand new (just out a couple of weeks), so should be available in the brick-and-mortar book vendors, and the on-line guys are offering it at about a 25% discount. I just wish that *I* were in a better position to put the info in here to use!

Notes:

1. http://btripp-books.livejournal.com/167658.html
2. http://bit.ly/365giving
3. http://amzn.to/1KvC39I
4. http://dorieclark.com/
5-6. http://amzn.to/1KvC39I

Saturday, May 23, 2015[1]

Fascinating stuff ...

This seems to be something of a theme in recently-reviewed books here, but this title also took a somewhat circuitous route into my hands. I had requested Jonathan D. Moreno's _Mind Wars: Brain Science and the Military in the 21st Century_[2] in the May 2012 "batch" of books being offered in the Early Reviewer program over on LibraryThing.com. However, I didn't win it (instead the "almighty algorithm" deigned to match me with _Death Metal Music_[3] that month), although I was interested enough in it that I'd put it on my Amazon "wish list" with the anticipation that one day I'd order a copy. However, in August of 2014, Moreno's _Impromptu Man_[4] came up in LTER, and I requested and won it. The current book came with _that_ as a "throw in" from the publisher ... I was amazed that "they remembered" that I'd wanted this (I wrote them, and it was actually purely happenstance), and that's how I got _Mind Wars_[5] - so it's "sort of" another LTER book.

If not uniquely so, Moreno is certainly well-positioned to have informative views on the subject of "brain science and the military in the 21st Century", having been described as _the most interesting bioethicist of our time_, and having served as a senior staff member on three presidential, and a number of Pentagon, advisory committees, as well as holding a chair at University of Pennsylvania in Medical Ethics, and being the US representative to the UNESCO International Bioethics Committee. He grew up in the Medical field, as his father was noted psychologist (see _Impromptu Man_[6] for his biography of his father), and the younger Moreno was familiar with many of the top researchers of the time.

This actually comes into play at points in this book ... as in researching it, Moreno discovered some very disturbing work that had been done by a couple of long-time "family friends", and he found it hard to reconcile some of the experiments that had been done by these otherwise much-respected scientists. In fact, the book begins in the 60's, where his father had a Hudson-valley location for his institute (and government approval for dispensing LSD), when Dr. Timothy Leary notoriously opened up _his_ much-less-clinical operation just a couple of dozen miles north in Milbrook, NY. While popular culture, understandably, associates LSD with the hippies and related movements, its origin (and initial supply) is much more closely linked with mind-control experiments of the military. This is the "rabbit hole" that Moreno first jumps into. The copy that I have is the second edition ... the first, in 2006, really broke new ground, showing:

> ... that the security establishment's interest and investment in neuroscience, neuropharmacology (the study of the influence of drugs on the nervous system), and related areas was extensive and growing. However, no one had attempted a systematic overview of developments in neuroscience as they might affect national security, nor had any-

> *one raised the many fascinating ethical and policy issues that might emerge from this relationship.*

His work lecturing on the initial edition of the book also seemed to have loosened up channels where he'd previously been "hitting walls", his *"prediction that neuroscience would be of increasing interest to national security agencies"* was not only borne out, but

> *... matters moved more quickly than I had guessed. To my surprise, within two years after the first edition of* Mind Wars *I began to receive invitations to participate on intelligence community advisory committees that have provided important analyses of the state of the science and its future prospects.*

While a lot of this book is "gee whiz!" looks at what is being worked on (systems that let users operation machinery – be it a replacement arm or an attack drone – with just one's thoughts, scanners that can "read" the content of thoughts, etc., etc., etc.), a substantial portion of this is rather into the nitty-gritty of the brain, and the details of how they're coaxing *that* machine to work with *machine* machines ... and with a philosophical overlay across the whole work, putting all this *science* in the context of the related ethical issues. On this point, here's a bit that I bookmarked in the first chapter, "DARPA on Your Mind":

> *It is ironic that discussions about national security often fail to involve the optimal means of ensuring that people are safe to live their lives: keeping the peace. The sad fact is that there is a specific marketplace for the material of war, not of peace. Even though we might like to think that military and intelligence assets ultimately keep the peace, the fact is that it's a lot easier to monetize and market firepower than peaceful easy feelings.*

While essentially, un-illustrated, there is one page with diagrams of the brain which I found *very* useful, especially the one on "the forebrain and brain stem", which details several systems and subsystems and eventually nearly a dozen specific points – many of which I was only familiar with the name. Moreno almost waxes poetic in his introduction of the brain: *"Weighing only about three pounds but containing one hundred billion nerve cells, or neurons, with more possible connections than stars in the universe, the adult human brain is evolution's greatest achievement."* Of course the poetry exists in an environment that is largely funded by DARPA (the Defense Advanced Research Projects Agency), so the *first* use of most of this new tech is so that *"ultimately, human abilities may be augmented so that combat soldiers could have vastly more powerful and faster robotic arms and legs, and pilots could control vehicles through intentional thought alone."* Making quadriplegics get up and walk, or thinking your microwave oven into operation, are only happy by-products of the research.

In a discussion of proprioception (from Wikipedia: *"the sense of the relative position of neighboring parts of the body and strength of effort being em-*

ployed in movement") and how we might get feedback from machines, there is this fascinating section:

> Interestingly, tactile feedback may not even be a necessary part of the equation. The Brookings Institution national security scholar Peter W. Singer observes that the "sixth sense" of feeling bodily connected to the tools we use emerges over time. He imagines that controlling a prosthetic arm could become as second nature as driving a car, wherein one develops an intimate knowledge of its maneuverability and size through repeated experience. In the words of philosopher Robin Zebrowski, "it has been shown that our brains actually allot neural space to those tools which we take up consistently. The tip of the cane actually does become part of the person's body, to a degree never before realized. Each of us is bound, bodily, to the tools that we use in a deeply neurological way." Thus, in a limited sense proprioception may naturally incorporate prosthetics or other neurally controlled robotics as an emergent property, without needing to be engineered from the get-go.

Unfortunately, nothing in the middle five sections of the book, "Mind Games" (Abu Ghraib -like humiliation, *Manchurian Candidate*-like "brainwashing", U.S. LSD programs, Soviet ELF – extremely low frequency wave – projects, etc.), "How to Think about the Brain" ("remote viewing" programs that lead into a discussion of historical views of brain/mind duality, the "localism-holism debate", specific brain region/chemical functions, etc.), "Brain Reading" (various tests, systems, sensors, scans, predictive modeling, etc. that seek to get into people's heads), "Building Better Soldiers" (sleep issues, metabolism issues, reaction time, memory, and processing issues, fear/emotion issues, genetic enhancement issues, etc.), and "Enter the Nonlethals" (various non-killing approaches from drugs, smell, acoustic beams, microwave pain inducers, and the related legal/ethical arguments around these), had anything that jumped out enough to me for me to have flagged with a little bookmark, but I'm hoping the little "laundry list" of topics here will give you a sense of where Moreno was going in those parts of the book.

The final chapter, "Toward an Ethics of Neurosecurity", is almost a separate treatise in itself, and is pretty much Moreno taking all the details preceding it and giving it his "bioethicist" spin. Let me apologize in advance for the following lengthy quote, but I think it's a key point he's making, and I didn't feel that either my attempting a paraphrase or cherry-picking smaller bits did it justice.

> ... For those who are deeply concerned about the exploitation of science for military purposes, an obvious answer seems to be that the scientific community should simply swear off cooperation with the national security agencies, including ac-

cepting research contracts. Call this the purist approach. Based on some historical experience I shall elaborate, I believe the purist answer is short-sighted. In the real world, this kind of research is going to continue and it's best that university researchers be those who do it, rather than building top secret science fortresses with researchers who are not answerable to anyone but their commanders. It is critical for the well-being of our democratic society that the civilian scientific community is kept in the loop and that the rest of us can have at least a general idea of the kind of work that is being done, even though for legitimate reasons many of the details may not be generally available.

An important reason to keep the scientific process as normal as possible, including transparency in interactions among scientists, is that science sets an example for an open society in which secrecy is minimized. Secrecy makes it harder for our elected representatives to fulfill their constitutional responsibility of overseeing government-funded science, and for experts outside of government to contribute to sound policymaking. One way a democratic society can minimize secrecy is to keep national security agencies linked to the larger world of academic science. For the same reason, suggestions in Congress and elsewhere that DARPA should pull back on its external funding should be resisted. The link between the academic world and the national security establishment makes for a healthier society than if each were isolated from the other.

Now, I feel bad that I've only really been able to scratch the surface of all the amazing work that Moreno details in Mind Wars[7], but I hope the above gives you a good indication of what you can expect in the book. The new edition has been out a couple of years at this point, but it is still in print, so you at least have a sporting chance of being able to find it in your local brick-and-mortar book vendor. The on-line big boys have it, of course, but aren't cutting much off the cover price (which is quite reasonable for the existing paperback edition). The new/used vendors also don't have it for way cheap, but you might save half off of the retail if you went that way with a "very good" copy (and remember, paperbacks tend to lose condition a lot faster than hardcovers in the after-market).

I really liked this one, the writing is crisp and intelligent, and Moreno makes a valiant effort to make a lot of difficult concepts approachable. That said, there were parts of this that were somewhat of a slog, simply due to the density/complexity of the material involved. If you're interested in military stuff, mind stuff, tech stuff, heck, even drug stuff, you'll probably going to get a lot out of this. I'm excited to pass my copy along to my engineering student daughter, who is focused on robotics and was fascinated to hear me talk about the "thought control" elements detailed here!

Notes:

1. http://btripp-books.livejournal.com/167919.html
2. http://amzn.to/1JrYSu4
3. http://btripp-books.livejournal.com/136286.html
4. http://btripp-books.livejournal.com/161230.html
5. http://amzn.to/1JrYSu4
6. http://btripp-books.livejournal.com/161230.html
7. http://amzn.to/1JrYSu4

Sunday, May 24, 2015[1]

One a week?

This was another LibraryThing.com "Early Reviewer" program book ... that I was waiting for a *long* time (it was from the January 2015 "batch" but just arrived a week or so ago) ... and I got "faked out" by it, because it had been offered previously, and a bunch of LTER reviews were already up on the site ... leading me to assume that all of *those* folks had gotten their copies of Rachel Swaby's Headstrong: 52 Women Who Changed Science – and the World[2] and I hadn't (I contacted the publisher, Broadway Books, and they kindly sent me a copy of the recently-released paperback, which pretty much arrived simultaneously with the ARC – uncorrected proof "advance reading copy" – from the LTER offer). As regular readers of this space will no doubt suspect, the reason I was so hot to get a hold of this is that I wanted to get it read, reviewed, and passed along to my engineering student daughter ... figuring this would be inspirational to her (as it was, I gave her the "finished" copy).

As one would correctly surmise by the book's sub-title, this is 52 brief biographical sketches of women in the sciences, some "household names", but most not. The author opens up her thought process in selection to a remarkable extent in the introduction, noting:

> *Accomplishments alone could have warranted inclusion in a different kind of book, but to be here, narrative – a secret bedroom lab, an ocean-floor expedition, or a stolen photograph that helped solve the structure of DNA – needed to be the twin pillar of achievement. I didn't include scientists if I didn't feel like I could travel beyond the bullet points of a dazzling career.*

She also points out:

> *The scientists in this book aren't included because they were women practicing science or math in a time when few women did – although by that criteria, many would fit. They're included because ... their ideas, discoveries, and insights made earth-shaking changes to the way we see the world.*

Obviously, a book like this needs *some* sort of organization, and while it *could* have been done chronologically (admittedly, each section is arranged by year, but this causes a somewhat confusing "retrograde" flow of time periods), given that another of Swaby's selection criteria was that *"the book includes only scientists whose life's work has already been completed"*, it is by "field", with sections covering Medicine, Biology and the Environment, Genetics and Development, Physics, The Earth and the Stars, Math and Technology, and Invention. Personally (and this is a *minor* quibble), I found those categories a bit on the hazy side, leading to less clarity than there might have been ... but one understands that these women were not strictly siloed into handy categories in their lives.

There is a surprisingly expansive timeline here, going as far back as Maria Sibylla Merian (1647-1717), who is listed as a German Botanist, but is included for her detailed scientific illustrations of insects, and those primarily in Suriname (on the north coast of South America), to as recent as Stephanie Kwolek (1923-2014), an American Chemist, who, in a lifetime working for DuPont, invented Kevlar, and contributed to the development of Lycra and Spandex. It's also somewhat surprising that the list isn't dominated by 1900 dates, with about a third being 1800s or before (although some of these ladies were *very* long-lived, with nearly half the list living into their 80's and beyond).

Of course, in a book with 52 individual stories, there's not much of an "arc" to speak of, and so I'm just going to cherry-pick a few things that grabbed my attention (although, in the reading of it, I found it hard to add bookmarks, as nothing stood out as "essential" for the description). One that was mentioned in one of the quotes above, was the "dirty secret" of DNA ... which featured one of the less-long-lived subjects of the book, Rosalind Franklin (1920-1958), who was an English Geneticist ... Swaby says that (generally-credited discoverers of DNA) Watson and Crick *"simply wouldn't have made their discoveries when they did had it not been for two crucial pieces of information passed from Franklin's lab at King's College in London to Watson and Crick's at Cambridge **without her knowledge**"* {bolding mine}. The two pieces were an unusually clear photo of DNA that Franklin had calibrated and captured (she'd developed a very precise process for obtaining photographic images of these molecules), and an internal report summarizing her past few years of work ... these allowed Watson and Crick to correct a number of key errors they had in *their* data, and so publish the results before Franklin had a chance to synthesize her results into a submittable paper.

Another surprising story is that of Hedy Lamarr (1913-2000), more generally known as a *Hollywood actress*. Here she's an Austrian (born Hedwig Kiesler) inventor, who developed a frequency-hopping communications system (to help the Navy aim torpedoes, which were experiencing a 60% failure rate), the 1941 patent for which (that did not emerge from being "classified" by the military until two decades later) is the basis for *"Wi-Fi, Bluetooth, GPS, wireless cash registers, bar code readers, and home control systems"*. Swaby follows up with:

> *While she had a long career as a celebrated actress, Lamarr finally got the real recognition she deserved when she was awarded the Electronic Frontier Foundation's Pioneer Award in 1996. Her response: "It's about time."*

There are *some* famous names (as scientists) in here as well. One being Virginia Apgar (1909-1974), an American medical doctor who is likely familiar to any parents for the APGAR score for newborns, which she developed, but which was later cleverly re-worded by a resident to spell out her name

... A-Appearance (Color), P-Pulse (Heart rate), G-Grimace (Reflex irritability), A-Activity (Muscle tone), and R-Respiration. Prior to her coming up with the test, newborns weren't generally "examined" after birth, letting addressable issues turn into life-threatening situations. She later moved on to head the Congenital Malformations division at the March of Dimes.

Another name that anybody around in the 60's will recognize is that of Rachel Carson (1907-1964), and American Marine Biologist whose book on the disastrous side-effects of pesticide use, *Silent Spring*, was a major catalyst for the modern environmental movement. Her influence was felt both in the celebrations of Earth Day, and in the establishment of the Environmental Protection Agency.

Perhaps most media-known of this list would be Sally Ride (1951-2012), American Astrophysicist, and more famously, Astronaut. She beat out over 8,000 other applicants for her 1983 space mission, giving an icon for every STEM-loving girl on the planet.

Given that there are 52 bios in a 230-page book, none of these are particularly in-depth looks at their subject ... each running 3-6 pages – enough to give some background, provide those "narrative" elements that Swaby was looking for, and hit the high points of what, in a lot of cases, were long and distinguished careers.

There aren't any "boring" parts in Headstrong[3], the author's search for *stories* and the brevity of each topic assuring that, and it's a pretty breezy read. The cover features the pictures of a dozen of the subjects (none labeled, so after Sally Ride and Hedy Lamarr, I had no clue who was who), and one thing that I think would have improved the book would have been pictures in the chapters themselves ... although in some cases these might have been hard to come by.

This just hit the bookstores last month, so should certainly be available. I anticipate that this is going to be a classic for girls like my daughter, sort of a "vision board" for the whole spectrum of scientific achievement. The online big boys have it at nearly 30% off of (a very reasonable) cover price at this point, and that might be your best bet at the moment, unless your local book store is given to matching discounts. Aside from the "encouraging my daughter" aspects, I enjoyed reading this in the context of a fairly neglected "history of science" storyline. If your interests are in that direction (or in Feminism in general, I suppose) you'll find a lot to like here.

Notes:

1. http://btripp-books.livejournal.com/168017.html
2-3. http://amzn.to/1QQW91R

Saturday, May 30, 2015[1]

The sign points, the road falters ...

I really *must* stop believing in sub-titles ... I've had quite a run of books that purported (via the sub-title) to be about one thing, but never quite got there, or went in some completely different direction. On one hand, I'm kind of pissed off when this happens ... having devoted a chunk of time to actually *read* the book, in expectation that it was going to be going somewhere it really wasn't ... but I guess it's "my fault" for taking the sub-title at its word(s).

I'm afraid that Graham Hancock's The Divine Spark: A Graham Hancock Reader: Psychedelics, Consciousness, and the Birth of Civilization[2] ends up on that list. While there is LOTS about Psychedelics, and a bunch about Consciousness, the "tease" that got me interested in this in the first place was the "Birth of Civilization" part, which, while *referenced*, certainly does not play a significant part in the book.

Now, I've been a big fan of Graham Hancock for a long while, and have, fairly recently, been following him on Facebook, where I saw him discussing the book, and excerpting bits from *his* parts of it there. I reached out to Disinformation Books (which I was surprised to find is now part of Red Wheel / Weiser) for a review copy, which they eventually provided. The first thing to note about The Divine Spark[3] is that Hancock is primarily the *editor* of a collection of 26 papers dealing with (generally speaking) hallucinogens, their history, their sources, their chemistry, their use, etc. ... only 3 of which are Hancock's. The rest are a smattering of MDs, PhDs, familiar names like the solid Robert Schoch and the off-the-wall Russell Brand, plus a motley crew of drug enthusiasts and reality theorists ... with item lengths ranging from a very brief 3 pages, to nearly 30.

As long-time readers of my reviews will no doubt recall, I have a certain amount of experience in this sphere, having studied shamanism back in the 80's (with much of the entheogenic enhancements discussed herein in trips to Peru and elsewhere), as well as having the experiential resources of a near-classic "misspent youth". So, when *I* found the book a bit over-the-top in enthusiasm for psychedelics, it makes me wonder how it would be received by somebody whose interface with mind-altering substances was more in the tequila zone. Admittedly, in the past several decades I've been "clean & sober" and a non-participant in any chemical enhancements (I was very rah-rah when I read Hancock's story – included in this collection – about giving up his long-time intensive daily Cannabis use ... having had a couple of friends who completely *ruined* their lives with their dedication to that particular plant, at the expense of everything else ... and quite disappointed in his recent posts of having started smoking again, thanks to Colorado's new marijuana laws).

The book is broken up into five sections: On Consciousness, Expanding the Mind, Serious Research, Experiencing Psychedelics, and Supernatural. Individual pieces cover personal experiences with LSD, MDMA, Ayahuasca, even home-cooked DMT (*who knew?*), detailed notes from assorted scientific and quasi-scientific experiments dealing with psychedelics, to discussions of things as variable as the Casimir Effect (a method of extracting "free energy" from vacuum oscillations), stars being conscious (*"Perhaps the reason galaxies don't fall apart is because they are not dumb balls of gas reacting to nothing more than the laws of physics, but are instead joined-up communities of intelligent dynamic beings."*), the existence of Richard Dawkins as a proof of the existence of God (OK, so this is Russell Brand's blithering). And, there's lots of reports of things experienced when in altered states, especially working with Ayahuasca in assorted settings.

Again, I kept waiting to get to that "Birth of Civilization" stuff, and not finding much on the subject. There is work referenced here, in a couple of places, by a writer that I had not previously encountered, by the name of Michael Winkelman, who appears to be a researcher who *only* publishes into the text book channel ... meaning his books (several of which sound *fascinating*) are *painfully* expensive, with one appearing to have a *list price* of $132.00 (for just a 336-page hardcover), whose *Kindle* price is just shy of a hundred bucks! His work is touched on in at least a couple of these pieces and, again, seems to be the source of the concept that entheogens are what dragged early man up towards "Civilization":

> Winkelman uses the concept of psychointegrator plants to refer to experiential, phenomenological, or psychological aspects of their physiological effects. He suggests that the resulting mentation (how you think) and emotion (how you feel) may produce a holistic state of psychological integration and emotional growth. ... Psychointegrator plants are traditionally used across cultures in a religious, spiritual, and often therapeutic context and may enhance some of the innate capacities of consciousness, integrating various forms of information.

Needless to say, I was disappointed that these theories where not better represented in the text, as the idea that what we are as modern humans represents a dynamic interface between basic hominid "meatware", and the unique (albeit complementary) chemistry of this group of plants. If Winkelman's books were available in "mass market" editions (rather than the type of books you have to *rent*!), I'd have had an order in for 2 or 3 of them already.

Obviously, despite my disappointment in this (highlighted in the sub-title) subject not being covered more than in passing, there is quite a lot of very interesting material in The Divine Spark[4] ... although, again, I wonder how well this would come across to folks who haven't been exposed to these sorts of experiences. It will no doubt be *extremely* popular with fans of hallucinogens, as the book reads, over-all, as quite "druggy".

One piece really appealed to me as a libertarian ... a brief paper by Hancock called "The Consciousness Revolution" ... where the author looks at models of consciousness and how they, through religion and politics, become locked into particular *dogmatic and ideological views*.:

> *I refer here to the so-called "war on drugs" which is really better understood as a war on consciousness and which maintains, supposedly in the interests of society, that we as adults do not have the right or maturity to make sovereign decisions about our own consciousness and about the states of consciousness we wish to explore and embrace. This extraordinary imposition on adult cognitive liberty is justified by the idea that our brain activity, disturbed by drugs, will adversely impact our behavior toward others. Yet anyone who pauses to think seriously for even a moment must realize that we already have adequate laws that govern adverse behavior toward others and that the real purpose of the "war on drugs" must therefore be to bear down on consciousness itself.*

I do wish I was able to be more *enthusiastic* about The Divine Spark[5], as much of it is fascinating, but I kept getting that "designated driver" vibe reading it … like hanging out with one's *wasted* friends who are having a great time, and you're not. This has just been out for a month or so, and should be easy to find … the on-line guys have it (of course), and are currently knocking off about 20% from the cover price (heck, you could get it for 1/3rd of the price of the *cheapest* Winkelman book).

Notes:

1. http://btripp-books.livejournal.com/168309.html
2-5. http://amzn.to/1CETP3T

Sunday, May 31, 2015[1]

Struggling with Science ...

This was another of those LibraryThing.com "Early Reviewer" program books that I put a request in for due to my being the doting father of a daughter who is studying to be an engineer. These days, almost anything that deals with females going into the STEM fields gets my attention, as I'm (obviously) rooting for my kid to be the most awesome engineer ever, and anything I can do to make that less painful for her, I'm up for. Evidently, the LTER "Almighty Algorithm" is in sync with this, as Eileen Pollack's The Only Woman in the Room: Why Science Is Still a Boys' Club[2] is about the third or fourth book I've gotten from there that's more-or-less on the topic.

As those who have read many of my recent reviews, I seem to be in a zone of having issues with how the books I've been reading have presented themselves via their sub-titles. I am not the *first* person to note that "Why Science Is Still A Boy's Club" is not particularly representative of the actual thrust of this book. While being "thematically" accurate, this is largely an auto-biographical tale, focused on the author's experiences in attending Yale as a physics major, and not some in-depth look at the societal factors leading to the still-substantial difference in the gender mix in the sciences.

Not, mind you, that this material isn't *in there*, but ... and this is just my "gut feeling" ... it seems to have been added on in order to turn the author's *personal story* into something more "generally applicable".

I hope I'm not indulging in "spoilers" here, but Ms. Pollack opts to not go forward with a career in physics, and instead becomes an author and writing professor. It is, perhaps, a testimony to her skills in composition that I went through most of this book not really "getting" how long ago most the narrative happens ... as I ended up with a "huh?" moment when the dates finally sunk in – having felt that I was reading something far more *recent* in her life than the 30 years or so in the past this all occurred. Not that this is "ancient history" (she and I are only a year apart – so I probably have a visceral identification with her college experience, if in a very different context), but I was surprised about 2/3rds of the way through the book to find this was a middle-aged woman's recalling her grade school, high school, and college years.

Why surprised? Well, this is going to sound bad, but it's really hard to nail down with other words ... a lot of this is awfully *whiny*, with stories about how she wasn't appreciated at various levels, or how she got stuff, or didn't get stuff, or acted differently, or whatever, which read as a lot more *immediate* than revisiting long-past slights.

Of course, *I'm a guy*, and so probably don't have the appropriate sensitivity to how those situations impacted little Eileen ... but my ability to empathize

with her (despite being a "right-end-of-the-bell-curve" kid myself) definitely has a point where it drops off into less-sympathetic impressions.

Since the first 2/3rds of the book (which is convenient divided up into sections of her early years, her Yale years, and her revisiting things three decades later) is pretty much just a bio ... I guess it wouldn't hurt to do the broad strokes. The author was from a small town in the "borscht belt" of the Catskills in upstate New York, where her Jewish grandparents owned a small resort hotel, and her father was the town dentist. She starts the narrative very early on, when she is shocked that the stuff she's noticing (like *thinking*) at "age 3 or 4" isn't some major discovery on her part ... setting up a pattern of thwarted expectations that tend to recur throughout the story. She's described by one teacher as "obnoxious", and from her descriptions of her behavior at various points, that seems to fit. For much of the early part of the book, she's keen to point out how she was living in a wholly different reality than most of those around her ... she tells of a time when she was being tested for possibly skipping a grade (3rd?), and was in the office of the teacher who was putting her through various assessments. A pigeon gets into the office, the teacher freaks out, gets up on the desk, and is later quizzical why *she* didn't get more upset ... her response: *"Why should I be upset? This isn't my office. I'm not the one who needs to clear up after it."* ... which is obviously set up to show how "different" she was (even though she makes a point to say that she remembered what she said from 50 years ago ... how much dialog do *you* recall verbatim from when you were 8 or 9 years old?).

There's a lot of auto-biographical stuff here that, while adding "color" to the telling, probably doesn't do much to advance the supposed thesis of the book ... do we need to know about her crushes ... the nearly-inappropriate relationship she has with a high school teacher, which *does* have elements that impact the story, but it's just uncomfortable in the telling (she thought they'd get married, he turns out to be gay), etc.? And, do we *really* need to know about her hormonal imbalance (too much testosterone) that only got addressed (kickstarting her periods) with a visit to the doctor in college? These may make the bio more interesting, but don't do much for main point of the book.

So, the first third of the book sets her up as a brilliant, but unfocused kid. The second part of the book is her experiences at Yale ... and how she had to struggle through a wide assortment of difficulties that she (no doubt rightly) perceived as being things that a male would not have had problems with (from not wanting to speak up in class to ruining a pair of hose she was wearing in a lab). Again, a lot of this comes across as "poor me" rather than "this was a universal experience of all women on the Yale campus".

The last third of the book involves her going back to Yale (and her grade and high schools) to see how things had changed, or not. She was welcomed back by the various departments, etc., and set up with situations where she could interview students. This leads to the key *informational* part of the book ... after having interviewed (briefly, because she went to the wrong office initially) a female department head, there was a reception for the author, which ended up being attended by a large number of female students (and the department head), with the students raising a number of issues that the department head didn't realize were problems, resulting in her clearing her schedule and giving nearly full attention for the next several days to Ms. Pollack ... introducing her to a lot more contacts, etc. This provides the real "meat" of the book.

Anyway, The Only Woman in the Room[3] is not coming out until this Fall (it has a September 15 release date), so you'll have a while to wait if you want to check it out ... although you *can* pre-order it at the moment from the on-line big boys (at a 45% discount). While the book is well-written, and the story is engaging up to a point, it still feels like it's an auto-biography that ended up getting a sociological coda added onto it to make it appealing to a large enough market to get published. I had, when requesting this, hoped for something more integrated, and possibly more *informative* (not that there isn't a whole lot of data eventually presented here). I just didn't feel that the "Why Science Is Still A Boy's Club" theme was particularly advanced by the author's life story. Again, this may be my being a cynical "privileged" male brute, lacking the sensitivity to fully empathize with the tale ... so you might connect better with it than I did. Text

Notes:

1. http://btripp-books.livejournal.com/168580.html

2-3. http://amzn.to/1PZ7hao

Sunday, June 7, 2015[1]

Good News For "Type-A" Types ...

As I've noted here from time to time, books coming out from the LibraryThing.com "Early Reviewer" program do have a tendency to just be *"meh"* ... probably being due to being something of a "pig in a poke", where one requests review copies on a couple of sentences of description in most cases. However, every now and again there's a *"WOW!"* book and Kelly McGonigal's The Upside of Stress: Why Stress Is Good for You, and How to Get Good at It[2] is one of those. Now, I need to preface this all with a bit of a caveat: While Ms. McGonigal is a PhD (in Psychology from Stanford), I'm not sure how "grounded" her material is in a wider scope of research ... while much of this *is* referenced to various studies, I don't get the sense of it being exactly massively vetted, and I kept wondering if this was like some of the "newagey" stuff out there (albeit, pointing in a rather different direction) which cherry-picks bits of research, often out of context, to support a "revolutionary" stance. And, frankly, the central thesis of the book is sufficiently removed from the realm of "common knowledge" that it could well have been featured in Woody Allen's "Sleeper" ... where is character wakes up after 200 years in cryogenic suspension to a world where deep fat, steak, cream pies, and fudge are deemed health foods ... so why not "stress is good for you" as well?

The author describes how she used to be "like everybody else" in believing stress is bad for you, and taught classes and workshops to get folks to *"do whatever you can to reduce the stress in your life"* , but then she ran across a study that changed her mind. I'm having a hard time effectively paraphrasing this, so forgive the long quote – but this is the "launching point" for the book:

> ... In 1998, thirty thousand adults in the United States were asked how much stress they had experienced in the past year. They were also asked, Do you believe stress is harmful to your health?
>
> Eight years later, the researchers scoured public records to find out who among the thirty thousand participants had died. Let me deliver the bad news first. High levels of stress increased the risk of dying by 43 percent. But – and this is what got my attention – that increased risk applied only to people who also believed that stress was harming their health. People who reported high levels of stress but who did not view their stress as harmful were not more likely to die. In fact, they had the lowest risk of death of anyone in the study, even lower than those who reported experiencing very little stress.
>
> The researchers concluded that it wasn't stress alone that was killing people. It was the combina-

> tion of stress and the <u>belief</u> that stress is harmful. The researchers estimated that over the eight years they conducted their study, 182,000 Americans may have died prematurely because they believed that stress was harming their health.
>
> That number stopped my in my tracks. We're talking over twenty thousand deaths a year! According to statistics from the Centers for Disease Control and Prevention, that would make "believing that stress is bad for you" the fifteenth-leading cause of death in the United States, killing more people than skin cancer, HIV/AIDS, and homicide.

She obviously "connected the dots" and realized that her "anti-stress" work might well be *killing people*. She then looked at various health "crusades" that generally had backfired, from graphic anti-smoking materials to "shaming" strategies for weight loss, a lot of what passed for "common knowledge" in the medical community has turned out to be counter-productive when actually studied. And, just like smokers increasing their smoking in response to autopsy pics of cigarette-blackened lungs, or overweight subjects *doubling* their calorie intake in the wake of "eat healthy" campaigns, McGonigal realized that her audiences frequently were more depressed and distraught than before she "told them what to do" about stress. After digging into the subject she'd pretty much done a 180° turn:

> ... The latest science reveals that stress can make you smarter, stronger, and more successful. It helps you learn and grow. It can even inspire courage and compassion.
>
> The new science also shows that changing your mind about stress can make you healthier and happier. How you think about stress affects everything from your cardiovascular health to your ability to find meaning in life. The best way to manage stress isn't to reduce or avoid it, but rather to rethink and even embrace it.

Needless to say, this sounded like *great* news to somebody like me who's spent decades driving the body and mind to the limits of exhaustion – or in the Cowboy phrase[3] "ridden hard and put away wet" – nice to think I wasn't killing myself all that time!

One criticism I've seen about the author's work here is that she doesn't have a sharply-defined concept of "stress" … she does offer up a definition, however: *"Stress is what arises when something you care about is at stake."*, which one does have to admit is a bit wide-reaching and non-specific … and she does address the fact that covers a *lot* of ground. However, one person's major stressor might be another's minor irritation (she uses her personal fear of flying as an example which a lot of people would find laughable), and vice-versa, so having an "umbrella" that is big enough to cover "being out of cigarettes" and "death of a family member" is probably a good idea.

There's another key psychological field that plays into the main thrusts of the book, and that's "mindsets" ... *"Mindsets are beliefs that shape your reality, including objective physical reactions ... and even long-term health, happiness, and success."* ... and what's amazing about this work is that a single brief "intervention" addressed at changing one's mindset on something can seed seemingly permanent change. One study she cites was done with hotel housekeeping staffs, who were generally overweight with bad cardiovascular numbers ... much as if they were sedentary (and they believed that they "weren't exercising regularly") ... the researcher, Alia Crum (another Psychology PhD at Stanford), developed an information program (posters and 15-minute presentations) describing how their work *was* exercise, burning as much as 300 calories an hour, and exposed a test group to this. The test group's *mindset* was changed from seeing their work as "hard on their bodies" to being "intensive exercise", and, with just this shift, they began to lose weight, and improve their over-all health ... results not seen in the "control groups" which did not have the material presented to them.

Crum also did research on how one's expectations effected hunger hormones ... where what one had been told about a food, in this case a milkshake, determined the blood chemistry the subjects exhibited. She also developed a protocol for testing stress reactions, where subjects (including the author) went through a mock job interview, structured to be a horrible experience. One set of subjects first saw a 3-minute video about how stress can enhance performance, and the other set saw a video about how stress is worse for them than they thought ... and both groups were tested for the presence of two "stress hormones", DHEA and Cortisol, in their saliva during the experiment. Remarkably, the variable of which video was shown determined the ratio of these hormones, with the "stress is good" message providing a positive mix.

So, how did the "stress is bad" mindset get so established in the medical and psychological orthodoxies (let alone public opinion)? In 1936 Hungarian endocrinologist Hans Selye was doing a series of experiments involving injecting various substances into rats. He was noticing that the rats were having the same bad reactions no matter what he was injecting them with ... and eventually generalized a theory that the structure of the experiment (injections, etc.) was what was making the rats sick (and eventually dead), and came up with "stress" as the word for the cause. His definition of stress was *"the response of the body to any demand made on it"*, not (in the author's description) *"just a response to noxious injections, traumatic injuries, or brutal laboratory conditions, but anything that requires action or adaptation"* – leading to pretty much *anything* being a potential lethal stress-inducer.

His work became a world-wide phenomenon (he was nominated for the Nobel Prize 10 times), and he published and lectured all over the globe ... with the funding of the **tobacco industry**(!). Yes, back in those days, cigarettes were often marketed as a way to relax, and Selye even testified in Congress *"that smoking was a good way to prevent the harmful effects of stress"*. Also, most of his research (and those following) was based on investigations of lab rats, in hideous situations (the author describes it as

"*The Hunger Games* for rodents") that was then generalized to humans ... even though humans (thankfully) rarely are subjected to the extreme degrees of "stress" that the poor rats in these studies were.

One of the things glossed over in these experiments is that sometimes the rats sailed through with no bad effects ... which led other researchers to look at what might be "good" in stress. The author sums up these as: *"The stress response helps you rise to the challenge, connect with others, and learn and grow."* ... with specific examples of the various ways those happen. The stress response releases hormones that can be very beneficial, if "framed" properly, and this is where the "mindset" work comes in ... even a very brief re-framing of what one *expects* out of stress can make a remarkable difference in how that stress is processed – not only mentally, but in terms of one's bio-chemistry.

There's quite a lot in here about how various researchers have implemented mindset-shifting programs in numerous settings, from "last chance" inner-urban schools to video game players ... the subjects that got the messaging were able to re-frame threats into "challenges", and overcome what previously seemed insurmountable.

The author shows that there are a lot more dimensions to stress-response than the familiar "fight or flight" dichotomy ... she also proposes a "tend and befriend" aspect, which is typified by those who have been through horrific experiences frequently devoting their lives to help others. In this form, substances such as oxytocin, dopamine, and serotonin come into play, directly shifting how the brain is relating to situations around it.

A third modality she presents really hit home for me, the "defeat response" ... which I feel is more prevalent than one would want to think:

> *The defeat response is a biologically hardwired response to repeated victimization that leads to loss of appetite, social isolation, depression, and even suicide. Its main effect is to make you withdraw. You lose motivation, hope, and the desire to connect with others. It becomes impossible to see meaning in your life, or to imagine any action you could take to improve the situation. Not every loss or trauma leads to a defeat response – it kicks in only when you feel that you have been beaten by your circumstances or rejected by your community. In other words, when you think there is nothing left that you can do and nobody who cares.*

Yeah, it sounds like she's been reading my poetry!

The book is full of lots of stories from school systems, corporations, governmental programs, and psychological research which offer examples where the sort of mindset adjustment making stress appear as a beneficial factor in one's experience lead to vastly improved results versus "control" groups that got no messaging, or groups who were unfortunately exposed to "stress is bad" messages ... results that not only were notable in their statistics, but also appear to have long-lasting effects.

Now, the copy I have is an "ARC" – advance reading copy – which often does not represent the final format of the book ... I'm hoping that the published version (which came out last month) has set up the "exercises" in a more structured way, as they're easy to miss here, and they offer a lot of benefit ... it would be great if those were in "boxes" or somehow otherwise set outside the general flow of the text, making them easier to find and refer back to. That was one of my few gripes with The Upside of Stress[4].

As the author somewhat intimates at points, even *reading* the book may have the sort of mindset-shifting effect to move the reader towards a more positive interface with stress ... after all, if a 3-minute video on how stress can be a positive factor can change physical responses, how much more would reading a 300-page book with the same message help make those changes? While I'm not suggesting this is a "magic pill" for stress ... stranger things (NLP, placebos performing better than actual drugs, various spiritual practices) have happened. In any account, it's an interesting read, and I can't think of anybody whose existence is sufficiently stress-free that they wouldn't get something out of this. As noted, it's only been out a month as of this writing, so your odds are pretty good of finding it in your local bookstore ... and the on-line guys seem to have the hardcover for about a third off of cover price at the moment. I must admit, the caveats outlined at the top of this review still hang over this a bit ... I *hope* that what McGonigal is outlining here is *real* and that the research will eventually come to solidify this version of stress, replacing the "tortured rats" model of Selye and his followers ... but on some levels it has that "too good to be true" scent, making me hold off of a 100% endorsement of it.

Notes:

http://btripp-books.livejournal.com/168938.html

http://amzn.to/1cbZw3M

http://en.wiktionary.org/wiki/ridden_hard_and_put_away_wet

http://amzn.to/1cbZw3M

Thursday, June 18, 2015[1]

For those about to Tweet ...

So, this was one of those books that I got wind of on-line and dropped a note to the publisher to request a copy. Fortunately, it's another title from the good folks at Wiley, who are always quite accommodating of my asking for review copies.

To be honest, I've been using Twitter for so long (over 8 years ... I was one of the first 3 million users – out of nearly 650 million total users), that I wasn't particularly anticipating *learning* very much in this volume, but with enthusiastic referrals like that one ==> from Chris Brogan[2] (click here[3] for a bigger version ... he seems to be enjoying it!), I could hardly have not opted to give it a read.

Now, Twitter Power 3.0: How to Dominate Your Market One Tweet at a Time[4] isn't just a book about *using* Twitter, but about using it as a vehicle for building brands. In it, authors Joel Comm (who you may recall I've reviewed previously[5]) and Dave Taylor both set up (quite literally – the first third or more of the book is pretty much step-by-step on getting a Twitter account going) Twitter for those unfamiliar with it, *and* delve into their recommendations on how to use it for business.

The book starts at about a basic level as one could ask for ... explaining "social media", and how that's evolved, and why it's important ... then moves into looking at Twitter in the context of the whole social media environment. The book is extensively illustrated with screen grabs, so the reader doesn't have to use too much imagination to follow what's being detailed ... and among these in the early bits is even a shot of the fabled "Fail Whale" ... once a familiar and all-too-nearly-omnipresent "feature" of Twitter, now a semi-fond memory of the early days on the service (when was the last time *you* saw the Fail Whale[6]?).

Some of the things that the authors coach their readers on are things like picking a name, and the ways that can impact things down the road ... walking one through considerations that are well thought-out, and might have been missed by some "late adopter" deciding that it was time "to get on that tweety thing"). While I agree with most of the (very common-sense, really) material in this, I did have a *slight* disagreement with their blanket statement about putting numbers in your ID (ala classic AOL accounts) being *"something you should really try to avoid"*, with my counter-example (and, admittedly, this would only apply to a limited number of users) of Chicago Tribune's digital honcho Bill Adee having the rather clever Twitter handle of @Bill80. Perhaps the best part of the set-up chapters is how they walk the reader through the process as Twitter will present it, and suggest (sometimes quite strongly) things to skip (such as when Twitter wants to get into your email to let you know who's already on the service – which, if you use it right when you join, will result in a lot of contacts hitting your account, and finding pretty much nothing there ... so this is a step they recommend holding off on until you're gotten some "there" there in terms of content).

In my opening above I noted that I wasn't anticipating *learning* much about Twitter in general, but I was wrong on that count. For instance, if you're needing/wanting to set up multiple Twitter presences, but don't want to be having to follow a whole slew of mail boxes (I am *quite* familiar with this problem), you can use one Gmail account for them all (!) ... how? Well, Gmail ignores periods in the stuff to the left of the @ sign ... j.ohndoe and john.doe are exactly the same to Gmail, however, *to Twitter* those are totally different addresses and will let you set up new accounts on what is (on the other end) the same email, just but adding those periods. Pretty cool. They also follow this tip up with some other interesting Gmail hacks (that I may use eventually).

One odd feature here is that they hand "the mic" over to a Matt Clark of a design company called TweetPages for the fourth chapter. While "bringing in an expert" is a laudable concept, the book already has two "cooks" and shifting over to a third voice makes that section stand out. I really think this would have been better addressed if Comm and Taylor had sat down with a half dozen designers working with Twitter (I'm sure there are hundreds of consultancies out there who would have *loved* to be credited here), and presented a "processed" take on the (no doubt variable) information on "Twitter Setup and Design". This not to say that the material he brings to the book is trivial ... I bookmarked a number of things for my own use here, including where Clark says that, even with your profile pic, you should pay attention to the SEO value of the element ... he uses the example of renaming "IMG43879852895.jpg" as "TweetPages-Matt-Clark.jpg" as something that takes just a few seconds but could result in noticeable increases in search traffic ... and he provides URLs to a number of very useful things, from a tool that helps in identifying fonts, to one that will alphabetize lists, to another which suggests free (open source) alternatives to commercial software, etc.

If there's one thing that having the "guest" chapter does, it provides a "pivot point" for the book, as following that the book makes a significant shift in focus and tone, from the careful hand-holding of setting up one's Twitter presence, to nitty-gritty marketing advice on "Building a Following on Twitter" and "The Art of the Tweet". Now, I have some additional caveats here ... as so much of what they're talking about in these parts seem to me (who has been *using* Twitter for a very long time) as being "pie in the sky by-and-by" kind of results. I have never run, or been associated with a project using, a Twitter element that came anywhere *near* the sorts of following/responses/retweets that they talk about here. Maybe I'm "snakebit" when it comes to this sort of stuff ... but this reads to me like it's the "1%" telling the *hoi polloi* how things work on their end of the world. I seem to recall that I had a very similar issue when reading Joel Comm's *Ka-Ching* (about running on-line businesses) five years ago ... it sounded *great*, but represented results that neither I, nor anybody I knew, had ever been able to achieve.

The book then goes into "Connecting with Customers", "Team Communication", "Build Your Brand", "Drive Follower Behavior", and "Make Money on Twitter". Similar caveats apply here ... the theories seem sound, but I've never seen it work like this (an example: *"out of 200 followers, your {tweet} generates 12 replies, and you can see by searching for your username that it also picked up four retweets"* – I'm pretty sure there are lottery games with better odds than those sorts of numbers happening) ... although the authors have had a great deal of success in Twitter, so I suppose are case studies in how it *can* happen. There are some tips in here, though, which are golden ... such as following somebody you know is at a conference and the hashtags that are being used there to "virtually" attend. There have been dozens of conferences I wish I'd have been able to get to, that this would have been a great way to at least "listen in" to the chatter.

Twitter Power 3.0[7] closes out with some excellent additional useful info, with one section presenting a dozen third-party programs that work with Twitter, from the near-essentials of TweetDeck or Hootsuite, to things that follow trends or send alerts when selected key words are mentioned ... and a final chapter that features five pages of Twitter accounts that the authors believe are key for marketers to follow from their own lists (and a Twitter newbie loading these in when getting set up would "hit the ground running" on good info!).

This is brand new, just out a couple of months, so you should be able to find it in the stores catering to business/internet books, and the on-line guys have it at about a quarter off cover at this point. I found this an interesting read, tempered by the above-noted caveats (my jealousy at their results?). Certainly if one was totally new to Twitter, this would provide a great starting point, and it has enough useful stuff in it to make it a worthwhile read to even "old hands" on the service.

Notes:

1. http://btripp-books.livejournal.com/169107.html
2. http://btripp-books.livejournal.com/155126.html
3. http://ic.pics.livejournal.com/btripp/2663/423841/423841_600.jpg
4. http://amzn.to/1PQScx5
5. http://btripp-books.livejournal.com/96293.html
6. http://ic.pics.livejournal.com/btripp/2663/424297/424297_original.jpg
7. http://amzn.to/1PQScx5

Friday, July 17, 2015[1]

Another job search book ...

{Hello, review/journal readers ... the following review is going to be awfully personal, with a lot of my deep inner neuroses and open-bleeding-emotional-wound stuff hanging out ... just to warn you that this is going to be even less pedantic than usual ...}

OK, so those of you who have been paying attention to this space over time no doubt know, I've been in a LONG job search ... an *insanely* long job search ... that just passed its sixth year mark in May. Needless to say, there's a level of *desperation* building, that wasn't necessarily there back when I was reviewing a lot of job-search books when penning The Job Stalker[2] blog on the Tribune's ChicagoNow site a few years back (when I stopped writing that, I stopped requesting job-search books from the publishers, which is why you've not seen many reviews in that genre of late). I have recently thrown myself on the tender mercies of a local Vocational Services organization, which paired me up with one of their "executive coaches" (yes, I used to be an "executive" ... almost hard to remember those days), with the hope of trying some new things to get me back into the world of positive cashflow. One of the first things the lady said was "read this book" ... as it is the template that they use for helping people like me get hooked up with jobs.

So, two handy facts about this before we get going ... I would very likely *never* have picked up this book without it being "assigned" to me ... and I have certain significant "issues" with the job search paradigm being presented here (in a somewhat-non-PC phrase I use: *"asking me to do THAT is about a useful as yelling at a quadriplegic to take the stairs"* ... but it's smack dab in the middle of the "Brendan is not like the other kids" category), making me be a bit "reactive" when hitting those parts.

However, given those particular land mines, Orville Pierson's Highly Effective Networking: Meet the Right People and Get a Great Job[3] is a very informative, structured, and even easy-to-read book. The author uses a technique that I typically find irritating – the "real world story" – to good effect here, and, frankly, those parts of the book make it almost a *fun* read ... "humanizing" the instructions presented chapter-to-chapter (at the end of each there is a developing story about a friend of the author who comes to him for coaching in a new job search, which progresses as the various stages of the author's job-search model are discussed).

Now, obviously, it's hard to make a single book on the job-search be a "one size fits all" instruction manual, but Pierson at least makes a stab at it, with on-going asides to new college grads and other first-timers in the work world on one side and to CEO, etc., folks on the other. The main thrust of the book, however, is in the middle of that ... salaried employees looking either to change jobs or get jobs after having been downsized (the central character of the unfolding illustrative story is an engineering manager, for example).

The book has a somewhat odd structure ... while its over-all arc is reasonably direct through the author's system, individual chapters are presented as being in one (or two) of four "steps", which are part of a table of info that precedes each (which feel like they originated in another format – perhaps a PowerPoint that he uses to train people in his methodology?). These are defined in the second chapter as:

> **Decide** to network effectively.
> **Prepare** for job hunting.
> **Talk** to personal and professional contacts.
> **Land** a new job.

One of the things I found most commendable here is Pierson's realistic view on how hard the kind of networking he recommends can be ... and he sets a goal to make the process as comfortable as possible for all involved (he points out that the person being networked with in any given situation might be very uncomfortable with the discussion – expecting that he/she is being asked to provide something, such as a concrete job lead, that they are not capable of producing). The other thing that is fairly notable here is his insistence on (and instructions for) utilizing one's "non-professional" (or not in one's target field) friends & family connections, as they frequently know somebody who knows somebody who can put you in touch with a key connection.

Back to the "structure" issue ... I really wish he'd make one big chart with all the elements in it ... he seems to go from structural level to structural level with not the most linear flow ... for instance, in the chapter which includes the four "steps" noted above, he also has "The Four Goals of Networking":

> 1. Get the word out.
> 2. Gather information.
> 3. Meet insiders at targeted organizations.
> 4. Get in touch with Decision Makers.

These *precede* his definitions of the steps, and the steps are initially presented in another chart with various sub-steps detailed, *before* getting into the specifics for each. This level of complexity makes it hard to regurgitate this in a summary form here ... it reads through fairly logically, but is hard to condense. Before launching into the main part of the book, Pierson has a chapter on "networking myths", which tackles seven of the most common ones he's encountered. The specifics here are well presented, with his description of the "myth" and information that counters each. He also notes that there's a LOT of confusion about networking out there because so many books that have been written on the subject are for *salesmen* and not job seekers ... and he notes that MLM has further blurred the lines, as a lot of "network marketers" are trained to *sell* to any live body that gets within 3 feet of them, which means that a lot of one's contacts are wary about *any* approach that is goal-centered.

In the "Prepare" section the author defines "Real Networking", which consists of "An Authentic Conversation" (No gimmicks. Be Yourself.), "Common Interest", and "Information Exchange". Now, here's one of my "reactive" points ... I have never gotten *anywhere* in my life "being myself" ... the minute I start acting "authentically", everybody starts looking at me like I have three heads ... so seeing this here makes me *very* nervous. As a result, this is one of those places where I've mentally inserted a footnote "for Normals", and have to figure out how much "acting normal" is OK before it becomes a "gimmick".

He gets into charting networks at this point, which, again, seem to be something more naturally from a PowerPoint, but show how quickly connections can grow. He references the "six degrees" material, and notes *"job hunters usually succeed at the second and third degree of separation"*, i.e., it's not who *you* know, but who *they* know, and who those *other* people know. If your "network" is as small as 10 people (and most have several hundred - *"Your total network is everyone who will accept a phone call from you"*), that's 1,000 people on the third level. He further divides warm from cold contacts, and close (in terms of connection – former school mates, other members of organizations/churches, etc.) contacts in three categories:

> Active – contacts you talk to regularly.
>
> Dormant – contacts you used to talk to regularly.
>
> Passive – network connections that have not been activated.

In a part on "mapping your networks" he offers a list of a half a dozen categories of networks, and several dozen specific potential contacts. He then breaks these out one-by-one with discussion on how to approach them, etc. (in fact, in several places he even offers up sample "scripts" to use with the various types of contacts).

The place he loses *me* is in the "Project Plan" ... and, again, this is ME – with my particular psychological issues, I suppose ... but the first two of the three points of *"an effective project plan"* are right up there with the quadriplegic (or classic-era Dalek[4]) taking the stairs:

> Professional Objective - What kind of work you want to do.
>
> Target Market – Where you want to work.
>
> Core Message – What you want to say about yourself.

In my career, I've been a bit of a MarCom "generalist", competent/plausible in 10-15 different job categories ... and I've always preferred situations where I was "wearing a lot of hats" rather than being faced with a *"time to make the doughnuts"* kind of grind[5] (no matter how interesting the doughnuts in question might have been) ... so coming up with ONE thing to focus on is, cognitively, almost impossible (and I've typically been the guy who "picks the slowest line", so "pick one" is rarely a good strategy for this). And, in terms of WHERE, I have no clue ... and don't even have a good idea (even after reading this and other books insisting on this element) of how to GET a clue.

He goes on to define and expand on these, even at one point (as a section heading) noting: *your target list is just as important as your resume* ... which has me hitting a brick wall, as I've never been able to come up with one any more focused than "gee, I guess X company would be a cool place to work". Again, as far as *my* job search was concerned ... the wheels fell off the cart at this point, so much of the rest of the book was "looking at the stairs", and not being able to make any progress at integrating the materials. Pierson suggests numerous networking strategies to "get your message out", "gather information", "meet insiders", and "get in touch with decision makers" ... but always in the context of "Target Organizations". So, if YOU have a clear "professional objective", and a clear "target list", this will no doubt make a great deal of sense and be useful ... to me, they're like saying "use the third arm coming out of your back".

The next sections are about dealing with one's personal networks ... approaching "warm", "cool", and "cold" contacts on "inner", "middle", and "outer" circles, with sample scripts for ways to make useful connections with these various categories. One thing he notes is to NOT provide your resume before meeting with somebody, or while talking with them ... send it along *later*. This makes the discussion more about you and your search (and what sort of free-association info might come up in that talk), and not about the particulars on that piece of paper. Another interesting suggestion is to "map the networks" of decision-makers who might be in a position to influence your hiring. I found it odd, *especially* in this context, that the author doesn't much focus on LinkedIn (as this would almost be an *ideal* tool for this), but most of this is not more technologically advanced than making phone calls or meeting for coffee.

I suspect that for MOST people, Highly Effective Networking[6] would be a very useful book, as I'm guessing that the vast majority of people *don't* have the "blocks" I have for key elements of this, and would have *no problem* defining "what they want to do" and companies where they want to do it. For a book in this niche it is quite readable and even enjoyable. It appears to still be in print, and the on-line big boys have it for a bit off the cover price, while copies are available via the new/used channel for as little as a penny plus shipping. Again, if you're not *me*, this is likely a must-have for the job search.

Notes:

1. http://btripp-books.livejournal.com/169409.html
2. http://www.chicagonow.com/job-stalker/
3. http://amzn.to/1T5mZol
4. http://bit.ly/1I8Ud1Y
5. https://youtu.be/petqFm94osQ
6. http://amzn.to/1T5mZol

Saturday, July 18, 2015[1]

"No fun, no sin, no you, no wonder it's dark ..."

I guess the problem with a standard Liberal Arts education is that there's not enough time to get to *everything*, and I have discovered some glaring holes in *mine* that I've been trying to fill. I suppose had I done *one* major instead of *three* (with a "fourth" unofficially added in elsewhere during the summers), I might have pushed through more material in my English major, but I keep finding stuff that I know *of*, but really haven't *read*. Fortunately, there are the Dover Thrift Editions out there, making it *very* reasonable to plug those gaps ... and with a low cover price, they're ideal to "pad" on-line orders to get them up to the free-shipping promised land.

One of the more notable voices that I was familiar with, but hadn't specifically studied, was the notorious Oscar Wilde (and I'd even stayed at the hotel he lived at in Paris – The Hôtel du Quai Voltaire – also favored by Baudelaire, Wagner, and many other notables), although I *have* now caught up with a number of his famed works over the past few years. The current one is likely his most "pop culture"-known piece for the movies it's inspired, The Picture of Dorian Gray[2]. While I'd been aware of the broad strokes of this, in its various interpretations, I'd never ventured into the text itself. I had, however, picked up a copy with an Amazon order some time back, and decided to slot it into my reading list last month to have a bit of a break from the other stuff I'd been going through.

Wilde's writing is magnificent ... and I wonder how my own composition might have been affected had I read much of it in my teens and 20s. His books are also a window into a long-lost world of the English upper classes ... one that I must confess to be something of a "golden age" to me (being largely a product of old-line noble families) ... which is certainly not a popular concept in these dark days. This is the first caveat I'd offer for the book ... if you have little patience with the doings of Lord this or Duke that (or are of the neo-Jacobin demeanor so *de rigueur* in certain circles these days), you might find Dorian Gray[3] tiresome, as much of the book is the doings, discussions, and activities of the Victorian-era idle class.

Now (and I have to "go here" in those rare occasions when I'm reviewing a piece of "fiction"), if you are "spoiler-averse" (and somehow missed the basic story elements in pop culture), you might want to stop reading at this point. I am so used to reviewing non-fiction where the concept of "spoilers" doesn't come into play, that I have a very poorly tuned sense of what is and isn't TMI for the review reader.

The book is generally third-person narration from an unspecified standpoint (i.e., not being a specific character relating it), with large blocks of conversation between the main characters. Central of these, of course, is Dorian Gray – a beautiful youth who has become the "muse" of an up-and-coming painter, Basil Hallward, who is in the process of finishing up the title image.

The picture is unusually striking, and the artist has been planning to have it be the centerpiece of an upcoming exhibit of his work. A friend of Hallward, Lord Henry Wotton is visiting, and is charmed by Dorian, and begins to infuse in him his own "libertine philosophy" of living life for its pleasures (it is generally suggested that "Lord Harry" is a stand-in for Wilde here – having the best lines). As Dorian thinks through this … focusing on his beauty … he is suddenly saddened by Wotton's warnings on the fleeting nature of youth, and faced with the completed portrait, says:

> *"How sad it is! I shall grow old, and horrible, and dreadful. But this picture will remain always young. It will never be older than this particular day in June … If it were only the other way! If it were I who was to be always young, and the picture that was to grow old! For that – for that – I would give everything! Yes, there is nothing in the whole world I would not give! I would give my soul for that!"*

What is interesting, from a modern perspective, that there is *nothing* "supernatural" in this scene … just Dorian becoming aware, perhaps for the first time, that his beauty is a temporary thing, and being *horrified* at the prospect, and wants more than anything to avoid that fate. There is much agonizing and accusation between the three men, and Hallward, in desperation at the idea of losing his muse, grabs a palette knife and move to destroy the canvas, but Dorian stops him, as he is as enamored of the image as the other men. He arranges to have it brought to his house, where it is at first put in a prime viewing location.

Before moving through more of the story arc, I'd like to drop in some material that grabbed my attention while reading this as particularly illustrative of Wilde's writing. The first one is a description of Lord Wotton's (seldom seen) wife, "Lady Henry" …

> *She was a curious woman, whose dresses always looked as if they had been designed in a rage and put on in a tempest. She was usually in love with somebody, and, as her passion was never returned, she had kept all her illusions. She tried to look picturesque, but only succeeded in being untidy.*

A bit later she's quoted in regards to an opera that she and Dorian had both been at, albeit separately: *"I like Wagner's music better than anybody's. It is so loud that one can talk the whole time without other people hearing what one says."* … and one has to wonder if Wilde had a particular individual in mind as the model.

Another bit that I found of interest was this one dip into Lord Wotten's head …

> *Certainly few people had ever interested him so much as Dorian Gray, and yet the lad's mad adora-*

> tion of some one else caused him not the slightest pang of annoyance or jealousy. He was pleased by it. It made him a more interesting study. He had always been enthralled by the methods of natural science, but the ordinary subject-matter of that science had seemed to him trivial and of no import. And so he had begun by vivisecting himself, as he had ended by vivisection others. Human life – that appeared to him the one thing worth investigating. Compared to it there was nothing else of any value. It was true that as one watched life in its curious crucible of pain and pleasure, one could not wear over one's face a mask of glass, nor keep the sulpherous fumes from troubling the brain and making the imagination turbid with monstrous fancies and misshapen dreams. There were poisons so subtle that to know their properties on had to sicken of them. There were maladies so strange that one had to pass through them if one sought to understand their nature. And yet, what a great reward one received! How wonderful the whole world became to one! To note the curious hard logic of passion, and the emotional coloured life of the intellect – to observe where they met, and where they separated, at what point they were in unison, and at what point they were at discord – there was a delight in that! What matter what the cost was? One could never pay too high a price for any sensation.

The "mad adoration" he refers to is that Dorian had developed for a 17-year-old actress, who was evidently something of a Shakespearean prodigy, playing in a dingy working-class theater all the great female roles in the Bard's catalog, a different play every night. Sibyl Vane, discovered accidentally by Dorian Gray, had become his obsession, and he returned to the theater night after night to see her, eventually asking her to marry him. He then invites his friends to experience the remarkable acting of his love. However, his winning the heart of Sibyl, had "broken the spell" that had made her so exquisite on the stage … she had lived in a world where she was in love with the plays, in love with the stage, and totally immersed in that as in a dream … when her love shifted to Dorian, her ability to act crumbled, and on the night when he was to be showing her genius off to his friends, her performance was wooden, rote, and totally uninspired – which *horrified* Dorian, as he was in love with the *genius* of the girl, and not the person. He goes back stage and breaks off the engagement, and abuses Sibyl for her change. The next day he get word that she has killed herself … which does not affect him in the least, but he notices a subtle change in the portrait – a slight look of cruelty in the face.

He is given a book by Wotton, which inspires him to immerse himself in the pursuit of fine things, at first becoming a model dandy which fashion followed, and then for years traveling around the world, becoming an expert in scents, jewels, musical instruments, embroidery, etc., and racking up ever more changes in the picture, now ensconced in a locked room in the upper levels of his mansion. Some 20 years on from the opening scenes, Dorian is visited by Basil Hallward, the painter, who that evening is scheduled to depart for an extended stay in Paris. Hallward is there to present a whole litany of accusations against Dorian that he's heard over the years … wanting to have some response (denial?) before he leaves. Dorian is irritated at hearing these and tells Basil that he has "a diary" and brings him up to the hidden room. Obviously, the portrait is the record he's referring to, and the artist is *aghast* at the changes in it, making Dorian angry about being confronted in this way … and he ends up killing Basil. He blackmails a doctor to get rid of the body, and covers everything up.

One thing Dorian is in fear of is reprisals from Sybil's brother … a sailor … who first tracks him to an opium den, but is convinced that Dorian *can't* be the guy responsible for his sister's death, because of his apparent youth … Dorian escapes, but an old lady tells Vane that he hasn't aged in decades … setting Vane on a fresh search. In perhaps the weakest plot point, Vane is killed in a hunting accident (not by Dorian, but he's in the party), which is both a great relief to Dorian, and a cause for him to re-think the course of his life. He eventually convinces himself to destroy the portrait … but when he does, all the degradation that was infused in it, transfers to him, and he dies.

Again, the most appealing aspect of The Picture of Dorian Gray[4] is the splendid writing of Wilde … there are certainly "plot holes" here which in lesser hands would be glaring, but this is a delightful read … and a splendid look into another time. Because this is a "thrift edition" book, it has a minimal cover price of $4, and is currently on sale at Amazon for half that … so it's one of those things to put on a list of low-priced add-ons for when you're just shy of free shipping!

Notes:

1. http://btripp-books.livejournal.com/169581.html

2-4. http://amzn.to/1LNqcnX

Sunday, July 19, 2015[1]

Walking out of the jungle ...

I have known Alberto Villoldo for a very long time, having first journeyed with him down to Peru before he founded his Four Winds Society[2], and having done many of his programs/trips back in the 80's and 90's. Unfortunately, while his organization was getting bigger, and more formal, my finances were dwindling (yeah, starting my own publishing house was *awesome*, but we never managed to break even over the years of my running Eschaton[3]), so we sort of drifted apart over the past decade or so.

Of course, those of you keeping way too close tabs on these reviews will know that I've at least been keeping up with Alberto via his writings, having read/reviewed most of his stuff. I got early word about this coming out (following favorite authors on Facebook does have its advantages), and contacted the publisher for a review copy. I apparently had never reached out to Hay House before for one of their books, as I was quite blown away by the media kit they sent out ... pretty much the most deluxe thing that I've gotten from a publisher yet (well, at least since the fun "KaChing" button that came with Joel Comm's book[4] of the same name)!

Anyway, I didn't really know what to expect from Alberto's new One Spirit Medicine: Ancient Ways to Ultimate Wellness[5] ... I initially thought it was going to be something of an amalgam of various culture's "ancient ways" for Medicine/Wellness, but was fairly surprised by what it ended up as. The key point here is explained in the introduction:

> Apparently, during my years of research in Indonesia, Africa, and South America I had picked up a long list of nasty microorganisms, including five different kinds of hepatitis virus, three or four varieties of parasites, a host of toxic bacteria, and assorted nasty worms. My heart and liver were close to collapse, the doctors said, and my brain was riddled with parasites.

Now, I can't say that I'm surprised by *that* news ... I had frequently lobbied for doing Shamanic work in nice climate-controlled hotel function rooms (which *is* possible - I've "mentally generated" a roaring bonfire for a fire ceremony in a suburban banquet hall) rather than out in nasty hot, humid, bug-infested, muddy, if picturesque locales ... and it gave me pause as to what *I* might be carrying around from my trips with Alberto.

He further notes: *All my test results indicated I was dying; the doctors had even said, "You should already be dead."* ... which is a pretty sobering thought. He got this news while at a conference he was keynoting down in Mexico ... and his wife was heading off to run a expedition to the Amazon immediately after. He says:

> I stood in the departure wing at the Cancún airport, staring at my options: Gate 15, the flight to Miami where I would be admitted to a top medical center for treatment, or Gate 14, the flight to Lima and the Amazon, where I would be with Marcela in the land of my spiritual roots. ... Miami was the logical choice. But in that moment I summoned up the courage to put my future where my mouth was – to live what I had taught so many.

Of course, Alberto is no fool, and he basically felt that he was quite likely heading off to his death. He quotes from his journal:

> There are no guarantees here, Alberto. There is a difference between curing and healing. You may not be cured; you may die. But regardless of what happens, you will be healed. You will not walk out of the jungle into your old way of being.

There was no "magic wand" in the Amazon, he continued on to a few other locations for scheduled events, but eventually ended up back in the U.S. for medical treatment. The worst part was what was happening with his brain, the meds killed the worms, but the dying worms released *their* parasites into his system, flooding it with all sorts of toxins. He found that he couldn't play Scrabble, as he could no longer find the words ... leading him to begin to wonder what was going to happen to him in terms of consciousness and self. His return to health took over a year, and involved Shamanic treatments, standard medical approaches, spiritual disciplines, cutting-edge techniques in brain science, and a drastic regimen of dietary adjustments.

Now, I need to insert a significant caveat here ... one of the things that surprised me the MOST in the book was this latter element ... I have never held "food fetishists" in particularly high regard, and there are *so many* "unusual diets" out there which are hawked/championed by a wide assortment of very devout believers, each contradicting the next, that I've always felt, in a similar mode to the late Christopher Hitchens' adage for religions *"Since it is obviously inconceivable that all {food fetish diets} can be right, the most reasonable conclusion is that they are all wrong."* Needless to say, this preconception/prejudice on my part made the section of the book dealing with dietary issues *very* hard to deal with ... I was even getting snarky reading it, with mental commentary like "I didn't expect Alberto to turn into Martha Stewart!" when he's suggesting menus, ingredients, spices, and cooking methods.

Fortunately, that was just *one* section of the book, and the others I was in considerably better *simpatico* with. The structure here is four sections, which Villoldo recommends working through in order:

> Part I: Discovering Your Inner Healer
>
> Part II: Shedding the Old Ways
>
> Part III: Overcoming the Death that Stalks You
>
> Part IV: From Stillness Comes Rebirth

The first of these, generally deals with Shamanic realities, both historically, and theoretically, from how native peoples Alberto encountered in the Amazon didn't have the sorts of diseases that the West deals with, to ideas like the Mayan concept of "acquiring the jaguar body", and new-age (albeit utilized by the shamans) things like the "Luminous Energy Field" ("the LEF", though most of this), and even off into the Jungian "collective unconscious". Here also is the concept that "the mind is mad", and suggesting that the shift from hunter-gatherer diets to grain-based agricultural diets were essentially "sugar-based" ... thus appealing to the "limbic brain", but not conducive to working with spirit ... *"The neocortex thrives on One Spirit Medicine; the limbic system, driven by sensation, pleasure seeking, and emotion, does not."* ... and countering this with "good fats". The rather trendy concept of "neuroplasticity" (yeah, you've heard the commercials) comes in here to set up the idea that OSM (I suppose I can use an abbreviation too) works by *"Upgrading the information in your luminous energy field, eventually allowing new neural networks to form."*

Oh, one other caveat on the book ... in parts of this Alberto uses "One Spirit Medicine" in nearly every paragraph ... almost like he's trying to "brand" a wide spectrum of shamanic, spiritual, and scientific material with the label. It becomes irritating because he's simultaneously trying build a case that all these disparate elements pull together to MAKE "One Spirit Medicine", while labeling everything with the name ... it's like one were talking about developing an alternator, but constantly referring to it by the model of car it's eventually going to be a part of.

The second section is the one that I had the "food fetishist" issues with, although it starts out well enough, discussing the "second brain in your gut" – the 100 million neurons involved in the alimentary canal – and how Serotonin is chemically linked to DMT (synthesized by the pineal gland, and a component in ayahuasca and other psycho-active plants used by shamen). Where this takes the turn into the "iffy" area is when Alberto asserts: *"Research now shows that most of the diseases of modern living begin in the gut and are related to our diet."* ... in no way have *I* researched this, but my ... uhhh ... "questionable assertion" meter was certainly going off when I read that. He does a good job backgrounding environmental microorganisms and how we've evolved over millennia to interact with these, and a reasonable bit on "environmental toxins" ... but this leads into the popular manias on genetically modified foods, and the "toxic effects" of grains and sugars. Suddenly we're being told *"if you want to upgrade your brain to support One Spirit Medicine, you'll need to avoid all processed grains"* and insisting on *"cutting out fruits like watermelon and raisins, which have a higher glycemic index than a Popsicle"* ... which then turns into strict regimens of fasting and micro-managed meal schedules, menus, and supplementation. Something tells me that the Amazon shamans are not waking up and taking 250mg of Pterostilbene, 1g of S-acetyl glutathione, 500mg of Trans-resveratrol, and 1g of Curcumin (in its liposomal form), among a long list of other enrich-the-health-food-store supplements. The rest of this section gets into "super foods" and what to eat and not eat when (for instance, he recommend *not eating fruit* except in its growing season). Among the many issues I have with this section is my perception that one could probably *not afford* these regimens unless one was bringing home a solid six-figure income ... needless to say, you may find this section just *brilliant*, and maybe it might have the benefits that Villoldo is suggesting it does, but I found it "out of character" for the author, and it rings like his having "found religion" in the "food fetishist" world – perhaps being the main element of coming out of the jungle into something other than his "old way of being" – although, as I frequently have to say, "your mileage may vary" from my reactions here.

Moving on, the third section deals with health issues on a more basic level … the "death clock" on a cellular level, and how things in the system start breaking down around age 35. He spends a number of pages discussing the mitochondria in our cells, and how the mitochondrial DNA is passed down through the mother's genes so "represents the feminine life force recognized by the ancients", then gets into recommendations for "aerobic exercise", "healthy fats", and "fasting" for ways to support the internal recycling of cellular waste … and to lessen "oxidative stress". He outlines a number of enzymes that he supplements with, BDFN ("brain-derived neurotrophic factor"), Glutathione, and SOD ("superoxide dismutase"), which are supposed to help with various of these "stressors". This then shifts to looking at psychological stresses and "limiting beliefs". One bit I found particularly interesting is:

> From television and the Internet alone, we're exposed to more stimuli in a week than our Paleolithic ancestors were exposed to in a lifetime. And we're continually running to keep up with new information, to the point that we're chronically exhausted. I can't count how many times I have heard someone say, "If it weren't for caffeine, I wouldn't get anything done!" Nature designed the brain to deal with one lion roaring at us at a time, not the entire jungle turning against us.

This is in the context of the "HPA axis" (Hypothalamus, Pituitary gland, and Adrenal glands), and the hippocampus, which he suggests is "the thermostat of the HPA axis". He cites research that, among teenagers, the incidence of anxiety and depression is five to eight times what it was just 50 years ago, and then goes into the body chemistry, including adrenaline and cortisol, "stress" steroid hormones released by the HPA axis, and recommending omega-3 fatty acids to re-set the balance in this (which dovetails with the info on fish oil that I wrote about being very helpful with my own struggles with depression in my recent review of one of Dr. Weil's books[6]). The chapter shifts from how one can avoid the fight-or-flight trap, and into some more psychological spaces … making free time (the hunter-gatherer societies tend to have only 3 hours a day of "work", something that exploded into long hard days when agriculture took over), "pondering" and/or daydreaming, etc. This also leads to less fear of death and unseen things. *"The invisible world is unified, nonlocal, and beyond space-time. Though omnipresent, it is invisible to ordinary perception: we know it only through its manifestations."*, yet, the limbic brain *perceives separation rather than unity*, creating fear, perception of threats, etc. and a significant part of OSM seems to be shifting experience away from that.

The fourth section takes up as much space as the first three, which is a good thing, as I was on much more "agreeable" ground here, as it deals largely with the concepts of "mythologies".

> *The values and beliefs contained in myths are so stong that once you find your personal guiding myth, you feel compelled to change your life to conform to it. Change the myth and your values and beliefs change – and the facts of your life change accordingly.*

Villoldo notes that the Judeo-Christian tradition has engrained myths that *"operate in the psyche like computer programs running continually in the background"* but that *"at this point in our history, it's pretty clear that the human species needs to be more collaborative, creative, and cooperative – qualities that are aspects of the archetypical mother figure"* ... which suggests that a "Mother Earth"/Gaian mythology would be more beneficial today. At this point, the classic shamanic tool of the Medicine Wheel gets put in play:

> *Though the practices associated with the medicine wheel vary among the different indigenous groups of North and South America, the way I was taught by my teachers in the Amazon, we begin in the South, with the journey of the healer and healing our past wounds. We then move to the West and the journey of the Divine Feminine, facing the fear of death. From there we move to the North, the journey of the sage, where we learn to be still, like the surface of the lake that reflects everything and disturbs nothing. Finally, we reach the East and the journey of the visionary, where we practice dreaming the world into being and participating in creation.*

The South is represented by the serpent, with the implied parallels of "shedding skin" with growth and change. In an odd twist to the typical narration of this, Alberto brings in the myth of Parsifal and the Grail, with the overtones of the feminine force. The West is represented by the Jaguar ... and here the author asserts that this, in its indigenous American context, represents healing power much the same way that the caduceus does in European traditions. In the West, we meet the Goddess and face the fear of death. Greek myths are referenced here, Orpheus and Eurydice, Eros and Psyche (the latter in substantial detail). Alberto notes:

> *All initiation involves a journey to the ream of death and a meeting with the Divine Feminine from which you return renewed. ... There is no rushing the journey of initiation. Mastering the fear of death is a lifelong process. You may be challenged and tested many times, although with each time the way becomes easier.*

In the North is the realm of the Sages (this relates to certain "topographies" of the "otherworld") and is represented here by the hummingbird (although in other traditions, such as the Lakota, this is represented by the buffalo), with the sense that the hummingbird can hold still mid-air, and exhibits a calm within frantic action (hovering while its wings are rapidly beating). *"In the North we learn that what we call reality is an illusion, albeit one we are jointly re-creating every instant."* To provide a second perspective on this, Alberto brings in the story of Arjuna from the *Bhagavad Gita* ... where it's revealed that *"everything we do can become an offering to the divine and that we shouldn't be fixated on achieving specific results"* ... and with the suggestion that in stillness we can be guided by Spirit.

The East is represented by the Eagle, and the theme is that here *"you come to see that the consciousness that observes your experience is an inextricable part of a larger consciousness"*. Appropriate to that, the myth that is presented from another culture is that of Siddhartha, becoming the Buddha.

The last part of this section is an extensive piece on the "Vision Quest" ... in this Villodo discusses the turning points for a handful of his previous patients, whose difficult life situations were overcome, largely through doing a vision quest. He presents a plan for a 3-day vision quest in which one finds a "power animal":

> *In shamanic cultures, when you do a vision quest, traditionally a power animal will appear to you in a dream or waking vision. The word <u>animal</u> comes from the same root as <u>anima</u>, Latin for soul, breath, the life force. Carl Jung used <u>anima</u> to refer to the feminine principle. An animal, then, is an expression of the feminine aspect of the soul of the world. ... When you connect with a power animal you are in effect connecting with the psyche or soul of nature.*

This is followed by the "conclusion", in which Alberto ties up the various parts of his OSM "system", putting them in context of a number of settings, from healing to inner harmony, and evolution and brain development. Again, One Spirit Medicine[7] is a shift into new areas for Villoldo's teaching, while certainly grounded in what he's been working with over the past 30 years, it's moving into a whole new space – evidently based on his experiences with nearly dying from the various ailments that he'd picked up on his journeys.

Obviously, I have some issues with the new stuff, but this is, I think, the most "organized" form that he's generated yet. I may be misremembering, but it seems to me that up till now, he'd been good with people interfacing with his teachings to the extent that they were called to ... and this has changed to something more structured and linear (although he does preface his *"I recommend reading the chapters in the order in which they're presented and trying the practices and exercises."* statement with a *"to get the most out of the process"* caveat). Needless to say, I have significant disconnects with the new material he's inserting in the middle of that process, and I wonder how many people would be willing (or able) to go to the extremes of diet modification (and extensive supplementation) that he outlines therein. This has only been out a couple of months, and so should be available in the local brick-and-mortar stores carrying metaphysical titles, but the on-line big boys have it at the moment at a whopping 45% off of cover price, which is probably your best bet for picking up a copy.

Notes:

1. http://btripp-books.livejournal.com/169780.html
2. http://thefourwinds.com/
3. http://eschatonbooks.com/
4. http://btripp-books.livejournal.com/96293.html
5. http://amzn.to/1Fe4rbE
6. http://btripp-books.livejournal.com/162217.html
7. http://amzn.to/1Fe4rbE

Friday, July 31, 2015[1]

An interesting journey ...

If I were a judge, and this was a case, I'd probably have to recuse myself, as I have long-time familiarity with the author, who was among the early crew over on LiveJournal ... and so has been one of my "pixel people" for well over a decade. Unlike many of those on-line contacts, I have actually *met* the author on one occasion, last fall, and *almost killed him with my bare hands* then (he'd asked me to take part in a film somebody was doing about his "Concrete Shamanism", and at one point – standing out on the beach with the cameras rolling – he insisted that I choke him "for real" ... I grabbed a hold of his wind pipe and waited for him to look real panicked to let him go). Needless to say (no doubt to the relief of other authors), that's the only time THAT's happened!

Anyway, aside from the Shamanism, the author and I also had the writing/publishing overlap, especially when I was still running Eschaton Books full time. This brings up another point where I should probably take a step back ... I am a *terror* when it comes to formatting issues (and typos, and lacunae, and assorted related errata), and this book is *full* of them ... to the extent that I *asked* the author over on Facebook[2] about what lay-out program he'd used for it, thinking that the one consistent, highly irritating, "issue" in the book was an accidental artifact of some quirk in that system. He identified this, but assured me that the formatting "issue" was an intentional design element (all through the book, where a paragraph breaks across pages, the resuming text block has an indent like *new* paragraphs have, albeit coming mid-sentence). Unfortunately, this was hardly the only "odd element" in the book, and only *one* really stood out as being an intentional design element (the header/footer stylings on page 82).

So, the book in question is ALL THINGS GO: How I Became A Shaman[3] by Eric Durchholz / Patrick John Coleman ... the latest in the author's varied output of nearly a dozen titles. As one can guess from the sub-title, this is a book about transformation, but it's more "how Eric Durchholz became Patrick John Coleman" than about him "becoming a shaman". Frankly, despite his "branding" what he's doing as "shamanism", it seems to me that his path has much more to do with the Lakota figure of the Heyoka[4] than a "medicine man", "curandero/brujo", or other Shamanic manifestations (an example of this is his use of a partial pack of children's alphabet flash cards for divination, and other toys as shamanic "tools").

If I posit that the author is a Heyoka, it frees him of any of the linearity, structure, consistency, and logical progression that I would otherwise be looking for in a narrative like this. So I hope that he "owns" that as an alternative handle to "shaman". One would not be surprised if a Heyoka stopped a chapter mid-topic (heck, mid-sentence) and launched into the next thing on the facing page ... one would not be surprised if there were "missing" bits that were none-the-less identified in the text (in terms of graphics, etc.) ... one would not be surprised if the use of QR codes was irregular, with many of them leading off to inaccessible material (such as "private" YouTube videos[5]) ... and one would almost *expect* there to be odd formatting like that noted above. A Shaman, even a "Concrete Shaman", would *"have some 'shplainin to do"* about why things were the way they were in the printed piece ... a Heyoka, not so much (and, given that his books are self-published through Lulu.com[6], he doesn't have an Editor to answer to).

The book is an auto-biography of sorts ... although not particularly linear. Eric (I've known the "Eric" persona a lot longer than the "Patrick" entity) has had a rough life on a lot of levels, and the backstory of much of that appears in various points in this. For the broad strokes: he was *born* "Patrick John Coleman" in Chicago, but was adopted by a family from Kentucky and re-named "Eric Durchholz", his adopted family are "narcissists" (in his terms) and found it very hard to deal with him being both artistic/creative and gay. Living in a small town in the bible belt, his upbringing was fraught with traumas, and he attempted to run away on multiple occasions. By 1999 (the year his best-known novel, *The Promise of Eden* came out) he was living in Nashville, TN, and having a reasonably integrated life with his particular social scene there. However, in 2010 he lost nearly everything he owned in area flooding, and "freed" from the encumbrances of material things (which he cites at one point as "having way too much stuff to be able to move to Chicago"), he re-located to Chicago, and began working in Comedy, at Second City and other clubs. Then ...

> *In April of 2013 I was dragged into the spirit world and told I would be a "psychic, medium, healer and helper" and I was terrified by the experience. I was told by unseen spirits that I had died of a brain aneurysm in my new apartment that was situated between two huge graveyards. ... When I returned to life after an intense and horrifying period, I found I was very different. I knew things I should not have known. ... And my mind was a jumbled mess so I decided to figure out just what had happened to me. ... In my case, I did not choose to be shown the inner workings of the Universe and what humanity is and what we truly are and the one thing that keeps coming is that my perspective is not valid. ... We are all human beings viewing life through our own prism. Everyone's perspective is valid. This is a true thing. ... Another true thing is that I can access alternate and parallel realities to gain knowledge, get lessons and find ways to heal myself in this one.*

And ...

> *I did not choose to be a shaman but my perspective as a shaman is just as valid as your perspective. ... Just listen to what I have to say and draw your own conclusion. Or you can do what I do. I prefer to have no beliefs or opinions and just ac-*

> *cept things as they are. Because when aliens show up in your apartment to give you energy-field upgrades, what are you going to do? Tell them to leave?*

As I mentioned, the book jumps around quite a bit ... at one point being a scenario from 2042 ... parts of it written as Eric, parts of it written as Patrick ... parts of it written as plain expository material. There are also sections on Jane Roberts / "Seth", Esther Hicks / "Abraham", and Edgar Cayce (the author sees a lot of meaning on his being raised close to Cayce's home), as well as back-and-forth between the "Eric" and "Patrick" personas.

As I noted, there really isn't that much stuff about how the author *becomes* "a shaman", aside from the mental/spiritual turmoil involved with having the one persona leave and the other come in ... he pretty much encapsulates the "becoming a shaman" part as:

> *I did not choose to be a shaman. I was pretty much bopped on the head, pulled into the spirit world and told I was a shaman. One day I was working on comedy and the next I was figuring out the mystery of my own existence.*

He notes that he "began practicing" in August of 2013 ... so most of the "transition" is happening in the months from April to August of that year.

While I've followed Eric's on-line presence for well over a decade, he also delves into auto-biographical material here that I somehow hadn't noticed ... specifically that dealing with his becoming HIV positive. He copies a lengthy post (9 pages here) that he made to Facebook back in August of 2012 which details his discovering this and beginning to come to grips with it. I'm, frankly, amazed that I'd missed (or somehow forgotten) this on-line data point (it certainly is a substantial sub-theme of the book), but I guess my radar in this case was set more for the books/shamanism axis of the author's life, and not really registering the gay/HIV aspects (although at one point in his on-line "career" it was certainly hard to avoid that).

So, basically what you get in <u>ALL THINGS GO</u>[7] is a bunch of stories of Eric's life, a bunch of looks at things that have influenced him, a bunch of information about Patrick and how he came to be "in" Eric, and assorted material on things like "formlessness" and "walk-ins", all tossed into a cement mixer, bounced around, and poured out (see what I did there) as the author's coming to practice "concrete shamanism". I enjoyed parts of this very much, was made quite uncomfortable by others, driven *nuts* by some of the formatting, and fascinated by little sparkling bits of otherworldly wisdom that show up randomly through it.

Would I have been reading this if the author wasn't one of my "pixel people"? I don't know. And, in this lies the crux of my wondering if I really would recommend it to somebody who *didn't* have over a decade's familiarity with the author. It's a *strange* book, for sure. It's a reasonably "easy read" (the "uncomfortable" bits notwithstanding), but it's ultimately a look at one man's odd journey. If the uncommon mélange of stuff that I've described above sounds of interest to you, by all means pick up a copy. As noted, it's published via LuLu (so might be a challenge to find a copy in a retail outlet), but Amazon has it as well ... and throwing this in on a larger order will avoid shipping costs (which I recall are pretty hefty through LuLu).

Notes:

1. http://btripp-books.livejournal.com/170205.html
2. https://www.facebook.com/patrickshaman
3. http://amzn.to/1MlWcBV
4. https://en.wikipedia.org/wiki/Heyoka
5. https://www.youtube.com/user/ericdurchholz
6. http://www.lulu.com/spotlight/concrete7
7. http://amzn.to/1MlWcBV

Saturday, August 1, 2015[1]

Claiming Your Personal Power ...

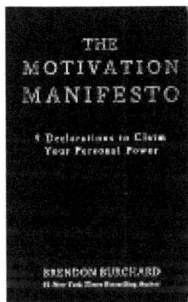

I have a very mixed impression of Brendon Burchard ... I first encountered him in the context of building up an "information business" (his Millionaire Messenger[2] book), and have found him on one hand very *informative*, with material that is, generally speaking, actionable in a fairly esoteric niche, but on the other hand way too into the "inspirational" - "believe it and it will happen" - zone for my tastes (see his Life's Golden Ticket[3]). Among the "info biz" guys, he's pretty open and giving (this book was "free with shipping"), with a lot of material not requiring one's credit card, but there's always seemed to be that "yeah, but ..." thing in play, that, like in MLM, a lot of people will aspire to making a living at it, but most never have a realistic shot.

His new book, The Motivation Manifesto: 9 Declarations to Claim Your Personal Power[4], is a bit different, as it *is* "a manifesto", and so is very "opinionated". I was *extremely* enthused with this when I started reading it, having been frustrated by a number of people in my daily life who are advocates (some *impassioned* advocates) for mundane, average, non-achieving, and *common* results, lifestyles, and goals (yes, I've been *berated* for reading/reviewing as much as I do as it "by implication" makes others feel bad because they can't/don't make the effort ... the reality of Diana Moon Glampers[5] is just another Alinskyite administration or two away). This is a call to excellence, to *striving*, to reaching beyond what we think we can achieve (let alone what the TV-numbed slugs settle for) ... or at least it is in the first section.

The book is in two sections (well, an introduction and two sections), the first being "On Human Nature", which looks at Freedom, Fear, and Motivation. Reading this (and the intro) had me wanting to stand on street corners and "spread the word" ... it's that powerful. The second part, however, the "9 Declarations", suffers somewhat from trying to "systematize" the call-to-arms of the first part into something more ... well, *marketable*? Not that it's not full of great stuff, but I felt it bogged down in places, and there were bits that I was mentally going "blah, blah, blah" about, and other parts that were generating a significant amount of resistance. The only bookmark I found I'd put in while reading this was in that part of the book, however, in Declaration VIII - "We Shall Inspire Greatness" where some of the specific types of things I noted above are addressed.

I'm a bit frustrated working on this review, because I usually have a dozen or so little bookmarks tucked in where I've found particularly juicy bits to bring to you here ... but in the case of The Motivation Manifesto[6], the "good bits" tend to run on for *pages*, not sentences. I'm going to dig through this and see if I can pull out some particularly representative paragraphs, but it's not going to be easy to do.

First of all, though ... let's get to what the "9 Declarations" are:

    I.   We Shall Meet Life with Full Presence and Power

- II. We Shall Reclaim Our Agenda
- III. We Shall Defeat Our Demons
- IV. We Shall Advance with Abandon
- V. We Shall Practice Joy and Gratitude
- VI. We Shall Not Break Integrity
- VII. We Shall Amplify Love
- VIII. We Shall Inspire Greatness
- IX. We Shall Slow Time

Obviously, this isn't your basic to-do list ... "reclaiming agendas"? ... "slowing time"??? ... "advancing with *abandon*"? Burchard is writing in an abstract mode in much of this, with, for instance, in the "time" one, the phrase *"We are not supposed to miss this moment."* repeats itself several times, yet there are accompanying (meditative/breath) exercises to practically adjust the perception of time.

Here's a bit from the "Motivation" section of the first part of the book ... it will give you a bit of the flavor of the writing's tone (which is rather "styled"), and show why I'm having a hard time here, as key points tend to unfold over several paragraphs, and are difficult (if not impossible) to condense out into bullet points.

> *The long evolutions of philosophy, psychology, and neuroscience share a common thread of unlocking human potential by leveraging <u>reason</u> and the full power of the mind. Reason is the secret to developing a motivated and independent identity. <u>I think therefore I am and I do</u>. Motivated people seize this truth. The great artists, leaders, and innovators use the entire force of their reasoning faculties to become their highest selves and do their highest good. They express who they truly are and pursue goals they find meaningful. They strategically contemplate their direction and values; they weigh what will give them the greatest sense of vibrancy and fulfillment in every major decision. They select from life's abundant array only the courses that suit their nature and their intention to be free and to serve. They are resolute in calling forth their greatest character traits and wrestling their lowest impulses into submission. They appear, in the eyes of the mindless masses, to be the lucky ones, the chosen. In fact, they decided to <u>choose</u>.*

Each of the "declarations" has similar looks at the thematic elements, and layers of information, where the "time" one has exercises, the first one splits out various "roles" that motivated individuals play in their lives, and within the "demons" one, it takes "internal enemies" and defines them as a demon "Defiance", which has three heads, "Doubt", "Delay", and "Division", and details how these hinder our efforts, and how we can overcome them.

Again, this is hard to condense down to a few nuggets ... most of the material comes packaged in runs of several paragraphs like the above ... it is, however, worth the effort of working through.

Physically, The Motivation Manifesto[7] is "deluxe" with a black leatherette cover with gold-stamped text, rounded cut corners, and a red ribbon book mark. It's available via the on-line big boys, but apparently is still being offered on Burchard's site[8] for "free" (a $7 shipping fee), which also includes a 12-week on-line course (I've not taken advantage of the "extras" like the course as yet). Needless to say, this is quite a deal, and is considerably less than the other options out there (even the used channels at this writing).

While "inspirational" books like this are hardly "my thing", it's hard to not value something with statements like this:

> Nor can we allow apathetic, small-thinking men and women to lay waste to our future. We mustn't let social pressures to poison our potential. Surely, we have warned other from time to time that we do not care what they think or that their judgments of us are unwarranted. We have often complained, made kind requests of others, or reminded people of the circumstances that made us want to improve our lives. We have appealed to their magnanimity to be gentler or more supportive, and we have asked them as kindred spirits to stand with us against those who interrupt our charge. Yet too often others have been deaf to our true voices. They didn't believe in us or support us or cheer us on when it mattered most. We must, therefore, not await their assistance or approval any longer. We must hold them, as we hold the rest of mankind, enemies in battle should they stand in the way or our dreams, but in peace and assistance, friends.

Notes:
1. http://btripp-books.livejournal.com/170268.html
2. http://btripp-books.livejournal.com/138306.html
3. http://btripp-books.livejournal.com/144832.html
4. http://amzn.to/1TfvL3O
5. http://www.tnellen.com/cybereng/harrison.html
6-7. http://amzn.to/1TfvL3O
8. http://www.motivationmanifesto.com/

Sunday, August 2, 2015[1]

Introducing "Quantum Biology" ...

Here's another of those books that have come my way via the LibraryThing.com "Early Reviewer" program ... and it's another good science book, of which there have, fortunately, been quite a few of over the past couple of years. Life on the Edge: The Coming of Age of Quantum Biology[2] by Johnjoe McFadden and Jim Al-Khalili is a fascinating look at an evolving field.

Now, I have to admit, this is one of those books that I have had a certain amount of "oh, *really*?" response to, as, frankly, the consistent uncovering of quantum operations involved in "everyday" events seems a bit ... well, like when fundamentalists attribute everything to *God* ... and I'd feel better if I'd seen more on this topic in my other reading, rather than having it all show up in one book like this (hey, I've read *lots* of books[3] that were based on just the author's lunatic take on the universe!). This is not to say that the concept of quantum activity being key to various biological processes is totally new to me ... I recall having read some things about how *photosynthesis* is achieved, at its most microscopic levels, by an energy transfer described as a "quantum walk", where an *exciton* (according to Wikipedia: *"a bound state of an electron and an electron hole which are attracted to each other by the electrostatic Coulomb force"*, or, elsewhere: *"an excited electronic state delocalized over several spatially separated molecules "*) is mobilized, via quantum coherence, across the pigment-protein elements to where its energy potential is eventually utilized. This is covered in Life On The Edge[4], but in a particularly idiosyncratic way (the section of photosynthesis is framed in a *Fantastic Voyage* scenario of shrinking the observer down, through various dimensional frames in the plant, until they're looking at molecular/atomic levels).

Like this, it appears that there are MANY biological functions that we've known *about* for ages, but have had substantial lacunae in the *how* these worked ... and these go to as basic things as how we smell scents, or how we move our muscles (really, it would appear that we just either didn't *ask* how these things happened, or simply skipped over the details) ... and this book picks apart these at the finest levels and looks at how quantum mechanical events play a key role in the "how".

I'm somewhat irritated with myself that I didn't put in my usual couple of handfulls of little bookmarks in this (I found *one*), as it makes it a lot harder to condense the sense of the book for you here ... but the *Fantastic Voyage* factor is at play all through the text ... lots of "story telling" flowing in and out of specifically scientific bits (which very quickly get quite complicated), and not a lot of "Topic One ... Topic Two ... Topic Three", etc. ... which I, oddly, found bothersome. The book starts, in the introduction, with a rambling piece about a robin, "getting ready" to migrate from Sweden to North Africa ... which at times brings to mind the cocoanut-carrying swallows of Monty Python fame. One thing that I sort of took offense to in here is how the authors disparage the work of Rupert Sheldrake ... dissing him on several occasions ... which (obviously) comes up when looking at how birds get around (something that Sheldrake has published work on). I think there's an old adage about living in glass houses that the authors might have kept in mind when presenting material as "out of the mainstream" (or at least "established") as this is.

Anyway, as to that European robin wanting to get out of the cold ... how does she navigate as accurately as she does, going from Scandinavia to the other side of the Mediterranean (and back again) on her migration? Well, nothing is straight forward here (I think I'm getting to the "why" of there not being my usual mass of bookmarks in this), and something will start off with a colorful story about a robins migration, then veer off into historic theories, alternate modern research, the work of various scientists that have worked on *parts* of what comes together in the bird's navigation, assorted similar elements, the underlying physics (both classical and quantum), vectors off into biological topics, and sometimes dropping threads, only to pick them up several chapters later. It turns out that the bird has a magnetic "sense" built into its eye that uses a particular quantum process within a chemical reaction dealing with a pigment, which allows it to "see" the *angle* of the lines of magnetism around the planet ... and by reading that angle, the bird can tell where it is. No, really, it's a LOT more complicated than that, and the details are half the book apart.

I wish I'd be able to easily walk you though this, but it's a jungle in there. To give you a taste of how this plays out, here's a bit from another "Fantastic Voyage" look into something – in this case, how a tadpole changes into a frog:

> ... *These nanomachines of nature are performing, at a molecular level, a carefully choreographed dance whose actions have been precision engineered by millions of years of natural selection to manipulate the fundamental particles of matter.*
>
> *To get a closer look at the cutting action, we descend into the enzyme's jaw-like cleft that holds the substrates in place: the collagen protein chain and a single water molecule. This is the <u>active site</u> of the enzyme – its business end that is speeding up the breaking of peptide bonds by bending the neck of the energy hourglass*. ...*
>
> *... the enzyme is restraining the peptide bond in an unstable transition state that has to be reached before the bond can be broken. The substrates are tethered by weak chemical bonds, ... which are essentially electrons that are shared between the substrate and the enzyme. This tethering holds the substrates in a precise configuration ready for the chopping action of the enzyme's molecular jaws.*
>
> *As the jaws of the enzyme close, they do something far subtler than simply "biting down" on the bond: they provide the means through which catalysis can take place. We notice a big positively*

> *charged atom hanging directly beneath the target peptide bond being swung into position. This is a positively charged zinc atom. If we consider the active state of the enzyme to be its jaws, then the zinc atom is one of its two incisors. The positively charged atom plucks an electron out of the oxygen atom from the substrates to stabilize the transition state and thereby deform the energy landscape ...*
>
> *The rest of the job is carried out by the enzyme's second molecular incisor. This is one of the enzyme's own amino acids called glutamate, which has swung into position to hang its negatively charged oxygen atom over the target peptide bond. Its role is first to pluck a positively charged proton out of the tethered water molecule. It then spits this proton into the nitrogen atom at one end of the peptide bone, giving it a positive charge which draws electrons out of the peptide bonds. ... drawing the electron out is like pulling the glue out of a bonded joint, causing it to weaken and break*

* this is a conceptualization of how "quantum tunneling" is enabled.

And, that (obviously) doesn't even get into the *quantum* elements involved in the process ... these stories swirl in and out of the description and through the background science ... citing all the big names, and lots more whose research is either more obscure or sufficiently recent to not be as recognizable. I must admit, there was material in here by the likes of Shröedinger, Planck, Feynman, and others that I'd not encountered previously ... but that's probably due to this "quantum biology" stuff running off into less-explored corners of the physics involved.

I'm hoping that this book isn't finding its way into the textbook channel, as it is *so* convoluted that it confuses as much as it explains ... I almost *never* re-read books, but this one tempts me to triage the time just to make sure I got everything straight. Needless to say, it's chock-full of *fascinating* material, but much of it is fairly challenging, requiring at least a familiarity with several disciplines to really understand what's happening there (and a lot of this really pushes the envelope vs. "standard knowledge" or general experience).

As one would expect for an "early reviewer" book, Life On The Edge[5] is brand new (only officially coming out just this past week!), so is likely being featured in the brick-and-mortar stores delving in to physics. The on-line big boys have it at about 1/3rd off of cover, which is probably your best bet at the present for picking up a copy.

While I had a number of "gripes" with the book, both in how it was presented and in some of the details, it was more of a "wow, that's *amazing*" reaction most of the time. While I would have preferred something more linear (although, with all the material coming in from various disciplines, that might not have been practical), and less "cutesy" (really, I didn't need the "now you're shrinking down" stuff), it's quite an eye-opening look into a brand new area of science.

Oh ... and you can thank me for *not* titling this review "*... and a few swabs from Bono too*".

Notes:
1. http://btripp-books.livejournal.com/170590.html
2. http://amzn.to/1esUqC2
3. http://btripp-books.livejournal.com/165201.html
4-5. http://amzn.to/1esUqC2

Tuesday, August 11, 2015[1]

A love letter to an abiding urbs ...

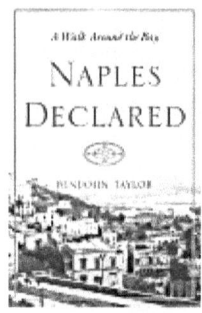

I've been having a string of fairly good luck with volumes from the dollar store of late ... while not being "pig in a poke" buys exactly (I *am* able to look them over and get a sense if I want to read them or not), they typically come unanticipated, not recommended by anybody or any citation, and pretty much "by accident" of the book being on the shelf on a day that not only had I made it out to one of the dollar stores I have access to (all requiring at least a significant subway ride to get to), but additionally on a visit where I had time to dig into the book display. Needless to say, however, walking out with even *one* nice "like new" hardcover for a buck (instead of $26.95 in this case) feels like a substantial "win"!

Benjamin Taylor's Naples Declared: A Walk Around the Bay[2] is a bit of an odd duck, however ... it's not *really* a travel book (I never quite got enough geographical bearings to make any sense of its sub-titular "walk around the Bay", other than to note that the city is, indeed, on a bay), nor is it centrally a *history* of Naples, and it's only peripherally an autobiographical telling of the author's on-going relationship with the city, its people, its background, and its other visitors. While I'm not much given to quoting from the accessory sections of books, a bit from the "Acknowledgments" at the end of the text would put this in its creative context:

> *This is a book of memory and reflection, not reportage. Over the course of sixteen years, during eleven stays in Naples, I talked to hundreds of people; nobody, however, was "interviewed" for these pages. I took only sketchy notes, and none in line with good journalistic practice. What I did instead, year after year, was to let the interesting, sometime funny or poignant thing learned from near-strangers settle down in me, and only now have I made the inventory.*

Frankly, the book has an "evergreen" feel to it, not being notably of a particular time, so it could have been written any time in those sixteen years. However, it just came out in 2012 in hardcover, with a paperback edition following a year later (which has its own web page[3]). But the author's approach, being hardly *linear*, presents me with challenges on how to convey the general sense of the book to those reading my review here. Taylor throws history, art, food & wine, architecture, religion, crime, politics, autobiographical snippets, war, and even a smattering of sex into a basket and gives it a whirl, grabbing random handfuls of the mix to apply to the word picture he's painting for the subject at hand in each part. Also, while the book *is* illustrated, it is not *extensively* so, with 30-some-odd ≈ 2x2" b&w pictures throughout the text, and an 8-page insert of color photos, starting with a skeleton from Herculaneum, and a swastika-banner-festooned *Piazza de Plebiscito*, awaiting a visit from Adolf Hitler, to some snaps of buildings, etc. mentioned in the text, and a number of large renditions paintings discussed in a long-ish look at some art trends (which, personally, I didn't think needed to be included, as a link to an on-line version of these images would have easily sufficed were somebody *really* interested enough to see what he was referencing).

Naples, it would appear, is a *very* old place, with the author citing burials of pre-Greek neolithic indigenous peoples dating to 5,000 BCE ... and its *historical* lineage goes back as far as 1,800 BCE when Mycenaean traders established an island outpost in the outskirts of the Bay, followed by other Greeks from various areas, with the city itself being founded around 600 BCE. The book starts with a long "highlights of history" *Chronology* taking a dozen pages to go from those early dates on up to political happenings as late as 2011. In these listings an amazing roster of conquerors, combatants, and ruling cultures appears ... from Etruscans, to Samnites, to Lombards, to the Angevin empire and their competitors from Aragon. Of course, in the midst of that, Rome conquered the Italian peninsula, and absorbed a *lot* of the Greek culture via Naples. Oh, and there's the matter of Vesuvius ... sitting square on the Bay, this volcano is notorious for wiping out its human neighbors every now and again, most recently erupting in 1944, and badly damaging the region with earthquakes in 1980.

I really do wish I could more successfully grab bits and pieces here to quote .. but, Taylor, in a matter of a scant few pages, riffs off of some historical factoid about some Roman ruin, and will suddenly be talking about opera, and then veering off to something from his youth, where a neighbor took the very young author under his wing and introduced him to a touring opera production in *Dallas*, of all places, only to have that move back to ancient history, and the art still visible in certain ruins in and around the city.

Much of the history of the city is *quite* bloody, from the well-known cruelties of assorted Roman emperors (some of which favored Naples as a vacation home, if not second capitol), to the back-and-forth of various dynasties from other places in Europe over the centuries, which frequently resulted in public beheadings and less-public poisonings. Plus there was plenty of famine, disease, and war sweeping over the region, including having much of the city leveled by Allied bombers during the Second World War. He also discusses the notorious sway that organized crime has had in the region ... an issue that appears to be on-going.

There are additionally tales here of modern artists, musicians, and writers ... many of them in the past century seeking a haven for their homosexuality when the cultural setting of the USA was less than welcoming. He discusses meeting with some over the years, and having been influenced by others.

Naples Declared[4] is still in print (in the paperback edition, as well as a Kindle version), but used copies of the Hardcover (and paperback) are available in "very good" condition for as little as a penny (plus shipping) from the on-line big boys' new/used vendors ... which if you can't get yourself to a Dollar Tree (I saw a couple of copies of this still at the one I usually go to this past week), is probably your best bet. I enjoyed reading this ... it is chock-full of fascinating detail from a wide scope of disciplines ... and the writing (while, as noted, somewhat chaotic in its focus), is quite engaging.

I'd pretty much recommend this to all and sundry ... being one of those books that one doesn't *have* to read in any particular genre, but is so broad-based that you will be glad to have gone through it, pretty much what your particular interests are.

Notes:

1. http://btripp-books.livejournal.com/170906.html
2. http://amzn.to/1eH4Y06
3. http://naplesdeclared.com/
4. http://amzn.to/1eH4Y06

Sunday, August 16, 2015

From an impressive leader ...

As I pointed out in the previous review, I have been having a run of good luck in finding interesting books over at the dollar store, at, of course, the amazing sum of *a dollar* ... having been (as I know I've bemoaned way too much in here) "out of [paying] work" for the past six years, the ability to walk out of the store having paid a buck plus tax for a nice hardcover with a $27.95 cover price is pretty sweet!

Needless to say, the current title is one of these that I found on those shelves. As is frequently the case, this is not something that I might have picked up at a regular bookstore, or on-line, the dollar availability creating a serendipity that stirs up my reading habits (a good thing, yes?) a bit. Our Last Best Chance: The Pursuit of Peace in a Time of Peril is a book by King Abdullah II of Jordan which stands out firstly by simply being a book by a sitting monarch ... something that I, at least, am not particularly aware of being "a thing". It is also, obviously, a window into the politics and cultural forces in the Middle East that has almost no equal in terms of access to the "back stories" of pretty much everything happening in that arena.

It must be noted that, within his own family, this was not a unique entity, as the author's father, the famed King Hussein of Jordan, had penned an autobiography in the early 60's, and this is referenced as something of a touchstone for this. As far as niches go, this is not just an autobiography, albeit it *is* formatted on the arc of the author's life (and he is still a young man at age 53), but endeavors to provide an analysis of many factors gripping his country's region. This starts off on a bitter-sweet note, with the Preface starting with:

> ... when I started writing this book, I hoped it would reveal the inner workings of how, against great odds, the United States, Israel, and the Arab and Muslim world had brokered peace in the Middle East. As I write these words, however, I can only say that this is a story about how peace has continued to elude our grasp.

Of course, King Abdullah II's family, the Hashemite lineage (the current King being a 43rd generation descendent of the Prophet Mohammad), is notable in the region for both its Western sensibilities (with British and American educations featuring in their development), and its willingness, even *eagerness*, to make peace with its neighbor Israel. This stands clearly apart from other entities in the region, such as Hamas, whose *raison d'être* is the "elimination" of the Jewish state.

This is not to say that he isn't *critical* of Israel. It is often too easy for those of us in the USA to see the region in very black & white terms, with Israel being the "good guys" and everybody else being threats to their existence.

The author's view is, understandably, rather different, and while he *appreciates* certain aspects of Israel, his view is that there are factions within Israeli politics who are every bit as dead-set against a negotiated peace as Hamas is from the other side. One thing that was quite the eye-opener his was his experience with the Bush administration. He had seen a good deal of progress in the days of the Clinton administration, but the neo-cons in the Bush White House seemed to have little interest in hearing Jordan's side of things – despite the author's frequent overtures. It appears that the die had been cast early on in the *Zeitgeist* of the American government leading up to the overthrow of Saddam Hussein … and making even middling efforts to "play nice" with the Palestinians was *not* part of that, being that they were clearly an "enemy force" in that world view.

Speaking of world views … it's a frequent jab at Americans that we don't have particularly much awareness of what happens in other parts of the globe, and one thing that King Abdullah II refers to here is "Benelux", which is an economic union of Belgium, the Netherlands, and Luxembourg within the E.U. that I don't believe *I'd* ever previously heard of … he holds this out as a model:

> *My dream is that we will link the economies of Israel, Palestine, and Jordan in a common market – patterned on Benelux in western Europe. We could combine the technical know-how and entrepreneurial drive of Jordan, Israel, and Palestine to create an economic and business hub in the Levant. The potential for joint tourism is massive, as it that for foreign investment. The possibility for cooperation is immense. The Israelis are world leaders I agriculture, but lack land and workers. We could work together to make the desert bloom.*

Personally, this is the most rational, and *logical* suggestion that I've seen for peace in that region. Unfortunately, politics (and religion) keep getting in the way. Another thing that I don't believe I'd read of was the "Arab Peace Initiative" that Jordan was instrumental on reaching an agreement on (endorsed by 22 members of the Arab League) … unfortunately, it came at a time (in 2002), when things on both sides were spiraling into chaos and conflict. I certainly hope, however, that the author has not abandoned the vision of a "Benelux in the Levant".

Again, this is also an autobiography, and so there is a lot of personal information in here. I am skipping over all the details about his schooling in the UK and the US (which *is* interesting), but do want to highlight a couple of bits from that aspect of the book. On one hand, you get a real sense of how *dangerous* running a country "in that neighborhood" can be … among many leaders who were assassinated over the past century there was the author's great-grandfather, with his father standing next to him. One of the precautions that his father, King Hussein, had made was to name the author's *uncle* next in line for the succession. While this created some "issues" later, it shifted the target from the author's back, and allowed him to grow (in the relative obscurity of the military) into the leader he would become. On the other hand, there are the stories such as:

> *My father used to tell me how when he wanted to take the pulse of the country, he would wrap a traditional checkered head scarf around his face and drive around Amman at night in a battered old taxi, picking people up. He would ask every new passenger, "How's the economy going? What do you think of the Palestinian-Israeli situation? What do you think of the King's new policy?"*

It is hard to imagine even the Mayor of a major American city successfully doing this, but this shows how manageable a country such as Jordan can be. Taking a cue from his father, the current King has made a habit of visiting various government offices in disguise, and making sure things *changed* when the people were being mistreated by officials. Sure, it's his own story about himself, but it's hard not to like the author as depicted in these stories!

Another interesting "window" here is on the various wars in the region, and the interactions he (and his father) had with the main players in these conflicts (such as very uncomfortable visits with Saddam's notorious sons, Uday and Qusay). While the Jordanians have been strong allies of the USA, the author is certainly no "yes man" for American interests, and his perspective on the whole convoluted morass of political, military, religious, and regional elements is quite educational.

I would definitely recommend Our Last Best Chance[3] to all and sundry, as not only is it a fascinating look at a really remarkable life, but a view of a globally important region that we certainly don't get from the press here – on the Left or the Right. As noted, I found the hardcover of this in the dollar store, but the paperback (which, oddly, has a different sub-title although just coming out a year after the initial release) is still available, and there are various other editions (international, large print, and, of course, ebook) also out there. I usually point readers to the "cheapest available" route to getting a copy of a book I'm reviewing, but books bought through retail channels have their proceeds going to support scholarships a the King's Academy – a top notch school that King Abdullah II established in Jordan (also discussed in the book), which is certainly something to consider.

Notes:

1. http://btripp-books.livejournal.com/171084.html
2-3. http://amzn.to/1UVnhj4

Tuesday, August 18, 2015[1]

When everything becomes nearly free ...

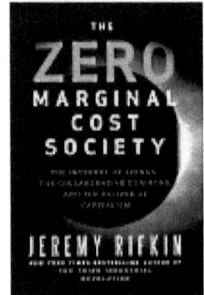

This book took one of the more *unusual* paths to get into my hands ... it turns out that the author, somehow, ended up reading my Green Tech Chicago[2] blog over on the Tribune's "Chicago Now" platform, and asked his office to send me a copy of his new book. The fact that the author is the global figure Jeremy Rifkin[3], just blows me away ... and I'm *thrilled* that he thought enough of one of my posts[4] to send out his latest book: The Zero Marginal Cost Society: The Internet of Things, the Collaborative Commons, and the Eclipse of Capitalism[5].

Now, I am pretty sure that, lacking this particular trajectory into my to-be-read piles, I would have been very unlikely to have obtained this title in my "free range" book shopping, as "economic theory" is *not* one of my favored genres ... although this has the clear connection to much of my reading in that it concentrates a great deal on how the Internet has changed the world. This is a follow-up to his The Third Industrial Revolution[6], the broad strokes of which are presented here as the concept linking energy and communications to the various jumps in industrial/societal change ... the first revolution coming via the development of steam power, paired with the printing press, the second being the development of the internal combustion engine (and the oil economy), combined with electronic communications (radio, TV, etc.), and the third, being the evolution of "renewable" energy (I'd prefer to think of neighborhood Thorium reactors, but the focus here is more in the wind/solar zone) combined with the global connectivity of the Internet (and the sub-titular "Internet of Things").

The "story" here starts in the feudal times in Europe, where most people had a totally subsistence lifestyle, which, through the effects of the water-driven mill, eventually evolved to a market economy, which moved people off the land and into the cities, eventually developing into Capitalism and vertically-integrated models:

> The solution {to new demands} was to bring production and distribution all together, in house, under centralized management. The vertically integrated business enterprise took off in the last quarter of the nineteenth century and became the dominant business model during the whole of the twentieth century.

To his credit, the author does note at one point that Soviet-style communism was no less vertical, just with different job descriptions at the various levels of management.

I don't think it's accidental that the printing press and broadcast media are used as the symbols of the first two Industrial Revolutions, as in the Third these are some of the first victims of the "zero marginal cost" reality. This has been a personal *bête noire* of mine, having been in the publishing biz at the dawn of the e-book phenomena. It was just back around 1999 (OK, for *me* that sounds like yesterday – no doubt "your mileage may vary" on that perception) when large colleges were spending the money to provide (relatively) high-speed internet services to their students ... once this was available, it was not long before "sharing" music (or "stealing" intellectual property, depending on which side of that chasm you resided) was a very common thing, with platforms such as Napster emerging to simplify the distribution. Whether or not it was "robbing the blind paperboy" or not, that distribution was an illustration of "zero marginal cost" ... if one person had a CD and could copy a song into an .mp3 file, potentially *everybody* who had an adequate connection (and back then "fast" was around 200kbps, and your cell phone now is about 25x as fast), could have that song *for no cost*. Needless to say, this created a generation which believed that *all* intellectual property should be "free" ... and it took quite a lot of legal ugliness to arrive at the current model of paid downloads!

Rifkin focuses a good deal on both 3D printing and MOOCs (Massive Open Online Courses). The latter of these is fascinating, as it grew out of a standard university setting ... but has developed to the point where it is threatening to "burst the bubble" of traditional college education. He notes:

> *The revolution began when a Stanford University professor, Sebastian Thrun, offered a "free" course on artificial intelligence (AI) online in 2011, one similar to the course he taught at the university. Around 200 students normally enrolled in Thurn's course, so he anticipated that only a few thousand would register. But by the time it commenced, 160,000 students from every country in the world – with the exception of North Korea – were sitting at their computers in the biggest classroom ever convened for a single course in all of history. "It absolutely blew my mind," said Thrun. Twenty-three thousand of those students completed the course and graduated.*
>
> *Although thrilled that he was able to teach more students in one virtual course setting that he could reach in several lifetimes of teaching, Thrum was struck by the irony. While Stanford students were paying $50,000 or more per year to attend world-class courses like the ones he taught, the cost of making the course available to every other potential student in the world was nearly nothing.*

An earlier book by the author is <u>The End Of Work</u>[7] where he argued that as technology makes for more efficient production, the number of workers plummets. An example he gives here is:

> *In the United States, between 1982 and 2002, steel production rose from 75 million tons to 120 million tons, while the number of steel workers declined from 289,000 to 74,000.*

Those are sobering numbers (unless one owns a steel mill, I suppose), with production nearly doubling, while the work force is at a quarter of its previous numbers. And, *that* is an example over a decade old, nearly predating the Web.

He goes on to paint a very dire picture for standard employment. Whole categories of jobs have disappeared, and the combination of "automation, robotics, and artificial intelligence" are threatening even classic white-collar gigs. Speaking personally, I've been out of (regular) work for SIX YEARS, and every year it gets closer to a world where even *writers* can be replaced ... there's even a program that will take the basic *data* of a sports event and write the news copy from that in a way that you'd never be able to tell there wasn't a human involved. And it goes almost everywhere ... one thing described here is a program for analyzing legal documents ahead of trials ... and *"one lawyer can do the work of 500 lawyers, and with greater accuracy"*. Scary stuff.

> *We are in the midst of an epic change in the nature of work. The First Industrial Revolution ended slave and serf labor. The Second Industrial Revolution dramatically shrank agricultural and craft labor. The Third Industrial Revolution is sunsetting mass wage labor in the manufacturing and service industries and salaried professional labor in large parts of the knowledge sector.*

What Rifkin foresees is a "Collaborative Commons" populated with "prosumers" (producer/consumers) ...

> *In a Collaborative Commons, sellers and buyers give way to prosumers, property rights make room for open-source sharing, ownership is less important than access, markets are superseded by networks, and the marginal cost of producing information, generating energy, manufacturing products, and teaching students is nearly zero. A central question arises: How is the new Internet of Things infrastructure that makes all of this possible going to be financed?*

I have a more practical question: if there are no professional jobs, how do I pay my condo's assessment fees and put groceries in the fridge? I have to admit at about halfway through here I sort of got lost ... lots of stuff about traditional theories of "the commons" mixed up with material about environmental issues, and various energy issues (I take it that the author isn't a fan of reactors – even of the GenIV variety – as these don't end up even being *mentioned* that I could tell). The "solution" in the short term that he proposes is that there will be TONS of jobs in the building-out of "the Internet of Things", but that's hardly a happy prospect if a "wordsmith" has to retrain to be a "wire twister".

The last parts of the book seemed to me to be quite pie-in-the-sky (pretty much projecting from the vectors involved in a wide spectrum of new technologies and business models), and somewhat hard to "take seriously" as there's a GIGO factor here ... making a guess at something 20 years down the road based on the "trendy" thing of the past month is hardly a reliable course to take. He does project a "philosophical" evolution, however, which has a certain plausibility ... how "forager/hunter" societies exhibited "mythological consciousness", the "great hydrolic civilizations" of 4,000-6,000 years ago developed into "theological consciousness", *in the nineteenth century, the convergence of coal-powered steam printing and the new coal-powered factory and rail-transport system gave rise to "ideological consciousness"*, and *in the twentieth century, the coming together of centralized electrification, oil, and automobile transport, and the rise of mass consumer society* evolved "psychological consciousness" (*living simultaneously in both an inner and outer world that continuously mediates the way we interact and carry on life*), leading (possibly) in the new model to an "empathic consciousness", or, in a massively connected world, a "biosphere consciousness" (unless, of course, the machines reach "the singularity" first - another concept I don't believe the author touches on).

He does, however, get into a lot of number shuffling over things like "carrying capacity" and various other similar grim scenarios, with warnings about climate issues and terror threats, but his closing points primarily deal with saying that we need to move past materialism and ownership of things. Having been in Marketing Communications (although only peripherally in the ad biz) my whole life in one form or another, I found the following "red flag" of particular interest:

> *For the materialist, advertising becomes the powerful drug that feeds the addiction. Advertising preys on one's sense of inadequacy and loneliness. It promises that products and services will enhance a person's personality and identity and make him or her more appealing, attractive, and acceptable to others. The German philosopher Georg Friedrich Hegel defined the new materialist man and woman coming of age at the dawn of the capitalist ethos. He argued that beyond its utilitarian and material value, property is an expression of one's persona. It's by forcing one's will into objects that one projects his unique persona on the world and creates a presence among his fellow human beings. One's very personality, then, is present in all the objects one claims as one's own. Our property becomes indistinguishable from our personality. Everything that is mine enlarges my unique presence and sphere of influence and becomes the means by which others know me.*
>
> ...
>
> *Advertising plays off the idea that property is the measure of a human being and pushes products and services as essential to the creation of an individual's identity in the world. For much of the twentieth century, advertising pitched the idea that property is an extension of one's personality and*

> *made deep inroads in reorienting each successive generation to a materialist culture.*

Needless to say, the author "is against it" when it comes to "materialist culture" and is, by extension, advocating for the sub-title's "eclipse of capitalism". As much as I can't stand the current state of advertising (I am incapable of listening to broadcast radio as *every* ad out there is blatantly anchored onto one or more of the Seven Deadly Sins, which I find extremely irritating), this does wander into a zone which is more about espousing far-Left rallying points that charting out actual solutions.

Anyway, The Zero Marginal Cost Society[8] is a very interesting read with a lot of fascinating takes on the economic evolution of the culture. As noted above, I was hardly in close alignment to many of Rifkin's projections, but the material he brings to bear supporting the over-all thesis is well worth reading. This only came out last year, so should still be on a shelf at larger brick-and-mortar book vendors, but the on-line big boys have both the hardcover and paperback at very generous discounts at the moment (close to 40% off), and copies *are* available in the new/used channels. This is hardly a book for everybody, but if you have interest in technology, history, or economics, you should find something to your liking in this (and if your politics are towards the Left you'll probably have less "aggravation points" that I found when reading it).

Notes:

1. http://btripp-books.livejournal.com/171323.html
2. http://greentechchicago.info/
3. http://foet.org/
4. http://www.chicagonow.com/green-tech-chicago/2014/10/energy-from-your-clothes-energy-from-your-walls/
5. http://amzn.to/1BIzTnh
6. http://amzn.to/1LflZLS
7. http://amzn.to/1EwaQjo
8. http://amzn.to/1BIzTnh

Thursday, August 20, 2015[1]

Some things are older than you may suspect ...

I have been aware of Robert M. Schoch for quite a while ... he has been one of those "alternative timeline" researchers dealing with the extreme antiquities of Egypt, and the one with the most impeccable credentials of that group of theorists. Not that others in that niche don't have impressive C.V.s of their own, but it seems that only Schoch got into it via what he has an advanced degree in (Geology and Geophysics, which he also teaches as a tenured professor at a major university). If you're not familiar with this area, Schoch's main "claim to fame" arose from being invited to consult on a project studying the Sphinx at Giza ... to give his opinion on what he felt the rock facings within the Sphinx enclosure indicated for the *age* of the sculpture, and, by extension, the whole Giza site. In his opinion, the type of weathering that is exhibited in these very old constructions could only have happened in a period when Egypt was subject to a great deal more rainfall than has been the case in the "canonical" timeline (which holds that the Sphinx was created in 2,500 BCE) and since ... his estimates are that the enclosure could not have been carved out any more recently than 5,000 BCE, and might date to as early a time as 9,000 BCE.

As I sat down to review this, I was having a hard time recalling what specifically spurred me to order it ... I still don't have a clear answer for that question, but I suspect this might have been referenced/plugged in Graham Hancock's Facebook feed (which I follow with great anticipation for the stuff he features). Anyway ... something must have gotten the idea in my head that I needed to get a copy of Schoch's Forgotten Civilization: The Role of Solar Outbursts in Our Past and Future[2], although I'm not sure exactly why ... as it's sort of in a "side issue" zone as far as my reading in the category has gone. It is fascinating, however, how this dovetails with other bits and pieces that I've read over the years.

The connecting theme in Forgotten Civilization[3] is the concept (as noted in its sub-title) of "Solar Outbursts", and how these may have deeply influenced civilization. Now, like Schoch's research on the Sphinx, there are several other threads of "heretical" material that points to there having been a global advanced civilization sometime about 12,000 years ago. From John Anthony West's theories of some of the older Egyptian ruins (such as the Osirion at Abydos) dating from that age, to various anachronistic sites in South America, India, and elsewhere, the "orthodoxy" simply scoffed and implied that all such theories were delusional at best. However, the recent discovery of the Göbekli Tepe site in Anatolia has changed the playing field, as Schoch notes: *"Based on radiocarbon analyses, the site goes back to the period of 10,000 BCE to 9000 BCE and was intentionally buried circa 8000 BCE."* ... meaning that we have solid evidence of an advanced culture (certainly in its sculpting[4]) dating to the same 12,000 years ago time period that was supposedly what the priests of Sais had told Solon (according to

Plato) was the fall of "Atlantis". Suddenly, all these *"Nah, couldn't be!"* advanced cultural artifacts dating from c. 10,000 BCE are harder to just summarily reject (although the vast majority of "doctrinal" archeologists – Zahi Haiwass certainly among them – still do). Schoch takes one chapter here to dig into the "accepted" timeline – which posits mankind being barely out of the cave in 10,000 BCE – and shows how much of this derives from the work of Gordon Childe, who in 1950 published a list of "ten basic criteria" that he held to be indicative of civilization. Childe's model has been the accepted paradigm for the past half-century, but has (when presented with examples like the Natufian culture in the Levant c. 13,000 BCE or Göbekli Tepe, etc.) some serious holes in it.

The book is in three main parts (although not specifically divided that way), first a look at three archaeological contexts, that of the Sphinx, Göbekli Tepe, and Easter Island, then a middle section looking at various scientific pursuits, ice ages (specifically the "Younger Dryas", a cooling period that happened about 11,000 BCE), sunspots and the lifecycle of the Sun, the Earth's magnetosphere, "cosmoclimatology", and off into such cosmic obscurities as "galactic superwaves", "gravity waves" (possibly triggering earthquakes), and even the possible effects of interstellar dust clouds … and then a third part where he's trying to link the theories he's worked up in the first parts to historical events and other "science stuff", followed by a handful of appendixes which seem to address particular issues that he's had brought up related to things in the book.

I've already touched on elements of the Sphinx and Göbekli Tepe … both apparently date from ≈ 10,000 BCE, with the latter being *intentionally buried* (much like the Pyramid of Kulkulkan at Teotihuacan outside of Mexico City) a couple of thousand years after its construction. The Easter Island material, however, is somewhat central to the book. It seems that the "moai" (the large statues) were quarried from pits that are presently well under water off the coasts of the island, this, with the fact the many of the maoi are deeply sunk into the ground, would indicate a possible very early date for their sculpting. The answer to the "so what?" question on the Easter Island material is that there are engraved tablets in an undeciphered script called "rongorongo" that Schoch (or, I guess, his wife Katie came up with the idea) feels is very similar to petroglyphs that a Los Alamos plasma physicist, Anthony L. Peratt, felt were similar (or a recording of) certain plasma phenomena that would likely happen in a major solar storm.

> *Powerful plasma discharges, much more powerful than the auroras observed in the present day, form structures known as plasma columns that can expand in some places and constrict or narrow in other places (due to "pinch instabilities"). In profile these plasma columns can form donut shapes and may look like intertwining snakes, a stack of circles, or even resemble human stick figures (the so-called "stickman" or "squatting/squatter man" figures …). In the modern day, powerful large-scale electrical discharges known as sprites occasionally occur in the upper atmosphere (about 80 to 140 kilometers above the surface of the Earth). Some*

> sprites take on stick figure forms and other shapes comparable to those of the plasma columns. Based on Peratt's models and experiments, in some cases the stick figure will have an upper cup shape (head) that has the appearance of a bird in profile. Peratt and his colleague W.F. Yao record that observers of the Carrington Event reported seeing "figures in the sky as if drawn with fire on a black background".

There are photo inserts in the book comparing the rongorongo script with various rock carvings, and plasma experiments. While there are certainly similarities between the script and the carvings, how many ways are there that a "stick figure" will appear? Unfortunately, I feel they were *really* stretching to attribute significant connections between the plasma patterns and the figures (making me wonder if this whole book is just a gesture to make Schoch's wife feel good). Anyway, those figures, and (in terms of chronology) that "script" (there was noted some *question* as to how old that actually was), are the main things linking extreme solar events with the archaeology of 10,000 BCE, with the rest of the book pretty much being "oh, and this!" add-ons.

One interesting thing in the above quote is the "Carrington Event", which was a major solar storm in 1859. This happened over a week, from August 28 through September 5:

> *In late August of 1859 a major sunspot group appeared. On or around August 26 and 27 a solar flare (although unobserved) may have occurred, as well as a solar proton event (SPE) and a CME {coronal mass ejection}. The CME may have taken on the order of forty to sixty hours to cross the distance from the Sun to Earth, arriving on August 28 and creating the first wave of outstanding auroras and the accompanying geomagnetic storm. ...*
>
> *On September 1, Carrington and Hodgson observed the solar flare. Given how bright it was modern estimates suggest the surface temperature of the sun at the point of the emission was close to 50 million degrees Celsius. An enormous amount of energy was released, not only as visible light but also as intense X rays and gamma rays that, traveling at the speed of light, hit Earth eight and one-half minutes later. A CME was also released from the Sun ...*
>
> *Protons were accelerated by the solar flare and the CME to incredibly high energy levels and penetrated into our atmosphere, creating a major solar proton event (SPE). According to one estimate, this reduced the stratospheric ozone layer by 5 percent, and it took years to fully recover. Furthermore, energetic protons hitting the nuclei of nitrogen and oxygen atoms created a shower of neutrons that*

> *rained down onto the surface of the earth. ...*

Schoch notes that this event, while major compared to "the usual" output of the Sun, was not as powerful as the Sun is capable of throwing at us (there have been CMEs that we've seen that have been huge, but fortunately pointed in another direction), and the suggestion is that something *significant* happened at the end of the Younger Dryas that threw the planet into a warming phase that created havoc for the civilizations that existed at the time.

One thing I found *very interesting* here is that Schoch is largely (in the current progressive terminology) a climate change "denier" ... for many of the same reasons that I have doubts about the current dogmatic theory. He rather archly outlines:

> *The accepted paradigm, the scientific dogma, is not to be fundamentally questioned. Small additions and tweaking, elaborations and expansions, and building on the accepted paradigm are acceptable and even encouraged, but questioning the fundamental basis of the paradigm is not allowable. Radically dissenting views and any data that challenge the accepted paradigm must be suppressed. Heretics are persecuted or ignored. (In past centuries, this might mean torture or death. In modern times it might mean exclusion from the scientific community by being locked out of jobs, publication outlets, and grant funding.) Ultimately such tactics constitute "cheating by concealment" and "discreet fraud" ...*

I've been aware of counter theories to the dominant paradigm for well over a decade ... going back to Richard Hoagland's "Hyperdimensional" physics material, which he's called on to explain why there has been *similar* "global warming" phenomena on Mars[5] and other planets happening simultaneously to the activity on Earth ... with a Solar cause being far more plausible than SUVs. Schoch cites:

> *In recent years there has been increasing evidence for, and acknowledgment of, connections between climate, Earth's magnetic field, solar activity, and related extraterrestrial and other "subtle" factors. Much of this work goes against the reigning paradigm, the common consensus that has solidified around the topic of global climate change (more commonly refereed to as global warming). The general consensus view, for instance, has been that increases in global temperatures seen in the twentieth and twenty-first centuries have been due primarily or totally to the actions of humans, most notably the increase of greenhouse gases (such as carbon dioxide) in the atmosphere due to the burning of fossil fuels and deforestation. Natural factors*

> *and cycles have been downplayed or ignored, despite the fact that changes in greenhouse gases have been correlated with global temperature changes for hundreds of thousands – even millions – of years, long before humans could conceivably have been causing such changes. Indeed, increases in carbon dioxide may in part be a consequence of global warming rather than a cause. Increases in temperature due to other factors (such as increases in solar activity) may warm the oceans, for instance, resulting in the release of carbon dioxide and an inability to absorb more carbon dioxide ...*

Obviously, I'm in agreement with him here, and, to be fair, he makes the "cosmic catastrophe" case very well, citing a lot of geological science (of course), from micro-diamonds in geological strata to odd cases of vitrification (where rock has been turned to a glass-like substance by extremely high heat) indicative of the possibility of ground-level (i.e. massive) plasma events. The down side of this is two-fold ... first, it's *quite* grim, and the sort of thing that you really can't do anything about, except to dig deep underground spaces to escape to in the brief warning period that one would have before something like this would hit (interestingly, there are "bunker-like" structures on Easter Island which he posits were created for shelters against the solar storms of 12,000 years ago), and secondly, we're WAY over-due (looking at ice cores, geographic strata, and deposits of assorted isotopes) for a big civilization-erasing event.

However, towards the end of the book he gets into some very strange spaces ... from instabilities in the galactic core that can result in periodic bursts of cosmic rays, which would not only effect Earth directly, but "throw gasoline on the fire" on the Sun, causing a whole alphabet of bad stuff, SPEs, CMEs, and even technology-destroying EMPs, to the possibility of our moving into an interstellar dust cloud that would be like throwing dry fuel into the Sun, with many of the same effects. He also pokes into some odd science, from the theories that water *"can form nanostructures with the ability to encode, store, and transmit information"*, to work that suggests that isotopes' decay rates are not *constant* but fluctuate in correlation with external factors: magnesium-54 fluctuating in correlation with solar flares, and silicon-32 and radium-226 exhibiting variations in decay rates that correlate with the changing distance between the Earth and the Sun.

While I found Forgotten Civilization[6] fascinating in the material it has at the granular level, it's a very odd book in the broad strokes, starting from an "alternative archaeology" tour of key sites that push civilization back many thousands of years before the dominant paradigm, to a look at how cosmic influences could be the driving force for both "climate change" and historical disasters, to pulling in a wide net of other materials which are only "sort of" to the point (as I see it, at least) ... and I doubt that was what I was anticipating when I ordered this! I'm also sort of surprised that this is only the first of his half-dozen or so books that I've picked up.

So, will you like this? I don't know. There is a ton of stuff *in* this that I was glad to have encountered (including theories I'd never even *heard of* previously, which is not a usual thing for me), but I've read a *lot* in the genre, and the over-all arc of the book put *me* off, and I suspect that it is likely to be a firehose of weirdness for readers coming to it without a substantial background in this material. Countering that perception, while it's been out for three years at this point, it hasn't gotten cheap in the new/used channels ... with the cheapest of those books still coming in higher than the discounted price (assuming you're getting free shipping) from the on-line big boys. I don't *regret* buying this, but I can only recommend it with that whole heap of caveats above.

Notes:

1. http://btripp-books.livejournal.com/171713.html

2-3. http://amzn.to/1IbRZO4

4. http://www.smithsonianmag.com/ist/?next=/history/gobekli-tepe-the-worlds-first-temple-83613665/

5. http://www.enterprisemission.com/warming.htm

6. http://amzn.to/1IbRZO4

Tuesday, September 1, 2015[1]

How to freelance ... starting TODAY!

OK, so I'm a member of IWOC[2] (Independent Writers of Chicago – kind of like Ewoks[3], but somewhat bigger and less furry), and have been pretty diligent in attending meetings. A month or so back, the presenter was one of our members talking about "Maximizing Your Freelance Income" ... a subject dear to my ~~heart~~ wallet. Her presentation was fairly useful, and she (of course) was eventually pitching her book on the subject. Now, after my years of penning the looking-for-work blog over on Chicago Now, The Job Stalker[4], (and reviewing numerous books for that) I have a certain cynicism about "how to" books, having found that the vast majority of these (especially in the job search niche – which this comes close to as a "finding work" book) are typically useless, unless one is in a particularly small slice out of the Venn Diagram of the author's experience (with some examples being sufficiently idiosyncratic to be of use to an audience of one). So, to a large extent, I ordered Diana Schneidman's Real Skills, Real Income: A Proven Marketing System to Land Well-Paid Freelance and Consulting Work in 30 Days or Less[5] "just to be polite", without any great expectations that it would be a help.

Fortunately, I found this to be one of those rare and wondrous books written by somebody who "has been in the trenches" and is not interested in blowing smoke up one's nether regions. Not that I'm going to be a *big* cheerleader for this either, as Ms. Schneidman is advocating a lot of processes that I have a *great deal* of resistance to (which is why I have never *aspired* to being a freelancer, but have only ended up needing to *be* one due to the notable paucity of full-time gigs for somebody in my demographic niche) ... but I can recognize solid advice when I read it, and this book is chock full of it (no doubt why it has a 4.8/5.0 star rating on Amazon).

And, while the book is structured on a very step-by-step arc (including stuff you want to do *now* and stuff that sounds like it might be important to do that can be basically put off until *never*), it's comfortably nestled into a continuing series of reminiscences from the author's own life ... starting with one of her (three that she was raising on her own) kids asking her, when she was coming home with tear-reddened eyes and a boxful of desk items, "You've been fired again, right?" ... a context that makes even the most resistance-producing instructions ring as true, and, perhaps, necessary. She notes right up front: *"You don't need passion right now. You don't need the answer to every question and comfort for every self-doubt to get paying work. ... Intelligent effort, applied consistently over time, will bring you success!"* ... and, as she further notes: *"If I can do it, anyone can do it."*

One of the things I liked most about how the book is set up is that there are these "to the point" sections at the end of each chapter which feature bullet points extracting the essence of the main action elements of each. They're not exactly the "Cliff's Notes" version that one could read through and pick up the basics of the book, but they function to "anchor" the main things you need to recall as you read through it.

Following the Introduction, she has a section called "Why Go Solopro?" (her term for the freelancer role here), with thirteen reasons … ranging from the basic: 1. Earn Money, to the somewhat esoteric: 11. Repair You Soul (which, frankly, spoke directly to me – in having been beaten down so much by job search frustration *"that you exude, and therefore attract, negativity"* and that the "small victories", or, as she puts them *"quick pats on the back"* [noting *"most people don't care enough to reject you!"*] can build back up confidence and positivity). Also, as a "solopro", you're not just a job seeker, you're a provider of *services*, and that's more positive as well.

In the first chapter she presents "three guiding ideas" for going solopro:

> – First, offer a service as similar as possible to what you did in your last good full-time job.
> – Second, contact the best prospects individually. And …
> – Third, get real! Let's define quickly as thirty days and not thirty minutes.

To this she adds what could be taken as "auto-suggestions" and their implementation:

> *Your most important personal belief is that your work and your service are exceptional. You care deeply about your clients and do the best you can for them. You deserve top rates.*
>
> *Are these your beliefs? If not, make them true or get out of the business. Are you exceptional? Then believe you will succeed. And if you don't believe you are exceptional? Why not?*
>
> *If this is something you can fix, <u>fix it immediately</u>. Need more training? <u>Sign up for it.</u> Spend money on it if necessary. … Need more experience? <u>Get it.</u> It may be worth your while to work for free or at a low rate for a volunteer organization or smaller company. …*

The second step is "Determine Your Service and Your Niche" … with a hint to *"Select a niche in which you can make a living."* she gives the example that she at one point was writing résumés – this didn't conform to her further advice to *"select one in which you feel comfortable charging an attractive fee for your work"*, as she found herself constantly trimming her bills trying to be a "Girl Scout" (*"if you don't have the guts to require payment for all the hours you work, you're a Girl Scout"*) – and eventually had to focus on doing writing for the insurance and asset management industries.

The third step is "Take a Grown-Up Approach to Marketing" … this chapter runs through quite a lot of material and situations, but one key element is under the heading *"Embrace what does not come naturally."*

> *If phoning is the most effective means of finding buyers for your service, and I'm here to tell you it often is, then you pick up the phone.*

> If you dread telephoning or any other direct interaction with prospects and clients, consider it is more efficient to push beyond your comfort zone than to constrict your marketing effort around your fears.

That last bit could just as well have been directly addressed to me … she even suggests the possibility of hiring a coach to help one start phoning. This takes us right into Step 4 - "Say "Hi" to Our Friend the Phone" … a chapter that is very dense with details, from sample scripts to pre-call checklists, to "philosophical" bits like:

> The authorities preach that _knowing_ and _liking_ must precede _trusting_, but that hasn't been my experience as a freelancer. I've found it easy to skip directly to trust. And to me, establishing trust is the essence of what I'm doing when I call prospects.

One of the essential things here is "the list" … which she discusses various ways of developing. If you're going to make her recommended call volume you'll need a _serious_ list, as she says "the secret" of getting solid, dependable, freelance work is to _call large numbers of people_ … and, yeah, I was _horrified_ when I saw the number she was thinking of … 1,000 … yep, a thousand names … did I mention "resistance"?

> You only need to make fifty calls a day. Then do that five work days a week for four weeks. At the end of four weeks you will have made 1,000 calls.
>
> …
>
> What's it like in practice to make 1,000 calls in a single month? Well, I still don't know. Every time work has slowed down … I've resumed marketing and have filled my plate with assignments way before I have completed 1,000. …
>
> …
>
> … The 1,000 number is for those who are highly motivated to earn money quickly. Alternatively, it is for those who are desperate . (The two situations can be pretty similar in real life.) Either way, it is a course of intense action to obtain paying results soon. … But the more calls you make, the faster you get work.

Now, how can you tell how you're doing? (I really hate this part too.) In terms of people who _are interested_ (not necessarily giving you assignments at this time), _"5% is tremendous, 2% is excellent, and 1% is acceptable"_. Schneidman makes the point that those 99-95% of essential "no" (or "null", as most of the time you'll simply be ignored) responses are NOT _rejections_ … of course, being the type of guy who wants to curl up in a ball under his desk after "no" number 3 (out of 1k???), that's hard for me to process.

Oh, and she recommends keeping a spreadsheet of your calls ... this not only appeals to my OCD tendencies, but it removes that "am I being a nuisance?" thinking ... if somebody tells you to not call again, you can make sure they're on your own personal "do not call" list.

Step 5 is "Price, Bill, and Collect for Success" ... in which the author delves into how much to charge (by the hour, by the project, or by the "value"), how to determine hourly rates (this is one thing I've fallen down on before), gauging competition and market rates, etc. ... and goes into pages and pages and pages on how to present, negotiate and stay firm on your fees. She also provides a sample invoice, and goes into detail on how to collect when the client isn't being financially forthcoming. She also insists that the *first* thing you do every morning is determine if you should be invoicing a client, and then getting that out to them (*"Never postpone invoicing more than twenty-four hours from the event that triggers it."* – I've been bad on this one as well).

Step 6 is "Manage Yourself: Do the Work and Manage Your Time" ... interestingly, this starts out in the "philosophy" sphere – with defining what you're doing – come up with an "I am" statement, "I am a writer", or "I design", or whatever your particular *thing* is. This is again one of those auto-suggestion kinds of approaches ... it solidifies the reality as opposed to a vague or future-looking phrase. The solopro has a challenge in time management, as there is *doing the work* and there is *getting the work* and only one of those is billable. She suggests that the *second task* (following getting the invoices out) is doing a top-priority task that one has determined (and written down) the previous evening.

Step 7 is quite a firehose of information ... it is "Start Fast! Get Up and Running in One Day" and is just what it sounds like – a step-by-step walk through of getting your solopro business up and running NOW. This is structured as a 15-item checklist that gives you the broad strokes of each element, the time estimation she figures for that, and a list of "next steps" for these (obviously, not in the one-day estimate). She has a section up front on this called *"Let me make many of your decisions."* which she does rather bluntly all through this (your logo will be *blue*, your font will be *Verdana*, she gives you a specific template for an email sig, etc.) ... which no doubt aids in being able to get all 15 elements of starting your business done in a day! This chapter also has a plan for Day Two ... which should include phone calls ... but also sets up a few things that might take a bit more time (a portfolio, a website, etc.). Which then brings us to Step 8 (which I sort of alluded to up top), which is "Stand Still! Postpone These Marketing Techniques Until Later ... or Until Never" and includes a list of 17 activities that she argues against. Some of these are practical (like don't email to info@ addresses – get the actual target email), some of them are, well, a bit odd (like "Don't attend networking meetings." – when I've been attending at least two a week for *years* – but given my success rate for finding a job, she might have something there).

The book ends up with a couple of Appendixes, first a very brief one with sample prospecting email copy, and then one that's written by somebody else on the subject of becoming a Virtual Assistant. I found this latter inclusion, frankly *bizarre*, as it kind of veered off into a whole different area (I suppose it could be argued that being a V.A. is *sort of like* being a type of freelancer, but *still*), and left me wondering what the author of that piece "had on" Ms. Schneidman to get it inserted in the book!

Anyway, as noted above, Real Skills, Real Income[6] is quite a system for getting somebody up and running as a freelancer FAST ... and nothing in it (except for the second Appendix) seemed off-kilter – even if frequently running counter to my own comfort zones. The cover price on this is pretty reasonable, and the on-line big boys have it at a bit of a discount. If you are considering going into the "solopro" channel, I'd definitely recommend you picking up a copy ... great "been there, done that" words of wisdom here!

Notes:

1. http://btripp-books.livejournal.com/171969.html
2. http://iwoc.org/
3. https://upload.wikimedia.org/wikipedia/commons/b/b1/Ewok_SWExhibition.jpg
4. http://www.chicagonow.com/job-stalker/
5-6. http://amzn.to/1LDrgOs

Wednesday, September 2, 2015[1]

The why behind those rose colored glasses ...

OK, so those of you who read my on-line blitherings with any regularity will realize that "optimism" is not one of my top mental states, so you can sort of imagine the scene at the dollar store when I found Tali Sharot's The Optimism Bias: A Tour of the Irrationally Positive Brain[2] provocatively staring at me from the always-enticing shelves of $1 books ... did I want it? Would it be *nauseatingly* optimistic? What was it about? Fortunately, a flip through its pages reassured me that this was a study of psychological and brain states, and not some Pollyannaish polemic about positivism, so into the cart it went. And, oddly enough, rather that "aging" in my towering to-be-read piles for an extended period, the prospect of reading a "neuroscience" piece seemed particularly attractive soon after, so here we are.

One of the things that, perhaps, created a connection here was that the author did *not* set out to do research on positivity, in fact, this book began in about as negative place as one could imagine, looking at how traumatic events – in specific the 9/11 attacks – served to shape memories. She notes: *"I was interested in how the brain tricks us into believing that our recollections of exceptionally emotional events ... are as accurate as videotape, even when we are utterly mistaken."*, with particular emphasis on what she describes as "flashbulb memories" (*"because of their sharp-edged, picturelike qualities"*), which are "unusually vivid" and "reluctant to fade away".

Sharot points to research which suggests that *"Optimism is prevalent in every age group, race, and socioeconomic status."*, which she then expands on:

> Many of us are not aware of our optimistic tendencies. In fact, the optimism bias is so powerful precisely because, like many other illusions, it is not fully accessible to conscious deliberation. Yet data clearly shows that most people overestimate their prospects for professional achievements; expect their children to be extraordinarily gifted; miscalculate their likely life span (sometimes by twenty years or more); expect to be healthier than the average person and more successful than their peers; hugely underestimate their likelihood of divorce, cancer, and unemployment; and are confident overall that their future lives will be better than those their parents put up with. This is known as the optimism bias – the inclination to overestimate the likelihood of encountering positive events in the future and to underestimate the likelihood of experiencing negative events.

She starts off by looking at other "illusions of the human brain" ... first describing another horrific air disaster, where an Egyptian crew was flying out of Sharm el-Sheik, headed to Cairo and on to Paris. In this crash, it appears that the pilot experienced "spatial disorientation", or a type of vertigo where one is unable to detect the position of the aircraft in relation to the ground, resulting in trying to "correct" things which are not wrong, this then resulting in a "graveyard spin" (she notes this is also the likely cause of the private plane crash that killed John F. Kennedy, Jr.). Our sense of positioning is largely due to liquid-filled tubes in the inner ear, which *"works extremely well when we are on the ground"* but can be easily confused in powered flight. She moves from this to some visual illusions, both fairly familiar and not so much, and shows how the brain is frequently easily fooled. From here she moves to "introspective illusions", where rather than truthfully reflecting inner mental processes, one inaccurately infers and constructs intentions of past mental states (in experiments where the subject chose one option, but was presented with a rejected option as being what they had chosen ... 84% of subjects defended their "choice" even when it *wasn't* what they had actually picked). *"The researchers dubbed the phenomenon choice blindness and the participants' disbelief that they could be fooled in this way was described as choice blindness blindness."* Optimism bias is a similar cognitive illusion, and not only are we blind to the illusory nature of it, we're blind to *being* blind to it.

A fascinating side-issue that is covered here is how the brain can rearrange itself for knowledge ... with examples given both of birds learning to hide food, and London cabbies learning "The Knowledge" (the vastly complicated mental map of the streets and locations that makes that profession as exclusive as it is). This is in support of the concept of "mental time travel", which refers to *"revisiting the past and imagining the future"*. This leads up to the following:

> While the capacity for both awareness and prospection has clear survival advantages, conscious foresight also came at an enormous price – an understanding that somewhere in the future, death awaits us. This knowledge – that old age, sickness, decline of mental power, and oblivion are around the corner – is less than optimistic. It causes a great amount of anguish and fear. ... {it has been argued} that the awareness of mortality on its own would have led evolution to a dead end. The despair would have interfered with daily function, bringing the activities and cognitive functions needed for survival to a stop. Humans possess this awareness and yet we survive. How?

> The only way conscious mental time travel could have been selected for over the course of evolution is if it had emerged at the same time as false beliefs. In other words, an ability to imagine the future had to develop side by side with positive

> biases. The knowledge of death had to emerge at the same time as its irrational denial. A brain that could consciously voyage through time would be an evolutionary barrier unless it had an optimism bias.

She takes a chapter to look at "self-fulfilling prophecies", from the way that famed horse "Clever Hans" read clues in his handlers to come up with correct answers, to how stereotypes can reinforce themselves by framing expectations that can, in specific situations, can be totally reversed by making shifts in context, to even how different people can have totally different results from negative experiences depending on the way they process those events. She also compares some rather odd things: *"Like Barack Obama's speeches, Shirley Temple's films mirrored a difficult era while at the same time promising a better future."*, while asking if these sorts of things trigger oxytocin release in their audiences.

Sharot also goes into material on comparative crime rates and the (usually wildly incorrect) perceptions of these, and lifestyle elements which are generally assumed to be positive (such as being married and having children), which actually, when studied, aren't, to even how more money has a limit, and actual dollar amount is less important than relative income compared with one's neighbors and peers. One thing that was particularly interesting was the idea of "depressive realism":

> In depressed patients, the rACC {rostral anterior cingulate cortex} fails in regulating amygdala function adequately. As a result, while healthy people are biased towards a positive future, depressed individuals perceive possibilities a bit too clearly. While severely depressed patients are pessimistic, mildly depressed people are actually pretty good at predicting what may happen to them in the near future – a phenomenon known as <u>depressive realism</u>. If you ask mildly depressed individuals what they expect in the upcoming month, they will give you a pretty accurate account. If you ask them about their longevity or the likelihood of having a certain illness, they will give you correct estimations. Could it be that without an optimism bias, we would all be mildly depressed?

I suppose, having been "mildly depressed" for *decades*, this probably explains why I (and folks like me) think that most folks are *idiots* because they think things which are plainly headed for disaster have a chance to turn out OK! This sets up a base for a consideration of financial issues … the optimism bias could well be at the heart of American's dire savings rates … people see upward trends where there are none, and spend in anticipation of those trends … pair this with an unwillingness to consider age and illness, and even the super-wealthy (she uses Michael Jackson as an example of this) end up in trouble.

A familiar concept is looked at from some different angles here, *cognitive dissonance*, and how decisions can be influenced … I marked the following as a particularly to-the-point example:

> *If you would like to increase your employees' commitment to your company, your students' commitment to their studies, your clients' appreciation of the service you are providing, remind them every so often of their freedom of choice. Remind them of their decision to work at this company, to study at their selected college, and to use the provided services. An airline I often fly with does just that.*

She then insists that the "we know you have many options" announcement instantly convinces *her* that "since I chose this airline it must be better than the rest" (I guess some folks have less sensitivity to manipulation than I do!). The function here is that being presented with equally valid choices tends to make us uncomfortable, and anything that enables us to frame one choice as superior (or inferior) to the other enables a decrease in the doubt that we're making the right decision. Needless to say, there is a great deal of interest in the marketing world of how to manipulate these sorts of issues, and Sharot goes into a lot of the brain chemistry that plays assorted roles in these functions.

> *After making a choice, the decision ultimately changes our estimated pleasure, enhancing the expected pleasure from the selected option and decreasing the expected pleasure from the rejected option. If we were not inclined to update the value of our options rapidly so that they concur with our choices, we would likely second-guess ourselves to the point of insanity.*

She then returns to issues around 9/11 for a while, looking at how memories formed – with both her own experiences on that day, and laboratory work on others' recollections. There's another section on how preferences form – in this case Lance Armstrong saying it was more important to be a cancer survivor than a Tour de France champion (disregarding, I assume, the realities of the doping penalties). Health issues come up here:

> *… If we underestimate health risks, our likelihood of seeking preventative health care and medical screening is reduced, and the likelihood of engaging in risky behavior is increased. … Underestimating risk can lead to an infinite number of medical issues that otherwise could have been prevented, costing our health system millions of dollars a year.*
>
> *Why would our brains be wired in a way that biases the process by which we learn about the world around us? Why would we develop a system that causes us to predict the future inaccurately? Could being irrationally optimistic have survival value?*

Well, as anybody who has been exposed to new age materials over the past decade or so will tell you, it turns out that optimism can increase positive results, as the irrational expectations can *still* be "self-fulfilling", so optimists heal faster than pessimists, live longer, etc. These benefits, interestingly, are primarily found with "moderate optimists", leading the author to suggest *"A certain underestimation of the hurdles in front of us allows us to jump forward with force."* ... while "extreme optimism" just leads to bad results.

The Optimism Bias[3] is a fascinating read, and hardly what I expected getting into it. The questions it raises in relation to human psychology are certainly of interest to anybody interested in how we function – be that in a marketing sense or a "Darwin Award" *"hold my beer – watch this!"* view of hominid behavior. This has been out for a number of years, and the hardcover (which I found at the dollar store) appears to be out of print, but there are e-book and paperback editions available. The on-line new/used guys have "good" copies of the hardcover for under a buck (plus shipping), which looks to be the best bet price-wise.

Notes:

1. http://btripp-books.livejournal.com/172064.html
2-3. http://amzn.to/1gVF5dU

Thursday, September 3, 2015[1]

No, that's not a Harry Potter character ...

This is yet another book that came my way via the LibraryThing.com "Early Reviewer" program. I was hardly surprised that I got matched to this having a bunch of Richard Dawkins, Sam Harris, Christopher Hitchens, etc., in my library, but I was quite surprised when I got into it.

It is generally considered "bad form" to use the ARC (advance review copy) as a measure of the book as far as basic editing goes ... but this was a bit of a doozy on that level – to the extent that I wrote to the contact on the promotional materials that came out with the ARC to ask if she could *please* reassure me that this was going to have a substantial editorial work-over done to it before the actual book hit the shelves. She noted that the not inconsequential delay in publication was due, in large part, to the publisher (Humanist Press) wanting to address those issues. So, I am *not* going to be detailing any of the typographical, editorial, or lay-out issues that were screaming off of the pages in the ARC (especially since she told me that the editorial team was seriously considering implementing one major lay-out change that I'd suggested – see, that decade of running my own publishing house *is* good for something).

However, this book has been an "outlier" on a lot of levels ... when I first got it from LTER there was virtually NO trace of it online ... not only was it *not* on Amazon, it wasn't even on the *publisher's* site (the latter has at least been rectified) ... with the only thing I could dig up at the time being a Google Books entry. This blew my mind, as getting books out to the Amazon (etc.) pipeline is pretty much a "first task" these days ... and with its nominal release date being under two months away, it's *still* not out there! Amazing.

Anyway, Godless Grace: How Nonbelievers Are Making the World Safer, Richer and Kinder[2] by David Orenstein, Ph.D. & Linda Ford Blaikie, LC.S.W. is also an odd duck for the *atheist* reader ... one of my main "take aways" with this was the question "Who is this book *for*?", as it is hardly in the realm of the above name-checked authors, nor is it a particularly "evangelical" voice for the movement. Frankly, the main subjects of this book reminded me nothing so much as what Michael Ironside's character in the original "V" series (back in the mid-80s – dating myself) called Marc Singer's character – "Gooder", as in "do-gooder" – a telling jab by a black-ops specialist (whose *one* quote on the character's IMDB page is the rather awesome *"Faith is for nuns and amateurs."*!) to a TV producer of bleeding-heart features (the two of them just happening to find themselves on the same side of an alien invasion). If Dawkins, Harris, and Hitchens are Ironside's character, the people profiled here are in the model of Singer's character ... and if you find social crusaders as irritating as I do, this is going to be a bit of an aggravating read – especially as *most* of those profiled here aren't *just* activists on Atheist issues, but are also agitators for a whole melange of popular leftist causes, from LGBTQ (yeah, try *that* under Sharia Law), to vegan diets.

Unfortunately, this means that the over-all thrust of the book appears to be to show that there are as many "do-gooders" among the Atheist ranks as there are in the "imaginary friend" ranks. One can only hope that the day will come when there are more folks out there like Dale McGowan (whose <u>Parenting Beyond Belief</u>[3] I reviewed a number of years ago) representing the Atheist cause. His <u>Foundation Beyond Belief</u>[4] is exactly the sort of organization that can be held up against the faith-based institutions (albeit funded at a tiny fraction of these larger groups), and serve as a model for more rational action.

About 1/3rd of <u>Godless Grace</u>[5] consists of profiles of "activists" around the world, from deeply Moslem Bangladesh to largely secular Holland, with stops on every continent except Antarctica. Another 20% or so of the book is based on the results of a series of interviews done with "Former Clergy and Nonbelieving Student Activists", which walks though a number of topics and projects. Here again, the book has an unfortunate *enthusiasm* for ex-Clergy, as though these were particularly valuable acquisitions for the cause ... I suspect toasting the "de-frocked" smacks (for most folks) of being something off on the LaVey side of the "religious" mix – a neighborhood that most "rational humanists" would likely not want to find themselves sorted into.

There certainly is a good deal of *interesting* material here ... once one disengages from the "gooder" elements ... but it's somewhat randomly distributed, and requires a bit of cherry-picking. Lucky for you, I was sticking little bookmarks in this while going through it. Here's one thing that I found worth considering (which had a big blatant editorial "fail" smack in the middle of it, which I have corrected, although perhaps not in the form present in the eventually published version):

> *In terms of potential atheist characteristics related to personality, 2013 saw new published research by sociologist Christopher F. Silver of The University of Tennessee. His research suggests that there is a spectrum of six fundamental personality groupings of those who claim to be nonbelievers.*
>
> - *Intellectual/Agnostics – who enjoy discussing their atheism;*
> - *Activist Atheists – the category of people profiled in this book;*
> - *Seeker-Agnostics – those who do not believe and do not challenge the faithful;*
> - *Anti-Theists – do not believe and do seek out and challenge the faithful;*
> - *Non-Theists – have no belief and do not think about believers much; and*
> - *Ritual Atheists – who do not believe but still participate in religious ritual on occasion and*

may even belong to a house of worship.

Of course, to me that hardly seems like a "spectrum", or the Anti-Theists would be at the top of the list. Tellingly, there's another list in here, in a fascinating section titled "Non-God Belief in History – Some of the Major Players and Ideas", which presents what the authors consider some of the leading lights in Atheism today ... and I'm flabbergasted that they *include* Sarah Silverman, but don't have the always amazing Pat Condell[6] there. Again, the bias for "gooders" and/or mainstream leftist activism is showing itself here.

This is not to say that the book is without hard-line "Anti-Theist" verbiage altogether, it just doesn't seem to come from the actual authors. Here's a choice bit from Sociology professor Dr. Phil Zuckerman's Foreword:

> *... Religious people project onto and see in secular people what is actually occurring in themselves: a lack of moral rectitude, a dearth or moral surety, an absence of a solid moral foundation. The fact is, religious morality is an extremely shaky thing: it all boils down to nothing more than obedience to an invisible, magic deity. That's it. Whatever this invisible, magic deity says concerning right or wrong or good or bad, one obeys, or suffers the consequences.*
>
> *An extremely shaky thing, indeed. And thus, I suspect that religious people, feeling insecure about their own frail construction of morality, turn around and – in order to alleviate their own insecurity – accuse nonbelievers of having no morals or no moral foundation. ...*

Another piece I found of interest was on the other end of the book, in the Afterword by the President of American Atheists, David Silverman (which I've selectively trimmed a bit for use here):

> *Business, like politics and entertainment, is reflexive, not active. Business (unlike businesspeople) has no bigotry – it seeks money. In 1977, nobody though atheism had any money, because nobody thought atheists existed. Now, after the explosive growth of the movement ... and the incredible increase in exposure we've received over the past few years, all that has changed, and we are being recognized as the influential and sizeable movement we are. For anyone wondering about the efficacy of our movement, you need only look at the change in the number of people who solicit our {he's largely referring to conventions here} business over the past few years ...*
>
> *... Nationwide, poll after poll shows that not only is atheism rising, it is rising faster than all religions, in all 50 states. Moreover, atheism as it is correlated*

> *to youth in most polls, shows that the younger you are, the more likely it is that you're an atheist. ... And this means that the growth of atheism is being helped by both the increase of information, and time itself. ...*

Oh, and speaking of polls, there's a chapter in here on demographics, with some tables that indicate how Atheism ranks around the world ... some of this is just what you'd expect (not much of it in Pakistan, for example), but some of it does come across as counter-intuitive. Also, there's an appendix which has nine pages of tables featuring info on organizations around the world, from things as mainstream as the ACLU to obscurities like the Trinidad-Tobago Humanist Association (sure, you were just looking for their contact info).

Assuming that Godless Grace[7] is going to be getting the editorial attention it so desperately needs between now and its release date, it's not a *horrible* book ... but it's not one that, say, big fans of Dawkins & Co. will find particularly engaging. If your tastes go towards "social activism" in general, you might find the slant of the material to your liking ... if you're *not* in that camp, you will likely find this (or at least its main parts of profiles and interviews) a bit irritating.

As noted up top, this is currently ONLY available as a pre-order from the publisher ... and I'll be back in here once it gets "released into the wild" to update those links so you can pick it up on Amazon.

Notes:

http://btripp-books.livejournal.com/172436.html

http://amzn.to/1kxhin4

http://btripp-books.livejournal.com/40484.html

https://foundationbeyondbelief.org/

http://amzn.to/1kxhin4

https://www.youtube.com/user/patcondell

http://amzn.to/1kxhin4

Friday, September 4, 2015[1]

So, that's how you get to be all those things ...

I've been following Wayne Allyn Root on social media for quite a while ... I'm not sure if he was particularly on my radar prior to his run for the Libertarian Party's candidacy for President (and eventual role as the V.P. Candidate), but I've certainly been paying attention since 2008. While my main point of intersection with Mr. Root has been in the realm of Libertarian political thought, he has a bunch of "irons in" various "fires" ... much of which is extensively detailed in his new book The Power of Relentless: 7 Secrets to Achieving Mega-Success, Financial Freedom, and the Life of Your Dreams[2] (a review copy of which I got via a direct request to his publisher, the good folks at Regnery). While the thrust of the book is his "relentless" life approach, this also serves as something of an auto-biography, as he illustrates the various phases (the "7 Secrets" of the subtitle) with examples out of his life – be that surviving his school years as a scrawny kid in a bad neighborhood, or wooing his former Miss Oklahoma wife (who he claims had been a "lead singer" with Emerson, Lake & Palmer – a data point I, frankly, could find *zero* support for). Oddly, the auto-biographical material reminded me of G. Gordon Liddy's Will[3], a favorite from my youth.

I doubt that anybody has ever accused Root of being a shrinking violet or overly modest ... and some of what he claims here is easily in the "a bit hard to take" file, from claiming that *"This book completes Think and Grow Rich, The Power of Positive Thinking, and The Secret."* {!}, to his further elaboration: *"What you are about to read is like the perfect marriage of Mike Tyson, Mother Teresa and Napoleon Hill!"*. If I wasn't a long-time fan (and familiar with his rather boisterous personality), I might have not gotten past that part of the Introduction ... so be forewarned that one really needs to approach this with a supply of salt to dole out "pinch" by pinch as one works through this, as one soon comes to assume that there is a level of elaboration in most of his stories equivalent to what appears that he's added to his wife's biography!

The book is pretty much in two parts – the 7 "Principles of Relentless": Heart, Chutzpah, Ambition and Goal Setting, Preparation, Branding, Storytelling, and Aggressive Action, each getting a chapter, plus a "bonus" add-on of "Energy, Contagious Enthusiasm, and Never-Ending Optimism" – and a list of what Root calls "Positive Addictions", of which there are 12: Early Mornings, Home and Family, Mindfulness, "Prayer, Gratitude, and Forgiveness", Affirmation and Visualization, Physical Fitness, Healthy Diet, Vitamins and Nutrition, Charity, Inspiration and Empowerment, Smiling and Saying Yes, and Motion. Needless to say, you can get the general arc of the book in this, with each element being more-or-less fleshed out by biographical stories.

He starts out with "Heart", which is primarily a story about how his ailing mother, on the east coast, had slipped into an essentially brain-dead state, and the doctors were telling him not to bother flying out, but his sister told him to come immediately ... his mom maintained a heart beat long enough for Wayne to get there from the west coast and say his goodbyes, as which point she flatlined. He has a rather worthwhile paragraph about "heart" here, but it's long and I'll leave it for you to check out.

The second "Principle" is the Yiddish term Chutzpah, which Root translates as "audacity" (I believe there is a subtle jab at one of his fellow Columbia poli-sci classmates in that word choice). He says that he's "a blue collar son of a butcher from a dead end street on the Bronx borderline" with no special talents, but with "relentless chutzpah", which he claims to come by naturally. He raises an interesting point, that I'd not been aware of regarding the Chinese ...

> *I am very proud of my Jewish heritage. I am also bursting with pride for the people of Israel. But the question for you is: Can <u>anyone</u> learn RELENTLESS CHUTZPAH?*
>
> *The answer is a resounding YES. The Chinese are obsessed with learning how to succeed and obtain wealth. Over one third of the books sold in China are about financial success. And a large portion of those books are about <u>Jewish success</u>.*

He then list several bestsellers in China that deal with *"the traits that have made the Jews so remarkably successful"*. I find it ironic that Root is "proud" about his Jewish heritage (and spends a couple of pages highlighting "remarkable facts" about Israel), but evidently converted to being a born-again Christian (no doubt for his wife's benefit, as he mentions that about her when describing their first encounter), although to his credit, he's not "preachy" about *that* stuff here. He goes on to present "The Nine Rules of Relentless Chutzpah", unfortunately, these are more discursive than bullet-points, so I'll just note that they range from "stop complaining" to "be fearless" and "take risks". Root holds that getting told "NO" is *"merely the start of a negotiation"*!

The third principle is "Ambition", and he's certainly a font of that. Early on in his career he wanted to be the next "Jimmy the Greek", and held onto that for a couple of decades, until there he was, co-hosting a show with his idol. However, the main illustrative story here is about his daughter Dakota, who was home-schooled but made it into Harvard (after turning down an early-admission offer from Yale) and Oxford. He introduces a 12-step process for goal setting, here, which has a lot of "standard" stuff on it (a "vision board", "write your own obituary", etc.), but has some rather unique elements as well, such as #6 – Keep a "Black Box" ... this is basically a journal that he puts in his *"mistakes, frustrations, rejections, failures, defeats"* on a weekly basis ... allowing him to review what *didn't* work and learn from it. Another good one is something of an extended "to-do" list, #7 – Make a Daily "Hit List" ... a charting of specific actions that you need to take, crossing off the ones you complete, rolling into the next day (ala the line from a recent movie: *"I always close my contracts!"*) the ones you don't.

In the fourth principle, "Preparation", Root details what he calls "The Relentless Triad", which is a scheduling regimen that he uses to start his day. This involves getting up early, and devoting a half-hour each to mental, physical, and financial tasks ... a half hour of reading, a half hour of exercise, and a half hour of career-centric activity (such as adding names to contact to the aforementioned "hit list") - but he only uses that time *"for creating new ideas, opportunities, clients or careers"*, rather than dealing with any current work. He notes that if you are able to average 4 *new* actions/contacts per day (six days a week), that's 24 per week, 96 per month, 1,152 per year ... and probably represents activities that are *not* being done by your competition. Root says that working from home allows him to devote an *hour* to each of those functions (from 6:00am to 9:00am) ... plus he recommends to schedule a 15-minute time for review of the day every evening. Yes, it sounds awfully driven, but that's where the "Relentless" thing comes in.

The fifth principle is "Branding", and the main story he goes into here was taking his wife's 92 year-old grandfather up on a request – he wanted Wayne to "make him famous" before he died. Root pulled out all his media savvy and "branded" a sky-diving adventure he was taking "Grandpa Norm" on as *Throw Grandpa from the Plane* ... the press ate it up, they got on a bunch of shows, and Norm got to meet a number of his favorite actresses in a whirlwind media junket. This chapter also talks about sports stars such as Floyd Mayweather, Joe Namath, and others examples such as Ralph Lifshitz (better known as Ralph Lauren), Matt Drudge (who runs his billion-dollar web site with just two employees), and even counter-examples such as the guy who was later lionized as "the father of legalized casino gambling" in Las Vegas, who shunned the limelight, and ended up dying penniless as a simple ranch hand. Root frames branding this way: *""Hooks" are how you stand out in a crowded field. The reality is that you are either a "talented hooker" or you're just screwing yourself! ... Your name, "hook", or brand is what people remember and pay for."*

"Storytelling" is Root's sixth principle, and by storytelling, he means "video". Personally, I *hate* that message, because I can "get the sense of" an on-line *text* article in 5-10 seconds of scanning, but when you hit a video (or audio, for that matter) posting, you're stuck with it until it either gets to the point or wastes a chunk of your day/life. However, I'm reminded of the famed Hunter S. Thompson quote: *"I hate to advocate drugs, alcohol, violence, or insanity to anyone, but they've always worked for me."* because, as much a I can't stand video, Root makes a pretty good case for using it in an extensive bit on "Ten Miracles Brought to You by Relentless Video", where he shows how he used video at various points in his life, from getting into Columbia, to getting his grandfather on national TV shows. He also swings into the political realm for a few pages, discussing how the current POTUS has used video to push his disastrous agenda on the country.

The final, numbered, Principle here is "Aggressive Action", which starts off with a rather choice bit:

> The greatest lie ever told is "Opportunity only knocks once." The truth is, opportunity doesn't knock at all. You have to search for it like a heat-seeking missile, attack it, knock it over the head

> with a club, seize it, and drag it home like a caveman!
>
> The real world is brutal. Opportunity is not sitting around waiting for you. It's not knocking. You have to create and seize opportunity by taking aggressive action. Nothing good comes from sitting still, waiting, or procrastinating. Good things only come from action and motivation.

Here Root discusses several individuals who took relentless action – from a family friend who was looking for a husband, to a New York realtor who was able to not only maintain her business, but *build* it, when *deployed in Kandahar, Afghanistan* as a Navy specialist. His "personal story" here is how he met his wife at a Grammy party at a nightclub in L.A. - she had a hard-and-fast rule to not date anybody she met in a nightclub, but Root was "relentless", and kept pushing, eventually the gal called up her best friend in New York, asking if she should break this rule … her friend asked the name, and *miraculously* it turns out that she was Wayne's *cousin* (making him "like family") … but his now-wife would never have made that phone call if he'd not been in "aggressive action" (which he notes is like advertisers having to consistently make impressions to keep their products in people's awareness) mode.

In the "bonus principle" chapter, the most notable thing is the "Always Say "Yes"" section:

> … I try to say "YES" to everyone, not just the media. If you say "NO", nothing good can happen. Good comes from the word "YES." Opportunity, wealth, or fame can never come from a deal you didn't do. "YES" doesn't guarantee success, but it does make it possible that magic can happen. There is always hope this time will be the home run. With "YES" there is possibility. With "NO" there is zero possibility.
>
> You just never know which deal you turn down was fated to be "the one" that would have changed your life, that would have made your dreams come true. So, I try to say "YES" to everyone.

Obviously, this goes against a recent trend (especially of those of us who spend most of our lives on the web) of trying to say "no" more … because it's impossible to sit through every webinar, read every blog, check out every video … but it's part of Root's philosophy. How *accurate* a part, I have some personal questions about … having tried to get answers from him on a couple of questions I had about an early part of the book, which not only went *unanswered*, but totally *unacknowledged* … hardly a "YES" move there.

Anyway, The Power of Relentless[4] was just released a couple of weeks back, so it should be out prominently in the bigger brick-and-mortar book vendors in your area. However, at the moment, the on-line big boys have the hardcover at a whopping 45% off of cover price, which is quite a deal.

While I had "issues" with parts of this, I really enjoyed reading it, and while I am (just being who I am) highly unlikely to implement the whole program Root presents, there are certainly bits and pieces that I'm going to be grabbing for my own purposes. While this is very much Wayne "tooting his own horn", with some parts of it being "bigger than real", it's a fascinating look at how a wildly successful guy sees as the path involved to getting him to that level of achievement – which he's set out in a system that you might very well be able to follow.

Notes:

http://btripp-books.livejournal.com/172545.html

http://amzn.to/1h5W0v6

http://amzn.to/1NSy1wC

http://amzn.to/1h5W0v6

Saturday, September 5, 2015[1]

"Change" as an euphemism ...

As a long-time Chicago resident, not much in this book *surprises* me ... I can well remember when groups like ACORN (for which the current POTUS was an "attack lawyer") were threatening area banks with bringing "redlining" (Community Reinvestment Act) suits against them (which would have frozen their ability to do basic business functions like opening new branches, etc.) unless they agreed to meet quotas of what were, to any *sane* observer, "suicidal" loans – providing money to borrowers who, by any but the most delusional gauges, were simply NOT going to be paying them back. People (and certainly the Leftist MSM) are all too happy to put the blame of the financial collapse of '07-'09 on the banks, but it was blatantly socialist/communist organizations that forced the "poison" into the system. This book is largely about how *similar* plans have been enacted by the current POTUS and his allies.

As those of you who have been reading my reviews over the years will no doubt have noticed that I have been reading/reviewing a *lot* fewer political books than I used to. This is two-fold, on one hand, psychologically, I have been trying to not be the screaming rage beast (a few gamma rays short of the Hulk) that contemplating what has been happening to America leads me to, and, secondly, trying very hard to pretend that if I don't accept that the current disastrous administration *exists* it will go away and I will awake to a Goldwater-esque happy land. To this later point, unless absolutely necessary (as in typing out this book's subtitle), I refuse to utter or write the name of the current POTUS ... even contemplating it makes me want to launch into a major rant!

Anyway, this is yet another of those dollar store finds ... albeit one that was hard to pick up (having a picture of That Person on its cover). This is by Stanley Kurtz (who had published a previous book on the current POTUS called Radical-In-Chief[2], and was one of many voices warning America about re-electing That Person, this time specifically looking at a bunch of organizations and strategies in play in the current administration ... Spreading the Wealth: How Obama is Robbing the Suburbs to Pay for the Cities[3]. Now, I am a life-long "city boy" and have nothing nice to say about suburbia, so one might think that "robbing the suburbs to pay for the cities" might be something that I'd gladly endorse ... but the picture that Kurtz paints here is of a form of Leftism that I'd not heard of previously ... that of "regionalism", which goes back to the current POTUS's political roots. It is *amazing* just how radical many of the top-level appointments in this administration are ... on a par (on the other side) of making somebody like a (KKK icon) David Duke the top figure on a cabinet-level post! Seriously, if this was a "mirror image" administration on the far-right, you'd be hard put to even find *names* of figures who were as radically right-wing as the circle of hard-Left ideologues around the current POTUS. How could this happen? Well, the movements leading up to this have been studiously working under the radar for *generations*, and the existing MSM wouldn't say "boo" about a

Leftist plot until they themselves were being sent to the wall (and, hell, *some* of them would no doubt still be making up excuses for the regime as the blindfolds were being tied on). While the book itself is focused on a handful of radical scams that the administration and its allies have been running, the most interesting parts are on how this band of anti-American monsters got into a position where they could enact their far-left schemes.

> The problem with this conservative debate over the political significance of Obama's radical Alinskyite past is that it completely ignores his radical Alinskyite <u>present</u>. The truly important political critique of President Obama is that right now, this very day, he is using his long-standing Alinskyite alliances and convictions to guide administration policy while keeping his radical goals from the public. The president's political history is an invaluable resource for making sense of these poorly known policies and future plans, of course, but the real problem exists today and tomorrow, not in the past.
>
> ...
>
> Yet it's just here that the radicalism of Obama's hidden regionalist agenda proves itself. It isn't just that Obama keeps his anti-suburban plans below the public radar because they confirm virtually everything his conservative critics have ever claimed about him. The deeper problem is that were the full truth about Obama's regionalist agenda to come out, it would split his electoral coalition. Obama's regionalist plans are nothing less than a direct attack on large sections of his own middle-class supporters. It's true that over the very long term Obama and his Alinskyite allies in Building One America[4] hope to reshape American attitudes, thereby creating a new and dominant redistributionist coalition of the left. In the short term, however, were Obama's plans to be revealed, they would show him to be substantially to the left of even his own party's center of gravity.
>
> The history of Kruglik's {Building One America's Executive Director Michael Kruglik[5]} long campaign for regionalism, extending back to his years with the Gamaliel Foundation[6], confirms this. Time after time, even after showing an initial receptiveness to his plans, Kruglik's mainstream liberal allies learned what Gamaliel's real agenda was, then ran screaming the other way. The same would happen to Obama were the full truth about his own radical regionalist goals to emerge too soon.

This book is a gem for how it traces back the influences to their roots. Over the years that the current POTUS has been "in the news", the name Saul Alinsky has come up frequently, but rarely with much detail ... here he and his groups and sub-groups are detailed. It was a shock to read:

> *Alinsky once bragged that the Communist Party saw his first community organization, the Back of the Yards Neighborhood Council, as the ideal united front. By "united front" or "popular front", the Communists meant groups that they quietly controlled, even if the membership included many non-Communists.*

... as I had worked with the now-called Back of the Yards Community Council in recent years on a project that I was a consultant on! On their web page they do mention Alinksy, but only as *"a colorful, professional organizer"*.

In a section titled "Without Consent of the Governed", the book looks at another current figure, David Rusk, whose writings have been the inspiration (or map) for the current administration's HUD "Affirmatively Furthering Fair Housing"[7] program.

> *In 2003, a decade after publishing his bold case for doing away with suburbs, Rusk offered a thought about regionalist political strategy: "The policy debate must be framed not as a choice between conservative and liberal philosophies, but as a choice between policies that work and policies that do not work.*
>
> *The swallowing up of suburbs by cities or by newly established regional governments (which amounts to the same thing) would signal a profound rejection of America's most cherished traditions of self-government. If there was ever a stark choice between liberal and conservative philosophies – American and European approaches – this is it. Yet adopting the rhetorical strategy favored by Obama himself, Rusk would portray this revolutionary shift of ideals as a merely pragmatic decision. Rusk's claims about what works and what doesn't when it comes to urban policy are questionable, to say the least. His policy answers stem not from pragmatic calculations but from his own redistributionist values.*
>
> *...*
>
> *Rusk certainly doesn't come off as a fan of freedom and democracy. He thirsts for redistribution by fiat: "Poorer communities have no way of tapping the wealth or richer communities without the intervention of a higher level of government." Rusk is out to annex your suburb and pick your pocket. If annoying principles like individual liberty, voluntary association, and self-government stand in the way,*

> *that's just too bad. The contradiction between hard-left redistributionism and traditional American freedoms could hardly be drawn more sharply.*

What is possibly the *most* shocking about the present administration's plans are that they involve government *control* over who can move where ... with quotas for race and income dictating whether you could buy (or even rent) that dream house across town, across the state, or even across the country ... if you did not meet the HUD guidelines, you'd be out of luck. Welcome to Soviet-style government (and better keep that picture of the Glorious Leader clean and prominently displayed).

Again, this book is a gold mine of information on the organizations and individuals in the inner circle of the current POTUS (he studied with many of these vermin, and "apprenticed" as a community organizer with others) ... here's a bit that names some more names:

> *Of course you don't have to be a socialist to favor the regionalist agenda. On the other hand, it helps. From Dreier's[8] {top ACORN supporter Peter Dreier} perspective, regionalist redistribution would appear to be a pragmatic way to advance socialism in the here and now. Dreier of course is an enthusiastic advocate of Myron Orfield's[9] redistributive regional tax base sharing scheme, which the Obama administration's alliance with Building One America is designed to promote.*
>
> *Dreier sees stealth as fundamental to enacting the regionalist agenda, chiefly because our majority-suburban country would reject a city-centric redistributionist agenda were it presented openly. Dreier praises regionalist programs that proceed "below the political radar screen." He also favors deploying regionalist arguments focused not only on "equity" but on "efficiency and the environment" although redistribution would appear to be his overwhelming concern. ... Dreier suggests that redistributionist measures ought to be "unobtrusive, and just one part of a larger package".*

Speaking of "larger packages" ... the book also takes a deep look into the "Stimulus", the "Affordable Care Act", and "Common Core" ... each of which is *packed* with ultra-left initiatives that would never survive being subjected to public scrutiny. Like the ACA (which the execrable Nancy Pelosi famously said *"we have to pass the bill so that you can find out what is in it, away from the fog of the controversy "*) these are deliberately *huge* programs, which make it easy for the Alinskyites to hide the reality of what they're looking to inflict on the country – without the light of debate (or consent of the governed).

Also covered in a good bit of detail is the personal history of the current POTUS, with his various stops around the globe in the hands of assorted socialists, communists, and black-power advocates. Special attention is given to his years of being radicalized at the feet of Frank Marshall Davis[10], who primed him for immersion in Alinsky's home turf of Chicago. The extent that the current POTUS is intimately linked with the most anti-American ultra-left radicals is shocking … and it's a *crime* that people don't know about this (the MSM, having long ago turned into a cheering section for all things Lefty, won't say a single "discouraging word" about That Person).

Like *many* of the books that throw a harsh light on the machinations of the Left, I really, *really* wish that all-and-sundry would read Spreading the Wealth[11] … it names the names, and connects the dots into a *damning* condemnation of the scam that's been perpetrated on our country. The biggest caveat I can present is that *nobody* will read this with their blood pressure in control. If you're a fan of freedom and traditional American values, this is like reading a police report about your sister being raped … if you're hoping for a "progressive" over-throw of everything that has defined the USA, you'll be mad that your Glorious Leader is being manhandled with the truth … in either case it's going to upset you. Parts of this *are* a bit dated, as the initial publication was up front of the last election, and there's a lot of framing the material here as "a warning" about what was to come were the current administration to get a second term – but that's easy enough to overlook (especially as blatant as the POTUS and his cabal have been in ignoring the Constitution and the rule of law since they got another four years in power). As I noted, I got a hardcover copy of this at the dollar store, and there may be more out there … but it's filtered down to the new/used channels for as little as 1¢ (plus $3.99 shipping) for a "very good" copy (it only seems to be "in print" at this point as a Kindle/Nook edition). Get a copy … the more people know about the machinations of the current POTUS the better prepared the country will be to fight back.

Notes:

1. http://btripp-books.livejournal.com/172860.html
2. http://amzn.to/1g2c9jD
3. http://amzn.to/1MrT7Bb
4. http://goo.gl/js36Pr
5. http://goo.gl/c8NfSu
6. http://goo.gl/RBBnnx
7. http://goo.gl/0GoFvD
8. http://goo.gl/NJbHP0
9. http://goo.gl/sZRtyh
10. http://goo.gl/xAdQWF
11. http://amzn.to/1MrT7Bb

Sunday, September 6, 2015[1]

"How soft your fields so green can whisper tales of gore ..."

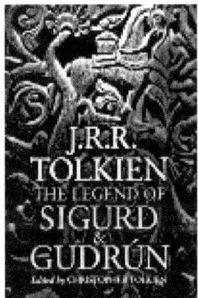

I, frankly, don't recall how J.R.R. Tolkien's The Legend of Sigurd and Gudrún[2] got into my to-be-read piles, as it has been floating around there for a *very* long time. I suspect that this was a dollar store find (although it's missing the marker swipe that most of those feature to signify a cut-out, as well as the register receipt that I'd typically stick in the back pages), but I can't imagine that I *ordered* it on-line (it's a bit obscure in relation to most of my reading), unless it was in one of those infrequent binges I have with a B&N clearance (which do tend to spark some "oh, heck, that looks interesting" pig-in-a-poke acquisitions). Anyway, this has been trying to insert itself into my reading stream for at least a couple of years, and managed to find both a slot where I was in a Monty Python-esque *"and now for something Completely Different ..."* mood, and looking for a "quick read" (which this promised to be with over half of it just being short lines of verse).

This is, of course, hardly the first Tolkien in my collection ... being of the age where everybody I knew read *The Hobbit* and *Lord of the Rings* in grade school. I wasn't, however, notably aware that the author's "day job" was as a philologist[3], who had a long career as a professor (in Anglo-Saxon and English Literature) at Oxford University.

I felt, in reading this, that the book should have been co-credited to his son, Christopher Tolkien (who has been executor of his father's literary estate), as an *author* rather than as simply being tagged as having edited the book, as there is probably a higher word-count of his *explanatory* copy than the actual translation/retelling of the texts by his father. He gives an on-going commentary both on his father's interaction with the material, and how it was pretty much rescued from obscurity to create the present book. This is a key part of that:

> My father's erudition was by no means confined to "Anglo-Saxon", but extended to an expert knowledge of the poems of the Elder Edda and the Old Norse language (a term that in general use is largely equivalent to Old Icelandic, since by far the greater part of Norse literature that survives is written in Icelandic). In fact, for many years after he became the professor of Anglo-Saxon at Oxford in 1925 he was professor of Old Norse, though no such title existed; he gave lectures and classes on Norse language and literature in every year from 1926 until at least 1939. But despite his accomplishment in this field, which was recognized in Iceland, he never wrote anything specifically on a Norse subject for publication – except perhaps the

> "New Lays", and for this, so far as I know, there is no evidence one way or the other, unless the existence of an amanuensis typescript, of unknown date and without other interest, suggests it. But there survive many pages of notes and draftings for his lectures, although these were for the most part written very rapidly and often on the brink of illegibility or beyond.

The specific material in the book are poems *"treating of the Völsung and Niflung (or Nibelung) legend, using modern English fitted to the Old Norse meter"*, which, until this (2009) publication, had never been released or quoted previously. The titles are *Völsungakvida en nyja* – "The New Lay of the Völsungs, and *Gudrunarkvida en nyja* – "The New Lay of Gudrun" (these are approximate here, my lacking an appropriate font for several Icelandic characters). The general theme of the story is vaguely familiar, being closely related to the narrative that runs across the four long operas of Wagner's "Ring Cycle", although the younger Tolkien notes that the German composer had taken substantial liberties in crafting his stories, and was working from Germanic versions of the source material, which appears to have varied a good deal from the Norse. The editor further notes:

> *To a large extent the spirit of these poems which has been regarded as (a branch of) the common "Germanic spirit" – in which there is some truth: Brythwold at Maldon would do well enough in Edda or Saga – is really the spirit of a special time. It might be called <u>Godlessness</u> – reliance upon self and upon indomitable will. Not without significance is the epithet applied to actual characters living at this moment in history – the epithet <u>godlauss</u>, with the explanation that their creed was <u>at trua a matt sin ok megin</u> ["to trust in one's own might and main"].*

The younger Tolkien also gets into some discussions of how the various language groups, Old Norse, Old Germanic, Old English, and assorted related forms, had noted similarities, which could be traced especially through cases where essentially the same stories (or elements of common stories) were preserved in varied linguistic contexts. In the case of the Norse materials, preservation is a major issue ... as Christian influence was spreading and, by about 1,000 CE, the presence of either writers/orators or hearers with enough knowledge of the myths and the language was nearly at zero, although:

> *... poetry became a profitable export industry of Iceland for a while; and in Iceland alone was anything ever collected or written down. But the old knowledge swiftly decayed. The fragments, much disjointed, were again collected – but in an antiquarian and philological revival of the twelfth and thirteenth centuries. Perhaps it would be more true to say, not antiquarian revival, but kindly burial.*

Not only did the Norse material suffer from cultural shifts, two substantial fires, one in 1728 in Copenhagen, and another in London in 1731, ended up destroying much of what had been collected, and leaving gaps in what survived. The poems that Tolkien is working from here were a later "compilation" of surviving materials, in a form that it suffers from … the editor again comments:

> *This author was faced with wholly divergent traditions (seen in the preserved Eddaic lays) concerning Sigurdand Brynhild: stories that cannot be combined, for they are essentially contradictory. Yet he combined them; and in doing so produced a narrative that is certainly mysterious, but (in its central point) unsatisfying: as it were a puzzle that is presented as completed but in which the looked for design is incomprehensible and at odds with itself.*

This point is largely why I've gotten over 1,000 words into this review without getting to any "content" per se. There were elements that I found fascinating … such as the character of *Atli*, or Attila ("the Hun"), and the Niflungs/Nibelung (somehow the same as "Burgundian" in modern English), in conflict with him, plus the Goths (in the pre-*Bella Lugosi's Dead* sense of the term) in the mix as well – all this happening somewhere around 436 C.E. (although one must wonder how *historical* the theft of the dragon's fortune – at the core of the story – is). Another very interesting thread here is how hard it is to be a favorite of Odin … Odin's favorites are the baddest-assed of all the bad-assed Norse warriors … and if he *likes* you, he's going to conspire to make sure you're going to *die* so you can be collected by the Valkyries to come be one of his warriors at Valhalla … needless to say, being "favored" this way is less than popular among most of the mortal warriors involved.

Anyway, I tagged a few bits in the poem to give a sense of how Tolkien's retelling (in modern English, but following the Old Norse poetic format) reads. This first one is from "The Lay of Gudrun":

> 100
> At the dark doorways
> they dinned and hammered;
> there was a clang of swords
> and crash of axes.
> The smiths of battle
> smote the anvils;
> sparked and splintered
> spears and helmets.
>
> 101
> In they hacked them,
> out they hurled them,
> bears assailing,
> boars defending.
> Stones and stairways
> streamed and darkened;

day came dimly –
the doors were held.

102
Five days they fought
few and dauntless;
the doors were riven,
dashed asunder.
They barred them with bodies,
bulwarks piling
of Huns and Niflungs
hewn and cloven.

One of the things that made reading this somewhat challenging was that the poetic parts were commented on *after* the end of the whole poem … and without markings in the poem itself to indicate where there were notes … so one had to be "reading in parallel" the notes (which referred back to specific stanzas, or groups of stanzas) and the poem to see what was being given clarification. This set of stanzas is part of a section that is noted to be *"totally independent of the Norse sources"*, and appears to be related to Old English poetic fragments The Fight at Finnsburg and Finn and Hengst, which goes to illustrate how fragmented the materials had become and how randomly re-assembled those bits and pieces survived.

This next bit is from "The Lay of the Völsungs – part V – Regin", which gets into the familiar Nibelung tale of the killing of the dragon Fáfnir (here referred to as "Hreidmar's son") … the notes for this section (which are found nearly 100 pages further on in the book!) indicate that the source material from these verses was also "patched in", derived "from a prose passage in *Fáfnismál*, closely similar to that in the Saga".

45
Round turned Sigurd,
and Regin saw he
in the hearth crawling
with hate gleaming.
Black spilled the blood
as blade clove him
the head hewing
of Hreidmar's son.

46
Dark red the drink
and dire the meat
whereon Sigurd feasted
seeking wisdom.
Dark hung the doors
and dread the timbers
in the earth under
of iron builded.

47

> *Gold piled on gold*
> *there glittering paley:*
> *that gold was glamoured*
> *with grim curses.*
> *The Helm of Horror*
> *on his head laid he:*
> *swart fell the shadow*
> *round Sigurd standing.*
>
> *48*
> *Great and grievous*
> *was Grani's burden,*
> *yet lightly leaped he*
> *down the long mountain.*
> *Ride now! ride now*
> *road and woodland,*
> *horse and hero,*
> *hope of Ódin!*

While the story is disjointed and somewhat hard to follow, and some of the issues in the commentary are obscure elements of history and linguistics, the over-all sense of reading The Legend of Sigurd and Gudrún[4] is of being treated to a culturally significant document which has been (to various degrees of success), wrested from the grip of oblivion. Not only (as touched on above – and more extensively in the book) did the ancient sources nearly disappear, the material by the elder Tolkien seems to have never been organized for publication by him, but was "rescued" by his son from lecture notes, letters to colleagues, and annotations of related survivals. While not being a "pristine" fifth-century literary document, this at least lets us hear the echoes (albeit in modernly readable English) of a long disappeared world.

This is still in print six years on (I'm guessing it might be in use as a text book, although its cover price is not in those inflated zones), so you might be able to find/order a copy through your local brick-and-mortar book vendor. The on-line big boys have it presently at a 37% discount, but there are "new" copies in the new/used sellers' offers that would bring the total (although there are no super-cheap listings – making me again assume it's in the textbook channel) to less than half of that figure, even with the shipping.

Obviously, this is not a "for everybody" book, as it does require a certain level of focus to get the sense of it. However, if you were an English major, or are a fan of Norse/Germanic mythology, you might find this of interest.

Notes:

1. http://btripp-books.livejournal.com/173245.html
2. http://amzn.to/1MT5XYb
3. https://en.wikipedia.org/wiki/Philology
4. http://amzn.to/1MT5XYb

Monday, September 7, 2015[1]

Woke up in a Soho doorway, a policeman knew my name ...

Well, that was enjoyable ... this is yet another great read showing up in my hands via the LibraryThing.com "Early Reviewers" program – not something that's "a given" in LTER, as there have been a *lot* of clunkers over the years – but this one was both informative and entertaining, and engaging throughout. The only "whuh?" element here was that it's not "new", really ... but the paperback version (officially coming out next week). I'm guessing that the hardcover of this was offered via LTER last year, as there are a whole bunch of reviews up for it already. This is Dataclysm: Love, Sex, Race, and Identity – What Our Online Lives Tell Us about Our Offline Selves[2] by Christian Rudder, the co-founder and in-house data wonk for the OkCupid dating site. I'm assuming that this (coming out only a year later) is substantially the same as the hardcover, but this is coming out with a new subtitle [previously: "Who We Are (When We Think No One's Looking)"], which always makes me wonder if there's been an update between the versions.

On one level, this is a bit of a "morality tale", sort of in the mode of Ryan Holliday's Trust Me, I'm Lying[3] (although in a *much* less sleazy milieu), where a master of a "dark art" comes clean about it, and tries to make amends. Unlike Holiday's "gaming" dang near the entire information infrastructure, here Rudder is talking about data ... and how it can look into our lives ... and eventually he ends up wringing his hands a bit (and noting that he does very little "social media", won't post pictures of his family, etc., in an effort to minimize how transparent his life is to the algorithms churning through that data) at how even with the slightest digital "trail of breadcrumbs", the number crunchers can find out remarkably accurate and personal information – typified by the story of how Target, by analyzing the shopping patterns of a teen girl, knew she was pregnant (and started sending out pregnancy-related fliers) before *her family* did ... or, more unsettling, the patent that Amazon has taken out for an "anticipatory shipping" system that will send out products that its analysis of the data indicates that you need/want, *before you even order them*. However, that's sort of jumping to the end of the story here ... the book is NOT a doom-and-gloom "the computers are going to rule us" dystopian tale, but a look *from the inside* of how all that stuff works ... although the cautionary element is certainly hovering over the book in its name – a portmanteau mashing up "data" with "cataclysm" – which echoes one mind-blowing factoid he has in here: as long ago as 2012, Facebook was collecting 500 *terabytes* of information *every day*!

Dataclysm[4] is set up in three parts, "What Brings Us Together", "What Pulls Us Apart", and "What Makes Us Who We Are", each with 4-5 chapters looking at specific elements thereof. It starts with the basics, gathering the data. Early on he puts up a caveat, true for most data sets involved (in academic studies), which have a tendency to be based on white American college kids ... he adds:

> *I understand how it happens: in person, getting a real representative data set is often more difficult than the actual experiment you'd like to perform. You're a professor or postdoc who wants to push forward, so you take what's called a "convenience sample" – and that means the students at your university. But it's a big problem, especially when you're researching belief and behavior. It even has a name. It's called WEIRD research: white, educated, industrialized, rich, and democratic. And most published social research papers are WEIRD.*

He adds in a footnote, from an article in *Slate*, that this profile only represents about 12% of the world's population, and differs from the others in *"moral decision making, reasoning style, fairness, even things like visual perception"*. While it's not exactly a case of GIGO[5], it certainly warns that when trying to extrapolate WEIRD data to a global model, you're probably going to be off from the start.

There is a *lot* of humor in this book ... an entertaining review could be whipped up by just repeating the jokes ... while this is *tempting*, I'll try to limit myself to a few choice ones. One that stood out sufficiently that it got its own little bookmark when I was going through this, was an odd footnote which reads: *"* Definition of true ignorance: getting your "what the kids are into" intel from the Securities and Exchange Commission"* ... OK, so standing on its own isn't quite the self-depreciating gut-buster it ought to be, so I'll have to "explain the joke" (trust me, I have a lot of experience in having to do this). This is at the very start of the "Writing on the Wall" chapter, which starts out talking about home-sickness among troops a century or more ago ... noting that *"in the American Civil War nostalgia was such a problem it put some 5,000 troops out of action, and 74 men died of it"*, and then suggesting that the best scientists of 1863, on "either side of the Potomac", were furiously working *"to develop the ultimate war-ending superweapon: high school yearbooks"* (assuming that this "cures" nostalgia). He asks if they still *have* high school yearbooks, what with Facebook around ... but then points out that in a recent FB quarterly report (hence the SEC angle) they noted a drop in use among the under-18 crowd, possibly requiring the printed book again. Yeah, it's funnier when you're reading through it.

This, however, sets up the issue of *writing* ... in less than a generation, *kids* are writing vastly more than any of their predecessor demographics ever imagined. Rudder cuts to the chase in terms of internet writing, and focuses on Twitter ... writing 140 characters at a time. Many commentators have bewailed how the web was going to destroy the language, and that we'd lose the use of longer, more sophisticated words. Here the author compares Twitter's list of most commonly used words with that of the Oxford English Corpus (all 2.5 billion words) ... in each case, the top 100 words are considered, which makes up half the writing. Counter-intuitively, the Twitter list has an average word length significantly longer than the OEC's ... 4.3 characters vs 3.4 (yes, there are a whole bunch of 2-3 letter words on those lists) ... and what's even *more* remarkable is that the average word length of something like Shakespeare's *Hamlet*, clocks in at a shorter word length than a similar word-count sample from Twitter (3.99 vs 4.80 – and that's with the @'s and #'s stripped out of the Twitter numbers). Another amazing source of data is Google Books, which has so far digitized over 30 million books, going back as far as 1800. Using that data all sorts of interesting things can be tracked, for instance, there's a fascinating graph in here which looks at mentions of food items ... things like "steak" or "sausage" go back to 1800, but the "winner" (currently peaking at over 8 mentions per million words) is "pizza", despite not noticeably appearing in the data until the 1940s.

Rudder similarly goes into the OkCupid data to see how message length relates to getting responses (which, after all, is the point on a dating site), and then flips into looking at "social graphs" (he uses examples of his own, plus his with his wife's data combined). To get an idea of how these look, check out a post[6] I did when LinkedIn was discontinuing its cool (but no doubt resource draining) "inMaps", where I included a copy of my (final) LinkedIn map. These can be very predictive, working in part off of Milgram's famous "six degrees" experiments. The author cites studies which show how couples' relationship longevity can be quite accurately predicted by how these combined maps develop.

Obviously, one of the biggest "big dogs" on the data end of the Internet is Google:

> Google has become a repository for humanity's collective id. It hears our confessions, our concerns, our secrets. It's doctor, priest, psychiatrist, confidante, and above all, Google doesn't have to ask us a thing, because the question is always implied in the blank space of the interface. ... What a person searches for often gives you the person himself.

An amazing example of how this "works" is that researchers using the Google Trends tool have been able to *"track epidemics of flu and dengue fever in real time"*, which has developed into "Google Flu", which follows searches for symptoms and remedies, and reports the trends to the CDC.

Going back to the OkCupid data, Rudder describes doing analysis on profile text ... and brings up a remarkable mathematical entity called Zipf's Law:

> {The} counterintuitive relationship between the popularity of a word (it's rank in a given vocabulary) and the number of times it appears is described by something called Zipf's law, an observed statistical property of language that, like so much of the best math, lies somewhere between miracle and coincidence. It states that in any large body of text, a word's popularity (its place in the lexicon, with 1 being the highest ranking) multiplied by the number of times it shows up, is the same for every word in the text. Or, very elegantly: rank x number = con-

> stant ... This law holds for the Bible, the collected lyrics of '60s pop songs, and the canonical corpus of English literature ... and it certainly holds for profile text.

He then presents a table with words ranked from 10 in various steps down to 29,055 out of James Joyce's *Ulysses* (to pick an example of "highly idiosyncratic" language) ... the "constant" here does vary somewhat, but are pretty close to a common number. One of the things he is able to do with this is to make comparative charts of how frequently words appear in different groups' profiles. The example he starts with is comparing the word rankings of "white men" with "everybody else", with the first few words being "the", "pizza", and (the band) "Phish". There's a diagonal which is the "common" line, and, not surprisingly, "the" and "pizza" are both on that line, and way up in the top/top corner. However, "Phish" is about 80% up on the "white men" side, and only about 30% over towards the "everybody else" side. He then adds another dozen or so words, with things like "orange" and "rollercoaster" showing up on the diagonal, and "snowmobiling" at about 0% for "everybody else" and around 60% for white men (on the other hand "Kpop" - Korean Pop, ends up at about 0% for white guys). He then starts breaking these down into various racial groups, with both men and women, and finds rather surprising stuff ... *"{These lists} are our shibboleths. As such they are something no one could generate a priori, by typing things into Google Trends or by searching millions of hashtags. Sometimes, it takes a blind algorithm to really see the data."*

One final amazing thing he holds for last here ... it's called "Parsons code" and it's the engine that enables the Shazam app to recognize music from very small samples ... *"... almost any piece of music can be identified by the up/down pattern in the melody – you can ignore everything else: key, rhythm, lyrics, arrangement ... To know the song, you just need a map of the notes' rise and fall. This melodic contour is called the song's Parsons code, named for the musicologist who developed it in the 1970s."* this is a string of letters, U for melody up, D for melody down, and R for repeated note ... he charts out "Happy Birthday" and "Yesterday" for examples. His closing paragraph is:

> Like an app straining for a song, data science is about finding patterns. Time after time I – and many other people doing work like me – have had to devise methods, structures, even shortcuts to find the signal amidst the noise. We're all looking for our own Parsons code. Something so simple and yet so powerful is a once-in-a-lifetime discovery, but luckily there are a lot of lifetimes out there.

Again, Dataclysm[7] was a delight, full of *"I did not know that!"* moments, entertaining stories, and some sobering realities. The paperback is just coming out in a few days, and right now the big boys have it for pre-order at a 45% discount (and this is evidently popular enough that used copies of the hardcover edition are still more expensive than the discounted rate on the new paperback). If you're a "web denizen" like me, or a math geek, or somebody interested in digging behind the surface of social realities, you will really enjoy this book. Highly recommended!

Notes:
1. http://btripp-books.livejournal.com/173339.html
2. http://amzn.to/1KOjprX
3. http://btripp-books.livejournal.com/165464.html
4. http://amzn.to/1KOjprX
5. https://en.wikipedia.org/wiki/Garbage_in,_garbage_out
6. http://btripp.livejournal.com/1191482.html
7. http://amzn.to/1KOjprX

Saturday, September 19, 2015[1]

Nice work if you can find it, I guess ...

It's probably a merciful thing that I've forgotten precisely what/who suggested that I check out Gretchen Rubin's The Happiness Project: Or, Why I Spent a Year Trying to Sing in the Morning, Clean My Closets, Fight Right, Read Aristotle, and Generally Have More Fun[2] ... I suspect that I read about it in some other book, as most folks who know me realize what an cantankerous, cynical, and generally pissed-off kinda guy I am, and would figure that this book and I were operating in wholly different universes. Frankly, for most of this book, I felt like Wednesday Addams being sent to the "Harmony Hut[3]", and wondering when it was going to *end*.

Speaking of divergent "worlds", I try not to read reviews of books before *I* review them, but in this case I was trying to decide if I was going to buy a copy, and found a recurrent theme in the more negative reviews. I'm not one to toss around the "privileged" tag a lot (although being now 20 years separated from a six-figure income in my on-going entrepreneurial impoverishment, it's an occasional temptation), but the author lives in a pretty high-end niche, with concerns (or lacks thereof) unfamiliar to probably most readers. She's a former clerk for Sandra Day O'Connor, a former chief adviser to the chairman of the FCC, and a lecturer at Yale, while her husband is a senior fellow at the Brookings Institution ... so you can imagine what their income level is. At one point she cites a study that *"suggested that getting one extra hour of sleep each night would do more for a person's daily happiness than getting a $60,000 raise"*. I have acquaintances who think making $35k/year is a princely sum and say that were they making (as little as) $50k/year they'd never bother with trying to better their positions! For these folks (and I think they're more common than not), "getting a $60,000 raise" is no more conceivable than having little green men walking out of a UFO to present the check ... yet the author throws this out there like it's an everyday possibility in her world. So, understand that the "happiness" being addressed here is *not* including being relieved to keep the lights, cable, and internet on, make rent, and buy some groceries in any given month.

I found it somewhat ironic that, towards the end of this, Rubin reports reading a review of her project (which had been unfolding on a daily basis on a blog) to her husband, and noting it was being called "stunt journalism". Given the inapplicability of her example to (what I assume to be) most readers, this is taking that to a "meta" level ... all but *admitting* the "stunt" aspect of this within the actual body of the work. Of course, there is a wide variety of works that fall under that (obviously somewhat snide) label ... from the sublime: Julie and Julia[4] – to the somewhat ridiculous: The Guinea Pig Diaries[5] (etc.) ... with this falling somewhere in the middle.

So, with those caveats, on to The Happiness Project[6] ... this begins with her taking a crosstown bus in Manhattan on a rain-soaked day and seeing a person just like her, *"trying simultaneously to balance an umbrella, look at her cell phone, and push a stroller"*. She notes:

> *I wasn't depressed and I wasn't having a midlife crisis, but I was suffering from midlife malaise – a recurrent sense of discontent and almost a feeling of disbelief.*

Amusingly, she relates this to the Talking Heads' song "Once In A Lifetime", specifically citing the line *"This is not my beautiful house."*, and then adds:

> *All these thoughts flooded through my mind, and as I sat on that crowded bus, I grasped two things: I wasn't as happy as I could be, and my life wasn't going to change unless I made it change.*

{Yeah, cue the tiny violins.} She jumped into doing research on "happiness", and started spinning out materials, a "scoring chart" based on that used by Ben Franklin, a list of categories and sub-categories (which became the basic structure of the book), a list of her own "Twelve Commandments", and what she calls the "Secrets of Adulthood" (among other lists of stuff), drawn from a wide array of sources.

Now, I really didn't sync with much stuff in here, so my little bookmarks of "choice bits" are few and not particularly illustrative, so I'm thinking the most *useful* way of presenting what's in the book is to fall back on giving you an "outline". The project was designed from the start as a year's enterprise, so is broken up by months, each month tackling a different area, with its own specifics, and action points. Here goes:

January – *Boost Energy* – Vitality
- Go to sleep earlier.
- Exercise better.
- Toss, restore, organize.
- Tackle a nagging task.
- Act more energetic.

February – *Remember Love* – Marriage
- Quit nagging.
- Don't expect praise or appreciation.
- Fight right.
- No dumping.
- Give proofs of love.

March – *Aim Higher* – Work
- Launch a blog.
- Enjoy the fun of failure.
- Ask for help.
- Work smart.
- Enjoy now.

April – *Lighten Up* – Parenthood
- Sing in the morning.
- Acknowledge the reality of people's feelings.
- Be a treasure house of happy memories.
- Take time for projects.

May – *Be Serious About Play* – Leisure
- Find more fun.
- Take time to be silly.
- Go off the path.
- Start a collection.

June – *Make Time for Friends* – Friendship
- Remember birthdays.
- Be generous.
- Show up.
- Don't gossip.

     - Make three new friends.
  July – *Buy Some Happiness* – Money
     - Indulge in a modest splurge.
     - Buy needful things.
     - Spend out.
     - Give something up.
  August – *Contemplate the Heavens* – Eternity
     - Read memoirs of catastrophe.
     - Keep a gratitude notebook.
     - Imitate a spiritual master.
  September – *Pursue a Passion* – Books
     - Write a novel.
     - Make time.
     - Forget about results.
     - Master a new technology.
  October – *Pay Attention* – Mindfulness
     - Meditate on koans.
     - Examine True Rules.
     - Stimulate the mind in new ways.
     - Keep a food diary.
  November – *Keep a Contented Heart* – Attitude
     - Laugh out loud.
     - Use good manners.
     - Give positive reviews.
     - Find an area of refuge.
  December – *Boot Camp Perfect* – Happiness
     - Boot Camp Perfect

One element that I found to be *mixed* at best was her inclusion of comments from her blog about these various items. These range from the vaguely interesting to the totally pointless … to the extent that I began to wonder if some were selected to simply be a shout-out to her favorite followers (although anonymously). Also, as self-focused as the book is, she indulges in a lot of "before" descriptions … and the over-all take-away is that she was not the most pleasant person to be around … she details a lot of ways she was one of those folks one tries hard to avoid in a social setting (hey, she was a *lawyer*, I guess it goes with the territory).

To hit some "highlights" … in January's "Toss, restore, organize." it turns out that she's a maniac for throwing stuff out … she even talks about *badgering* her friends to let her come over and *clean out their closets*. In February's "Quit nagging." it becomes pretty evident that this was a particular item she had to pay attention to. One has to figure when she starts out March with "Launch a blog.", she's talking about her situation, as blogging is not something that I'd recommend to all and sundry! Admittedly, she does frequently note that this is "her stuff" and that other folks need to figure out what's going to support *their* happiness, but a lot of this still comes across as "dictates" from on high. April's "Sing in the morning." really reflects her having two young daughters (ages seven and one) when writing this … I'm not sure that the same strategies would work with a surly 15-year-old. You'd think that somebody who was such an anti-clutter person wouldn't come up with May's "Start a collection.", but she makes an exception, and recommends that everybody have one "junk drawer" and one empty shelf. In June's "Don't gossip." Rubin tells more tales on herself, as this appears to have been a favorite activity for her at one point. One of the odder concepts here is July's "Spend out.", which is both related to giving/spending without expectation of return, and "using the good stuff" (be that napkins or perfume). One of the points that has widest applicability is August's "Keep a gratitude notebook.", which is pretty self-explanatory, and a very good idea. One that is hardly "for everybody" is September's "Write a novel." ... which starts out with somebody introducing her to NaNoWriMo[7]. October's "Meditate on koans." isn't quite as doctrinally Zen as one might expect (hope), as she notes having her own file of koan-like phrases from literature that she seems to prefer than the classics. November's "Give positive reviews." isn't just trying to be a Jedi mind trick on people like me, but is more admission on her part that she always was trying to "look smart" by tearing things down. Her "Boot Camp Perfect." in December was simply trying to do ALL these things all the time ... which I guess worked better than one might think.

Needless to say, The Happiness Project[8] was not the book for *me*, but I guess it (and the author's web site, and podcast, and articles in various outlets) is wildly popular with other sorts of people. If I was going to be really sarcastic, I'd suggest that the subtitle of this is "how a millionaire managed to minimize her ennui and call that being happy", but then that wouldn't let her name-check Aristotle and play up her Ivy League education, would it?

Since this *does* have its audience, it's still in print (in the hardcover, no less), and the on-line big boys have it at about a quarter off of its relatively hefty cover price. Fortunately (and, trust me, this is how *I* got it), the new/used guys have "like new" copies for a penny (plus shipping, of course). There were parts of this that I liked, but the "Eloise at The Plaza" vibe became frequently irritating. However, since I'm a cranky old guy who hates self-improvement books ... "your mileage may vary".

Notes:

1. http://btripp-books.livejournal.com/173646.html
2. http://amzn.to/1hZM3Qo
3. https://youtu.be/5Nkzbr-JaJU
4. http://amzn.to/1iESxo9
5. http://btripp-books.livejournal.com/135241.html
6. http://amzn.to/1hZM3Qo
7. http://nanowrimo.org/
8. http://amzn.to/1hZM3Qo

Sunday, September 20, 2015[1]

This is why Jefferson wrote of separation* ...

Geez ... I sure picked a swell time to have pulled Mike Huckabee's A Simple Government: Twelve Things We Really Need from Washington (and a Trillion That We Don't!)[2] out of the to-be-read piles (where it had been lingering since I grabbed a dollar store copy a year and half ago), didn't I? All the insanity around his support of that "won't do her job because of her beliefs" gal broke *weeks* after I got into this (honest!), and it really focused the problems I have with this book, and its author in general.

Now, let me apologize *now* if this ends up being more about my political philosophies and not so much about the book. There's so much more to write about Huckabee himself than what's in the book, frankly.

Huckabee is one of the clearest cases of where I have discomfort with my erstwhile allies on the conservative side of the political spectrum. His basic world-view (at least as expressed in A Simple Government[3] has a certain "Mayberry" vibe to it ... common-sense, Constitutionally-based, classic American populism ... which does, admittedly have a "church-going" tinge to it in the many real-world examples across the country. What amazes me is that the religion never seems to get "educated out" of guys like Huckabee ... it's like the water in his fishbowl, "just there" and never questioned. His arguments are typically of a Constitutional/common-sense (albeit not in the Paine sense of the latter!) vein, which I'm reading and agreeing with, until, suddenly he's justifying something or insisting on something, or whatever, based on some Christian (and not even *biblical*) basis, and I'm like "WTF, dude?!".

It shocks me that he, and conservatives like him, don't see the dissonance in that. Of course, in Huckabee's case ... he's been a fundamentalist from the get-go, having attended a Baptist college and getting a degree in religion, and then moving on to a Baptist theological seminary (which he dropped out of to go into Christian broadcasting). So, it's not like he was notably *secular* at any point in his life.

I, of course, am as deeply secular as anybody with as many religious credentials as I have (from Vajrayana Buddhism to tribal shamanic lineages, to assorted "western esoteric tradition" things, to even being a PK) could be, and have ZERO reference for how religion (or, more specifically, his particular brand of Baptism) permeates his life. The only parallel that I can sort of posit would be sports (although this is, admittedly, more "tribal" than "doctrinal") and my emotional connection with the Bears and the Cubs is about as close as I can get.

So, it seems plainly *bizarre* to me that he can so fervently support somebody like Kim Davis, unless he truly believes that one's personal take on one's religion (because, in reality, there is precious little "anti-gay" material in *the bible*, but a lot of *cultural* anti-gay sentiment in the fundamentalist Christian traditions) over-rides the law of the land. And, from what I see in Googling a bit, Huckabee even feels that one's faith trumps the decisions of the Supreme Court. Yet, I don't suppose that he is in favor of Muslim women wearing burkas in their drivers license photos. And, in the latter case, the individual hasn't *taken a job* that they're not wanting to perform because of religious beliefs, so is arguably less of an affront to the system (although certainly not something that should be allowed). It's like if I were a bartender and I refused service to a Packers fan, just for being a cheesehead.

Anyway, this sort of thing pops its silly head up over and over again in a book which (were one to purge the religion from it) would be quite a reasonable political read.

One note on the book ... it's yet another thing which came out during the last election cycle, looking at the current POTUS' first term and predicting (sadly, rather accurately) the horrors to come were said person given a second term ... so, much of it is somewhat dated and forward-looking to things that have (or haven't) already happened.

A Simple Government[4] is set up in 12 chapters, first about "Family Values" (making a point that the "most granular" level of governance is that in the family unit), then looking at a "Return to Local Government" (a very good idea), a look at managing budgets – comparing the state with the family budget, a look at taxation, a look at health care, a look at education, a look at environmental issues (which the author appears to be quite passionate about, but significantly argues that the Federal government is really bad at responding and really good at screwing things up), a look at immigration policy (and this was even before the insane policies of the current administration reached their present nadir), a look at terrorism, a consideration of our military policy, some discussion of America's place in the world, and a hopeful look ahead (again, written before the current POTUS had a chance to drive us further down his path of destruction in a second term).

I flagged a couple of bits that I thought were particularly sane in here, and figure I'll share this one:

> ... What if some stranger from the next town over came to your house one day and said he would take care of running your family for you if you gave him a certain amount of your income in exchange? You would have a say in the matter, but, oh wait, he'd also be in charge of a few other families – all different from yours – who would also get a vote. Would you trust him?
>
> My guess is you wouldn't. But this is what it's like at the federal level of government – a bunch of strangers take your tax dollars and figure out how best to put them to use. They don't know you, and they don't understand the needs of your community like you do. As a result, they set up programs and pass laws in an effort to please everyone (often pleasing no one), and you have very little say in what happens. And the bigger we allow our federal government to get, the worse the problem becomes.

> Every time Washington enacts a new law or mandate, you can be sure that the states, the private sector, and the people are left with less control over their destinies than they had the moment before that bill was signed. Politicians get so caught up in arguing the merits of a particular provision that we don't see the overall shift in power, especially when the bills are so large that we can't deal with their totality. Power is a zero-sum game. In other words, whenever the federal government accumulates more power, the state and the people inevitably lose some autonomy they previously had. Eventually, we can lose our way entirely.

There's a lot more "common sense" analysis of the various factors in play within the subjects under consideration in the assorted chapters, but this was at least a fairly contiguous block of material on this – that didn't shift into that (one's individual religious spin's) "faith trumps all" stuff (which, to be fair, is not pervasive through the text, but never far off-stage in the author's world-view).

Again, I might have had a somewhat different approach to reviewing this, had all that Kim Davis lunacy not cropped up in the past few weeks (and especially the author's championing the actions of somebody who is – in a secular view – *clearly* in the wrong). Will you want to read A Simple Government[5]? If you're a gung-ho Christian (or Southern Baptist, or however further down the fundy rabbit-hole you care to go), with a conservative bent (*ya think?*), you'll no doubt *love* this book ... but the farther apart from that demographic you are, the more you'll find stuff to be irritated with here. As noted at the top, I found this over at the dollar store about a year and a half ago, so it's been floating around out there for a while ... I was rather surprised to see that it's still in print (in a paperback edition), but the hardcover is available from the on-line big boys' new/used channels for as little as 1¢ (plus $3.99 shipping, of course) for a *new* copy. This is *not* one of those that "everybody needs to read", but it's a solid common-sense look at how screwed up the government is (if you can ignore the preachiness).

{separation}[6]

Notes:

1. http://btripp-books.livejournal.com/174078.html
2-5. http://amzn.to/1JK8tPG
6. http://www.loc.gov/loc/lcib/9806/danpre.html

Thursday, October 1, 2015[1]

Let the buyer beware ...

OK, so this *may* end up being one of those reviews which is more about my reactions to things *around* the book rather than the book itself. I had run into a mention of Marcus Buckingham & Donald O. Clifton's Now, Discover Your Strengths[2] (the odd formation of the title serves to imply that it's a follow-up to their previous *First, Break All The Rules*) in some other book I was reading (don't recall what that was at this point), and it sounded like a very useful read, as it offers the promise of helping me discover and focus on my strengths. So, as is my wont, I scurried over to Amazon and ordered a *used* copy ... no problem, right? WRONG! It turns out that the on-line assessment associated with the book involves a code (printed inside the dust jacket) that can only be used *once*, and evidently one of the previous owners of my copy had done the quiz and I was S.O.L.

Now, the core element here is THE ASSESSMENT ... "you can't tell the players without the program" and all ... and they (in this case "they" appears to be the Gallup organization) are *selling* these for as much as a new copy of the book about their "StrengthsFinder" ... and *that* will only give you your top five (out of 34 "strengths") – if you want to see the *rest* of the rankings, it will cost you *five times* as much. Needless to say, I'm not going to shell out $90 for that info, and, frankly, just getting the top five (although, admittedly, the cover, in rather small print, only promises "your top 5") seems like a gyp even if the code *was* working. I sent in a request to get a usable code (noting that I was going to be reviewing the book) and got ZERO response ... which further pissed me off.

I'm hardly the only one in this situation ... there's a rather interesting blog[3] out there which both addresses this, and has a *long* run of comments bitching about it. The blogger has the suggestion that *"If you're honest with yourself, you can achieve accurate results by self-reporting."*, and points folks to a form which lists the 34 strengths and lets you rank them to come up with your own list. Frankly, out of the 34, I probably wasn't saying *"yuck!"* to only 6 or 7, so I was able to narrow down the field quite a bit ... but this lacks the *precision* that having the actual quiz's dynamics involved.

So, on one hand I was angry for not being able to approach the book as it was intended, and on the other, a bit embarrassed that I'd once again fallen on the landmine of buying used books (with on-line components – more often an issue of stuff being "404" than being invalid, but still) ... however, six and a half years without a regular paycheck makes the odds of my *paying retail* for something like this pretty damn slim.

You might expect that I'd just throw some curses at the authors, their organization, their publisher, *and* the horse they rode in on, give you the broadstrokes about what the book's about, and wash my hands of it. But ...

The research involved here is pretty damn impressive. The Gallup Organization had done a thirty year (as of the time of the book's release in 2001 –

I don't know if it's been on-going since) "systematic study of excellence wherever we could find it", involving over two million interviews consisting of "open-ended questions". Out of this massive amount of data they started to find "themes", which eventually became the 34 "strengths" presented in this book – Achiever, Activator, Adaptability, Analytical, Arranger, Belief, Command, Communication, Competition, Connectedness, Context, Deliberative, Developer, Discipline, Empathy, Fairness, Focus, Futuristic, Harmony, Ideation, Inclusiveness, Individualization, Input, Intellection, Learner, Maximizer, Positivity, Relator, Responsibility, Restorative, Self-Assurance, Significance, Strategic, and "Woo" (which they say stands for "Winning Others Over", but could be just as well taken in the sense of "wooing").

One of the interesting things here is that they go against the "business as usual" concept of spending a lot of time, effort, and money on trying to "fix" one's weaknesses … here it's argued that this is, generally speaking, a waste, and we'd be much better served by focusing on honing our strengths. These are based on what they're referring to as "talents", which are defined in the analysis of the study as *"Talent is any recurring pattern of thought, feeling, or behavior that can be productively applied."*, with the emphasis on the *any*, as even some less-than-positive/helpful patterns can be framed as talents *if* they can be productively applied.

> *What creates in you these recurring patterns? If you don't much care for your patterns, can you stitch a new design? The answers to these questions are (a) your recurring patterns are created by the connections in your brain; and (b) no, beyond a certain age you are not going to be able to stitch a completely new design – your talents are enduring.*
>
> …
>
> *Your talents, your strongest synaptic connections, are the most important raw material for strength building. Identify your most powerful talents, hone them with skills and knowledge, and you will be well on you way to living the strong life.*

The authors are pretty adamant that these things are hard-wired in our brains, and that going against what's in there is pretty much like Heinlein's classic line about "teaching a pig to sing". However, there are inner signals that let you figure out where those talents lie … *"Spontaneous reactions, yearnings, rapid learning, and satisfactions will all help you detect the traces of your talents."*

The middle section of the book is simply a walk-through of the 34 "themes", each with just a single page, featuring a descriptive paragraph and 2-5 examples (framed as "X sounds like this:") featuring people from the study who fit that theme, with their relating something key to the concept. As noted above, reading through these does give one a fairly good idea of what are "your strengths", as they prompted a *"eww, that's not me"* reaction over and over again, except for where they didn't.

Again, without having the actual on-line test to go from, there was an irritating vagueness to this all. The listing of the strengths is followed by a rather interesting section called "The Questions You're Asking" which was pretty informative, if not including *my* #1 question: *why can't I take the damn assessment?!*. The next part is another 1-page-per look at "How To Manage A Person Strong In X", each with a half-dozen or so bullet points with fairly specific suggestions of working with that particular type of person.

The penultimate part of this got the majority of my little bookmarks, "Building A Strengths-Based Organization", which advances the authors' iconoclastic stance towards balancing strengths and weaknesses. One thing I found fascinating (given my own long job search) was:

> *Most employment advertisements loudly assert the need for certain skills, knowledge, and years of experience but remain mute on talent. It is ironic that they itemize qualities they can change in a person while ignoring the ones they can't.*

They include a number of additional assessment tools for managers, with lists of questions (*"these questions were selected from a list of hundreds because, when worded in exactly this fashion (complete with qualifiers ...), they predicted employee* {behaviors}) to be used in working with staff. There are quite a few eye-opening data bits here, such as that *eight out of ten* employees are "miscast", and that "job status" is more predictive than obesity, smoking, or high blood pressure when it comes to heart attacks!

Now, Discover Your Strengths[4] concludes with a technical appendix on the methodology, etc. of the research involved in developing the StrengthsFinder, which also includes some intriguing statistics on how various demographic categories differed (or didn't) in the results.

Obviously, it's hard for me to *recommend* this book via the used channels, since you *can't take the actual test*, but I'm not sure I liked it well enough to say "hey, money be damned" and saying it's worth paying retail for. If you're interested in this sort of thing as a *philosophical* discussion of types, sure, spending 1¢ (plus shipping) will get you a very interesting read about the work Gallup's done in this area ... but they're hell-bent on wringing every dollar out of organizations (who are the main target of this book), and aren't going to cut the people who might be trying to better themselves (again, check out some of the comments on that blog post ... some angry people out there!) any slack in the pursuit of that lucre. It's fascinating, but feels real sleazy once you've been jilted.

Notes:

1. http://btripp-books.livejournal.com/174165.html
2. http://amzn.to/1QMwnew
3. http://www.unsheeple.com/2008/11/free-strengths-finder-testkind-of-self-reporting/
4. http://amzn.to/1QMwnew

Friday, October 2, 2015[1]

Falling asleep in the sun ...

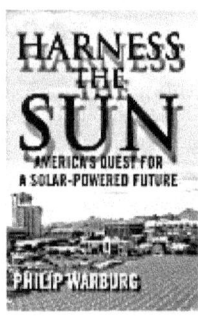

This is another book from the LibraryThing.com "Early Reviewers" program, and, unfortunately, after a string of quite good selections from LTER, this one is definitely back in the "meh" category. As you may recall, I also write a blog for the Chicago Tribune's "ChicagoNow" blogging platform, called Green Tech Chicago[2], so I keep an eye out for a lot of renewable energy stories, and I've come to expect a certain level of ... well, *interesting* ... which isn't front-and-center in Philip Warburg's Harness the Sun: America's Quest for a Solar-Powered Future[3]. Since finishing reading this, I've been trying to "put my finger on" what specifically I found unappealing with it, and I think I've finally figured that out. In most material on "green energy", there's a forward-looking aspect which promises great things in the future, often over-blown gee-whiz stuff, but hooks to get you excited about what's being discussed. This is true from GenIV reactors to mustard plants as a oil source, to tidal turbines, to solar satellites, etc. Those stories grip the imagination and pull you in to the tech involved. Not so much here.

For something subtitled *"America's Quest for a Solar-Powered Future"* (there I go again with taking exception with a book's subtitle), there's very little "future" focus here. Frankly, this reads like a series of very serious, diligently researched, but ultimately uninspiring newspaper stories ... if not a collection of excerpts from quarterly reports from various industry players. The ten chapters here look at different applications of solar technology – *as it's presently implemented* – and anchors the stories by featuring individuals involved in those businesses. If this was a series of "investigative journalism" pieces on "the state of solar", it would sort of make sense, but in this context they're just (to me at least) awfully bland.

Now, I will admit that I've probably read more about this stuff than most folks have, so things that are "new and exciting" to me are pretty thin here. I ended up with just two little bookmarks stuck in the book ... albeit one of them highlighting a fascinating system of using molten salt (a combination of sodium nitrate and potassium nitrate) to *store heat*:

> Heated to more that 1,000 F, the molten salt flows in large steel collector pipes down to the base of the concrete tower. From there it can be channeled to a heat exchanger that uses the captured energy to create steam for a power-generating turbine – if there's an immediate demand for electricity. Alternatively, there super-heated fluid can be pumped into a 3.6 million gallon stainless-steel storage tank just few dozen feet from the tower.

And the tower in question is an indication on how huge that project, Crescent Dunes, is ... it's as big as a 50-story building and stands at the center of 17,500 mirrors, each of which is about 140 square yards in size. I only wish there was that much "cool stuff" to note from every site the author visited.

Frankly, this might have been *intentionally boring*, as in the note sent out by the publisher with it, they say it's a *pragmatic report on the current state of affairs*, which would explain why there's so much stuff in here on government regulations (and give-aways by the current administration), supply chain and manufacturing issues, conflicts between the "green energy" folks and various environmental organizations (a lot of these installations have had to go to great lengths to make sure a wide array of critters didn't get disrupted), and assorted international political concerns (even going so far to suggest that having cheap Chinese solar panels destroy the American solar industry might be a good thing because it would accelerate the installed base of solar energy).

It could also be the case that the book just didn't appeal to me because its author is very likely the sort that I would dislike in person ... he's an attorney, a "community organizer" (like somebody else I can't stand), has worked for various governmental entities, and has been a lawyer for a handful of Environmental NGOs ... this is not a resume that speaks of "vision" – a Peter Diamandis[4] he's not. If the phrase "written by a lawyer" has the same icky negative vibe for you as it does for me ... you'll get the sense of what I see as wrong with Harness the Sun[5].

On the other hand, the material here is certainly well-researched, with a couple of dozen of pages of small-type footnotes supporting his arguments and assertions, and he includes a "selected bibliography" with over a hundred documents. If you wanted to have a "snapshot" of the solar industry today (it just came out a few weeks ago, so I'm guessing the info is as current as possible), this will give it to you. But ... it's not exactly gripping. Perhaps tellingly, even though this is brand new, the on-line big boys have it at a substantial discount, and the new/used vendors have *new* copies going for about 10% of the cover price. If you are looking for an overview of the solar industry, this is the book for you ... as it is an extensive look at pretty much all the types of operations in place in the US ... but if you're looking for something to get excited about, maybe not.

Notes:

1. http://btripp-books.livejournal.com/174560.html
2. http://greentechchicago.info/
3. http://amzn.to/1KI0AN5
4. http://btripp-books.livejournal.com/128282.html
5. http://amzn.to/1KI0AN5

Sunday, October 11, 2015[1]

Debates on freedom ...

One of the truly awesome things about the neighborhood I've lived in for 40 years in downtown Chicago is the presence of the Newberry Library, a research institution with a global reputation (for instance, the "originals" of the Popul Vuh[2] reside in their collection), which has a great love of books and free speech. These interests come together every summer in the concurrent events of the 4-day Book Fair, and (on Saturday) the Bughouse Square Debates (this coming from the nickname of Washington Square park in front of the Newberry). "Bughouse Square" has a long an colorful history, being a major "speakers corner" for the labor movement (and others ... including the characters in the famed Dill Pickle Club[3], a half-block down an alley from it) in the early 1900's, and today it is supposedly the only place in Chicago where one can host a protest without a permit – the only requirement being that the speaker is on a raised platform, even if that is simply "a soapbox" (hence *that* usage). The debates feature a "main stage" with guest speakers, but also a half-dozed "soapbox" stages set around the park where anybody can get up and speak their piece to the (often heckling) crowds.

One of the annual features is the awarding of the the *John Peter Altgeld Freedom of Speech Award*, named for former Illinois Governor J.P. Altgeld[4] who served from 1893-1897 and is best known for pardoning three of the Haymarket convicted bombers, and resisting the Federal government's efforts to crush the Pullman Strike. This summer, the award went to author Wendy Kaminer, an unusual selection in that she's not local. As part of the award presentation, the recipient gives a talk, and I was sufficiently impressed that I was wanting to check out some of her stuff, and found a copy of her 2002 Free for All: Defending Liberty in America Today[5].

Ms. Kaminer is a former ACLU board member, and that organization's "better angels" are exhibited in this book. While I had sort of been hoping for a Libertarian screed, what Free for All[6] features is more a "pox on both your houses" middle ground, with fingers wagging at both the Left and the Right, the Democrats and Republicans, and the Bush and Clinton administrations. As is the case in books dealing with "issues of the day", much of this seems almost amusingly dated (there is a lot of indignation being thrown at names that I'd not had run through my head in a very long time), and this book is collection of columns that were published primarily in liberal bastion *The American Prospect* (with some from *Free Inquiry*, *The Nation*, *Dissent*, and *The New York Times*) in the years 1999-2002. Needless to say, talking about liberty in relation to terrorism had a different palette prior to 9/11/2001 than after, and she notes that she edited some material here to reflect the changes brought on by those attacks.

Frankly, as this is largely a *philosophical* look at our freedoms, the "collection of columns" format weakens the book as a whole ... while an Ann Coulter is perfectly effective when pulling together thematically similar rants into a book, this feels a bit disjointed, and that's certainly not helped by jumping around within its timeframe. It is also topically a bit spread out, addressing 10 different areas, with some getting as few as just two columns, and others *eleven*. There are two sections on national security issues ("Homeland Offense", the two "bookending" this, starting with a "post-9/11" group of columns and ending with a "pre-9/11" set of pieces), one on public/private privacy dynamics, an extensive section on free speech, issues around religion, issues on law & order, two sections on "women's issues" (one "rights" and one "wrongs"), and two looks at "anti-individualism", one being offenses of the Left, and the other of the Right.

As you might suspect, this is not a particularly *uplifting* read, as it primarily is an exposition of how our rights and freedoms are getting abused ... and this is *before* the excesses of the current POTUS and his out-of-control administration. Personally, from a perspective of the recent "pen wielding" disregard of the rule of law over the past several years, many of the issues fulminated over in here seem downright *quaint*.

Anyway, the author somewhat sets up her perspective in the Introduction:

> *America's disloyalty to liberty is disheartening but predictable. Liberty leashes power and, right and left, people who find themselves in possession of power tend to resist restraints upon its use. Cynics don't care if they abuse power to advance their own interests; people who take pride in their own virtue generally manage to convince themselves that they exercise power virtuously (even when they exercise it harshly) to serve the public good. Powerful people convinced of their own goodness are as dangerous to individual liberty as powerful people for whom goodness is irrelevant.*

One of the pieces here, "Toxic Media", deals with the "big issue" (in 2000) of violence in games and shows, and the uproar of how this is targeted to children. When was the last time you saw hand-wringing over that on the Sunday morning talk shows? Here's how Kaminer closes out this piece, which I think does present some solid "philosophical" points that arise out of this:

> *It's unfortunate and ironic that amoral corporations, like Disney or Time/Warner, stand as champions and beneficiaries of First Amendment rights. As gatekeepers of the culture, they're not exactly committed to maintaining an open, diverse marketplace of ideas. Indeed, de facto censorship engineered by media conglomerates may threaten public discourse nearly as much as federal regulation. And, gratuitously violent media enriches neither our discourse nor our culture.*
>
> *But speech doesn't have to provide cultural enrichment to enjoy constitutional protection. We don't need a First Amendment to protect popular, inoffensive speech or speech that a majority of*

> *people believe has social value. We need it to protect speech that Lynn Cheney or Joe Lieberman considers demeaning and degrading. Censorship campaigns often begin with a drive to protect children (or women), but they rarely end there.*

One topic that *is* "up to the minute" is that of gun rights … and the author makes several very good points in the "Gun Shy" piece (the following is pulled from a couple of pages with about 2.5 paragraphs – that I felt was somewhat peripheral to the main argument – skipped):

> *Gun sales are said to have increased dramatically after September 11, to the bemusement of some who point out that guns won't protect us from terrorists armed with viruses or nuclear bombs. Still, it's long been clear that many Americans feel reassured by firearms, and if you fear the civil disorder that further attacks might bring, the desire for a gun is not entirely irrational.*
>
> *So, it's not surprising that people might assert their rights to own guns while they cede less controversial rights to privacy or speech by embracing electronic surveillance or supporting repression of dissent. It's debatable whether an increase in gun purchases will protect or endanger them. Armed with studies and statistics, advocates and academics on both sides of the gun debate argue about whether gun ownership deters and successfully interrupts violent crime or simply increases the chances of any assault becoming deadly, as well as overall levels of violence. People often choose sides in this debate reflexively (your views on gun control signal your position in the culture war), but questions about the practical effects of gun ownership aren't easily resolved. …*
>
> *…*
>
> *Constitutional scholars and historians right and left have been engaged in a lively debate about Second Amendment rights for some years. But outside the pages of law reviews, liberals tend to embrace gun control and scoff at the Second Amendment, asserting that it only ensures the power of the states or the collective right of "the people" to organize armed militias. The trouble is that the Bill of Rights was intended to empower individuals, not groups (and certainly not governments). It was intended to restrain organized majorities, not to arm them. Indeed, most liberal civil libertarians adamantly construe the First, Fourth, Fifth, Sixth, Seventh, and Eighth amendments[7] as grants of individual rights. (They'd construe the Third Amendment similarly if the government ever tried forcing us to*

> *quarter troops.) Still, they perversely single out the Second Amendment as a grant of collective rights, mostly because of a cultural aversion to guns. Liberals tend to disdain the right to own a gun the way conservatives disdain the right to read pornography.*

This is one of the most clear statements on the gun debate I've seen (certainly more nuanced than the popular *"What part of 'shall not be infringed' don't you understand?"*), and it's, if anything, a more key debate in 2015 than it was in 2002!

Again, Free for All[8] is a bit dated, but the discussions of our rights and freedoms within the contexts of some now "historical" debates is worth reading. As a testament to that, it is still in print in paperback, so might be out there in the brick-and-mortar book world, but the on-line big boys have it in stock *and* the new/used guys have it for as little as 1¢ (plus shipping) for a "very good" copy.

Notes:

1. http://btripp-books.livejournal.com/174593.html
2. https://en.wikipedia.org/wiki/Popol_Vuh
3. http://publications.newberry.org/frontiertoheartland/exhibits/show/perspectives/dillpickle/briefhistory
4. https://en.wikipedia.org/wiki/John_Peter_Altgeld
5. http://amzn.to/1KCb4r4
6. http://amzn.to/1KCb4r4
7. http://www.billofrightsinstitute.org/founding-documents/bill-of-rights/
8. http://amzn.to/1KCb4r4

Monday, October 12, 2015[1]

To sleep, perchance to dream ...

I was a bit on the fence about reviewing this, or even adding it to my LibraryThing catalog[2], as it's a free, extensively abridged, version of another book - Sudhansu Chokroverty's Questions & Answers About Sleep Apnea[3] — which is a 112-page book covering 100 questions, while the version I have is a 80-page book covering 20 questions (and, frankly, I was able to knock it out while waiting for my in-clinic sleep study). However, I went ahead and added it over on LT, so being the OCD-driven maniac that I am, I'm going ahead with grinding out a review.

As you might assume from the title, this is primarily a bunch of common questions about sleep apnea being discussed at various lengths (from a few sentences to a few pages). Sleep apnea is one of those "newer" diseases, having first been officially identified/defined in the 1950, although its first appellation was "Pickwickian Syndrome", based on the description of the (very public) sleeping patterns of a character in Charles Dickens' Pickwick Papers[4].

Initially treatment for this was rather invasive ... involving tracheostomy (putting a hole in the windpipe past the point of obstruction ... which couldn't have been particularly popular. However, in 1981 the "continuous positive airway pressure" (CPAP) approach was developed, with a machine that pumps air past the point where, in sleep apnea, the base of the tongue presses against the soft palate, closing off the airway, keeping that channel open.

The core issue in sleep apnea is that when the base of the tongue relaxes against the soft palate, you can't get air ... and as the CO_2 raises in the blood stream, the brain starts sending out signals to get some oxygen in ... waking up the sleeper. According to the author, 15-20 million people in the US suffer from this to some extent, and it ends up causing a whole array of health issues: cardiovascular (high blood pressure), metabolic (diabetes), and psychological (depression), let alone the mental strain of having frequently interrupted REM sleep. Of course, the snoring, gasping, aspects of the sleep apnea sufferer trying to get some oxygen *also* effects their partners ... I'd been long exiled to the living room for sleeping, due to "snoring like a 747 on take-off" so that my *wife* could get some sleep.

I'd never suspected just how *bad* I had this ... it turned out that I was waking up 58.6 times *an hour* before getting the CPAP machine, and since I've been using it (just a week or so at this point), that number has dropped to *under 1 time per hour*. Needless to say, the former number would indicate that I was getting no meaningful sleep, and probably had not had any noticeable REM sleep (or dreams) in a very long time.

There were some interesting bits and pieces in here ... like the "STOP" guide for determining if one might have sleep apnea:

S - Do you **S**nore loudly?

T - Do you often feel **T**ired, fatigued, or sleepy during the daytime?
O - Has anybody **O**bserved you stop breathing during your sleep?
P - Do you have or are you being treated for high blood **P**ressure?

Of course, in the span of 20 questions, not everything's going to be covered, but this book (and I assume the non-abridged 100-question version more so) does a good job of walking the reader from basic questions about recognizing the problem, defining the processes/symptoms, introducing the concepts around the CPAP machine, and answering key queries related to issues that might arise.

I feel fortunate that I've taken to this with little difficulty (I'm still finding myself having to get back up when I realize that I forgot to fill the reservoir for the built-in humidifier, but I assume that this will eventually become a "bedtime habit"), and look forward to the benefits (energy, weight loss, etc.) that everybody tells me comes with using the machine.

Again, the copy I have is a freebie from the clinic's literature rack, but the author's more extensive look at Questions & Answers About Sleep Apnea[5] is still in print and available via the on-line big boys, and used copies can be had for as little as a penny plus shipping. If you or your partner have some of the red flags around sleep apnea, you might want to pick up a copy of this to familiarize yourself with the symptoms, hazards, and treatments.

Notes:

1. http://btripp-books.livejournal.com/174962.html
2. http://btripp-books.com/
3. http://amzn.to/1WbzIwf
4. http://www.gutenberg.org/ebooks/580
5. http://amzn.to/1WbzIwf

Tuesday, October 13, 2015[1]

O Divine Poesy ...

OK, I'm stumped ... I know that *somebody* out in social media land strongly recommended this book ... I was thinking it might have been Chris Brogan[2], but I wasn't able to find the thing that said "this is the basic stuff" (or something along those lines) making Steven Pressfield's The War of Art: Break Through the Blocks and Win Your Inner Creative Battles[3] something that I had to pick up.

Now, I'd not been familiar with Pressfield previously, but he appears to be a very successful writer in what seems to be mainly historical fiction, having come out of screenwriting (where he had at least one major success after a lot of failure). On a surface level, this book is about the inner workings necessary to *be* a successful writer, with a special focus on doing battle against what he calls "the resistance". Frankly, his description of this is *very* similar to a concept (perhaps going by the same name) that I read in some other book, and for the life of me, I can't recall what that was *either*, so you're getting me writing this at perhaps at maximum frustration.

I really didn't have any particular expectations going into this other than it had been *highly* recommended by somebody whose opinions I trust. This *is* an odd book ... it's sort of autobiographical in a scattered way, with musings twisting around remembrances, interspersed with hard-won advice. There are lots of clichés about writers, and Pressfield embodies a lot of them ... from living in a van, and cranking out material on an old manual typewriter, to allusions to ideal relationships gone bad because the work for the muse trumped the work on the girl. The echoes of Bukowski and Hunter S. Thompson hang suggestively over this as well, although, having read this, I have not much more knowledge of the *person* Pressfield is, beyond small biographical tidbits like *"He is a former Marine. In 2003, he was made an honorary citizen by the city of Sparta in Greece."*

This is split into three "books": RESISTANCE - *Defining the Enemy*, COMBATTING RESISTANCE - *Turning Pro*, and BEYOND RESISTANCE - *The Higher Realm*. These are broken into dozens of pieces that range from a couple of sentences to several pages. He starts things out pretty straightforwardly, with an introductory section titled "What I Know", which reads:

> There is a secret that real writers know that wannabe writers don't, and the secret is this: It's not the writing part that's hard. What's hard is sitting down to write.
>
> What keeps us from sitting down is Resistance.

So ... that's what the writer (and other artists, or anybody trying to achieve anything worthwhile) is up against. On one level this is a "spiritual" book – the Resistance is somewhat personalized, and the Muse is certainly a real entity to the author ... before he begins writing he says "a prayer" which is the Invocation of the Muse from Homer's *The Odyssey* in the T.E. Lawrence ("of Arabia") translation[4]. The third part of this gets deeper into that zone.

When reading this, I ended up putting in more than my usual number of little bookmarks, but going back to them, the bits I flagged seem hard to extract from the flow of the book ... they were highlights in the process, but in several cases I can't really pull them out to bring to you here. I will make an effort, though. In a section "How To Be Miserable" he talks about being in the Marines, and how the Marines love misery, which he notes *"This is invaluable for an artist."*, as:

> The artist committing himself to his calling has volunteered for hell, whether he knows it or not. He will be dining for the duration on a diet of isolation, rejection, self-doubt, despair, ridicule, contempt, and humiliation.

Fair warning, I suppose ... this is very similar to the amazing introduction to the Best Screenplay nominees at the last Academy Awards, where Robert DeNiro described[5] the inner state of writers, and I wonder if whoever scripted those remarks was drawing from Pressfield's work, at least in spirit.

The concept of "genius" shifts back and forth in the book, between the Greek concept of the spirit which provides the individual's abilities, and the more modern sense of advanced competency (in contrast to mundane or "hack" work). This comes up in this discussion of mastering technique:

> The professional dedicates himself to mastering technique not because he believes technique is a substitute for inspiration but because he wants to be in possession of the full arsenal of skills when inspiration does come. The professional is sly. He knows that by toiling beside the front door of technique, he leaves room for genius to enter by the back.

One of the subtler themes here is that of evolution, not so much on the physical plane, but in the spiritual realms. A key conflict is the "Ego" vs. the "Self", with the Ego being an ally of the Resistance. The author puts it: *"I think angels make their home in the Self, while Resistance has its seat in the Ego."*. He goes on to define the Self more in this part:

> The margins of the Self touch upon Divine Ground. Meaning the Mystery, the Void, the source of Infinite Wisdom and Consciousness.
>
> Dreams come from the Self. Ideas come from the Self. When we meditate we access the Self. When we fast, when we pray, when we go on a vision quest, it's the Self we're seeking. When the dervish whirls, when the yogi chants, when the sadhu mutilates his flesh; when Native Americans pierce themselves in the Sun Dance, when suburban kids take Ecstasy and dance all night at a rave, they're seeking the Self. When we deliberately alter

> out consciousness in any way, we're trying to find the Self. When the alcoholic collapses in the gutter, that voice that tells him, "I'll save you," comes from the Self.
>
> The Self is our deepest being.

The book winds up in an interesting discussion of "hierarchy" vs. "territory", with the former being the playground of the Resistance, and the latter being the field of the Self.

You might well wonder what The War of Art[6] has to do with writing ... but there are, in fits and starts, a lot of direct-from-the-trenches advice on that level as well ... but it's more a spirit of fighting through the Resistance and staying true to the Muse than being a practical manual about being a writer. Perhaps the most telling thing I can say about this is that I suspect I will re-read it ... and reasonably soon ... something that only *very* rarely happens in my book consumption. This lacks linearity in the way Zen koans do ... and I suspect it will reveal more on subsequent reads.

This is still in print in the paperback, and it is *quite* reasonably priced in the Kindle format. While it might not be "for everybody", I'd recommend it to those who self-identify as writers, as you'll find it poking around in your head more than everything else you've read of late.

Notes:

1. http://btripp-books.livejournal.com/175283.html
2. http://chrisbrogan.com/
3. http://amzn.to/1JH4IG7
4. http://www.telstudies.org/writings/works/the_odyssey/invocation.shtml
5. http://hartwell.ganewz.com/wp-content/uploads/sites/11/2014/11/robert-de-niro-oscars-2104-quote-about-writers-672x372.jpg
6. http://amzn.to/1JH4IG7

Friday, November 6, 2015[1]

I did not need to know ANY of this ...

This was one of those dollar store finds that was in the "just as well it was only a buck" category. Dave Bry's (pronounced like "brie") Public Apology: In Which a Man Grapples With a Lifetime of Regret, One Incident at a Time[2] is an odd, and, frankly *uncomfortable* book. It is exactly what the title/subtitle suggest, a series of events for which he's apologizing ... most of which are embarrassing to various degrees.

This is set up chronologically, with sections on Junior High, High School, College, New York, and Adulthood. Each story starts off with "Dear (name):" and then runs with whatever bad behavior he's apologizing for – sometimes for many, many pages. Yes, through the course of this you get a pretty good scope of his history (and the sense that he's a bit of a jerk with substance abuse issues), but it's all one long icky read. Honestly, about a third of the way through this I was thinking "this guy *must* be doing one of those 12-step programs!" and he's working on step 8-9 where he'd make *"a list of all persons we had harmed, and became willing to make amends to them all"* and using this to at least *apologize* ... however, that doesn't get mentioned or even hinted at anywhere in here, so I guess this is just some sort of "airing of dirty laundry" in print. The author has been writing for several magazines and web sites, and he notes in the Acknowledgments that *"many of the apologies in this book were first published on The Awl"* (web site), so I guess he's decided that the embarrassing personal story is just "his niche". Ewwww.

Now, I almost *never* "give up" on a book, but about half way through this I was seriously considering not finishing it. Fortunately, the stories from his later life are less "triggering" than those of his earlier life ... and some of them even get into "poignant" territory (such as those around his father's death ... like picking up some comedies for the family to watch when they were basically waiting for his dad to finally succumb to brain cancer – one of which ended up being Woody Allen's *Hannah and Her Sisters*, which involves a sub-plot about Allen's character believing he has a brain tumor).

The subject matter of these stories is quite varied, from apologizing to friends of his parents' about what he wore to their son's bar mitzvah, to apologizing to Bon Jovi for having thrown empty beer cans over the rocker's fence and onto his lawn. There's apologizing for a graduation prank, and apologizing for dramatically spitting out the hamburger he'd been eating in a Paris bistro, when he discovered that it was made with horse meat. There's apologies to garage owners, gals at school dances, neighbors, and even to his son for letting him get lost in the park. Again, the earlier the stuff was, the more horrific the emotional load in the telling ... it's easier to let tales of him being an idiot around c-list rock stars (when writing for *Vibe* magazine) slide out of one's head, than those of him forcing grade school friends to "worship" a poster of Jim Morrison.

I have a hard time imagining how one gets to a place where the idea of writing these vignettes seems like *a good idea*, except, as noted, as some obsessive part of a 12-step program. Perhaps he should have written a postscript to the main part of the book apologizing to the those folks who actually *read* it. One would really have to be a particularly odd sort of a voyeur to *enjoy* this ... although I guess there are probably those out there who fit that profile ... but it's not *me*, and I'm guessing it's not *you*.

Not surprisingly, Public Apology[3] appears to be out of print (except for the ebook edition), and it's available on-line for as little as a penny in the aftermarket hardcover. As noted, it's in the dollar stores as well, but I don't expect anybody to go out *looking* for this. I guess we can chalk this up to "I read it so you don't have to" ... you're welcome.

Notes:

1. http://btripp-books.livejournal.com/175510.html
2-3. http://amzn.to/1WPJj6J

Saturday, November 7, 2015[1]

Evolving the city ...

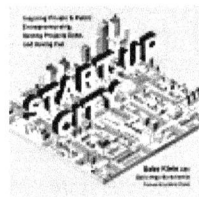

Back in September I was invited to cover the "Move Together"[2] 2015 National Shared Mobility Summit for my blog over on the Tribune's "Chicago Now" platform - Green Tech Chicago[3]. I wasn't able to attend the full conference, but was able to hit a couple of sessions on two days, and shoot an interview with the sponsoring organization's (the Shared-Use Mobility Center[4]) Executive Director, and sit through a discussion featuring the authors of a couple of new books. I was interested enough in these that I looked up their publishers, and sent out requests for review copies. This is how Gabe Klein's Start-Up City: Inspiring Private and Public Entrepreneurship, Getting Projects Done, and Having Fun[5] ended up in my reading pile.

Klein has a Chicago connection, having been Mayor Emanuel's head of the city's Department of Transportation from 2011 to 2013 ... although his C.V. is head-spinning for the number of things that are on there for somebody who hasn't quite hit 45 yet ... he was in a similar position in Washington, D.C., did a stint with ZipCar, and a car-sharing venture that Virgin was contemplating launching, ran a food truck company in D.C., and started his career in bicycle retailing following a hippie childhood (at age 10 he was in a rural Virginia yoga school/ashram).

When in the Emanuel administration, he was instrumental in the development of the Riverwalk, the BRT Chicago[6] initiative (whose dedicated bus lanes are still being created in the Loop), the DIVVY bike-share program, and the recently-opened Bloomingdale Trail, among numerous other projects variously familiar to my fellow Chicagoans. The book presents itself as "a helpful guide steeped in pragmatic realism", with chapter sub-titles such as "On managing others, empowering your team, and shamelessly promoting their accomplishments", and "Oh how to find funding where none seemingly exists, make the most of a slim budget, and get creative with the basics", etc. However, this is primarily a *memoir* of Klein's career (thus far), with occasional inserts of entrepreneurial "theory" spun off of his experiences in these assorted positions.

One thing that certainly flags Klein as "not your typical bureaucrat" is the sign he'd (I'm guessing tongue-in-cheek) suggested in place of the locally-well-known "Building A New Chicago" work signs that appear all over the city ... his version (which he had at least one done up, which hung in his office) read "Getting Sh*t Done – In Every M*th*r F*ck*ing Ward". If there is an over-arching theme here, it's that of using mind-sets and tool kits from entrepreneurial start-ups to help revitalize and spur development in cities:

> *You need to push boundaries and undermine the status quo, or your work reverts to the codes, regulations, and standards that have become the caricature of bureaucracies. What's worse is that these standards often fail us, as they did in this instance {his first attempt to install bike lanes in D.C.'s Pennsylvania Avenue}, because they fail to encapsulate*

> the dynamism of the city, the potential for engineers to creatively solve new problems, and the capacity of our citizens to see and embrace change.

Another odd thing about <u>Start-up City</u>[7] is its format ... it looks more like a travel book than a business book – in a 6x6" square lay-out, with lots of pictures, and strange illustrations that look like screen shots from some cartoon Lego world, and infographic-style graphics detailing assorted points. So, it's somewhat unsettling to flip through this and run into business-school insistences such as *"Embrace S.M.A.R.T. management and Six Sigma principles."* (the acronym standing for "Specific, Measurable, Agreed-upon, Realistic, and Time-based", and Six Sigma being an approach that *"says that anything less than 99.9999998 percent error rate, or 3.4 errors per million, is unacceptable"*). Needless to say, this isn't all about the "having fun" of the book's subtitle!

As you might have surmised by this point, a lot of this book is about "getting shit done" in the cities in which Klein has worked, but it also has "visionary" aspects, where he looks at concepts of how things will be evolving over time. One section that was particularly in line with the conference where I heard him speak looks at the his view on the future of cars:

> Vehicles today are only in use approximately 5 percent of the time. The rest of the day, they take up valuable space that could be put toward other public uses. That's a big sacrifice we've made, and I think that the self-driving cars are part of our opportunity to fix it. As mobility evolves from a private luxury into a subscription service in the "internet of everything" world, vehicles (in urban areas, at least) can be active 95 percent of the time while serving multiple customers rather than sitting around unused 95 percent of the time. As a result, societies will not need anywhere near as many vehicles as we have today.

As a life-long "city boy", I, naturally enough, found the stories of "fighting city hall" popcorn-worthy, whether it was Klein as an outsider fighting the unfair regulations against food trucks in D.C., or trying to correct programs in Chicago that were *"wracked by paranoia, which caused a series of gross inefficiencies"* (which, for example, led to using winter-formulated asphalt pothole patching material year-round, which would last about 2 days when the temperatures were above freezing!). And, there's a lot of that sort of conflict narrated across the stories here.

While <u>Start-up City</u>[8] is an engaging and informative read, it's ultimately a bit of a blur ... succeeding as a memoir, but not so much in its attempts to be a "guide". There is plenty of room here for the author to have bolstered the "business book" and "urban visionary" elements to be equal partners with the personal history narrative that's at the core of this ... it's not that those aren't *in it*, but they feel like they're less integrated into a three-way whole that they might have been. Klein closes out the book in the "visionary" mode, and here's a bit from the Conclusion:

> The future challenges and opportunities we face in cities are not just about the obvious – the advent of high-tech vehicles, apps, or even traditional transportation. How we configure our future neighborhoods and transportation systems will have profound impacts on climate change, on socioeconomic mobility, an on public health. The ground is shifting beneath us, and whether you're talking about energy or healthcare or climate, the landscape is evolving more quickly than we can even begin to anticipate. This is why our North Star cannot be about technology for the sake of technology alone. Instead, we must use the momentum of technological change as a force to help us create places that celebrate public life.

This has only been out a few weeks at this point, so it should certainly be available via the bigger brick-and-mortar book vendors, and the on-line big boys have it at nearly a third off of cover (and a very reasonable price for the e-book – although I wonder how much of the graphic presentation of this survives into the that format). I liked it – and certainly folks from Chicago and D.C. will be amused to see familiar places and get behind-the-scenes looks at local projects – but I think it falls a bit short from being all it could have been (or, perhaps, was envisioned to be).

Notes:

1. http://btripp-books.livejournal.com/175716.html
2. http://sharedusemobilitycenter.org/2015-summit/
3. http://www.chicagonow.com/green-tech-chicago/2015/10/moving-together/
4. http://sharedusemobilitycenter.org/
5. http://amzn.to/1L9cbjc
6. ..http://brtchicago.com/
7-8. http://amzn.to/1L9cbjc

Sunday, November 8, 2015[1]

America's traffic, cars, and roads ... and some things both mysterious and not ...

This is the second of the books that got on my radar from the "Move Together"[2] 2015 National Shared Mobility Summit (the other being here[3] – with more details on that event). There was a session I attended featuring the authors of two new books on city/transportation issues, and both sounded interesting enough for me to reach out to the publishers for review copies. The one currently being considered is Samuel I. Schwartz's Street Smart: The Rise of Cities and the Fall of Cars[4].

This is a book which, by all rights, ought to be very dry, and possibly tiresome. It's not. Heck, it's downright *entertaining*, and I'm tempted to attribute this to Mr. Schwartz's good humor (I seem to recall that he was "owning the stage" at the conference), but I'm wondering if this has something to do with the "with" credit (which is on the title page, but not the dust jacket or spine) of publishing-industry veteran William Rosen. In any case, between them, they have produced a book that's a great read, with (I'm guessing) wide appeal, in a subject area that one would not expect. I know it's unusual for me to praise a book before getting into the particulars, but I felt that this was, perhaps, the most *notable* element here – it's the text equivalent of hanging out with your favorite uncle who's had a fascinating life and is full of great stories.

I did have one gripe with this, however ... I really, *really* wished at numerous points that the book had been *illustrated* – preferably with a lot of photographs of the places being discussed. I wanted to *see* the collapsed section of the West Side Highway, the Cross-Bronx Expressway, the Williamsburg Bridge, and many other things mentioned here, along with maps, plans, etc. There are a few images here (less than a dozen, I believe), but the book would have been *greatly* improved if there were ten times that many.

The author is a first-wave babyboomer, and grew up in the shadow of Brooklyn's famed Ebbets Field ... before his beloved (Trolley) Dodgers up and moved to Los Angeles. His development was in the streets of Brooklyn in at time where you still could play stick ball without getting killed by traffic, and a lot of that sensibility informs this book ... especially the sense of how things have evolved over the years with the rise of the automobile. Oh, and he's also widely credited as being the person who came up with the term "gridlock" ... in a 1980 New York Transportation Department memo looking for ways to avoid that particular traffic manifestation.

Early on he defines the book's focus: it *"tells the story of a transformation in the common travel decisions made daily and weekly in the industrial world generally, and the United States specifically ... getting ourselves to work, to shopping, to social encounters, and to entertainment – how we've done so historically, and how we're going to be doing so in the future."*. And, one of the key concepts he frames as: *"Vehicles come and go. Buildings go up and come down. Roads last forever."*

Except, of course, when they don't. *"On Saturday morning, December15, 1973, the forty-year-old West Side Highway ... collapsed under the weight of a truck carrying more than thirty tons of asphalt. ... A day later, the road was closed indefinitely ..."* – leaving eighty thousand cars a day to find an alternate route. This is the first point when "things get weird" here:

> The predicted traffic disaster never appeared. Somehow, those eighty thousand cars went somewhere, but to this day we have no idea where. Or how, two years later, twenty-five thousand more people were getting into Manhattan's Central Business District.

He refers to this as "the counterintuitive phenomenon known as *disappearing traffic*", and notes that "lane closures not only cause traffic to decrease on the road's remaining lanes, *but only half the decrease reappears anywhere else*".

That sort of reality is a mystery to all involved ... but there are "less mysterious" things at work here too ... in many cases there were serious prejudices built into the available information – cables whose useful lifespan was being represented at 10% of the actual figure, while beams which were "cracked and perforated" by corrosion not even being considered in projections (this is what failed in the WSH collapse). This came up in the context of the Williamsburg Bridge, an 1909 construction that carried 350,000 people a day. Much like the mysterious disappearing traffic, there was a reality here that was surprising – narrower lanes were safer than wider lanes – and *fixing* the existing bridge (with narrow lanes) rather than tearing it down and replacing it with a "state of the art" bridge (which would have also required bulldozing *"two of the most vibrant and prosperous neighborhoods in the entire country"*, the Lower East Side in Manhattan, and Williamsburg in Brooklyn) is something the author had to fight strongly for.

Another unexpected change he notes is that of the driving habits of the Millennials:

> ... in 2009, Millennials drove 23 percent fewer miles on average than their same-age predecessors did in 2001. That is, their average mileage – VMT, or vehicle miles traveled – plummeted from 10,300 miles a year to 7.900 ... In every five-year period from 1945 to 2004, Americans had driven more miles than they did the half-decade before ... but by 2011, the average American was driving 6 percent fewer miles than in 2004 ... if all eighty million Millennials retain their current driving habits for the next twenty-five years ... per capita VMT ... will fall off the table.

This was a total surprise ... even as these trends started to manifest, federal Transportation Department officials were predicting a doubling of VMT over 20 years ... and, like in the case of bridge traffic, there were "experts" who flat-out rejected the possibility of the long-term patterns no longer being valid.

The author also argues that American "car culture" didn't happen by accident, but was created by government programs that encouraged suburban sprawl – *"houses whose cost per square foot was so much lower than that of the available housing stock in densely populated urban centers"* –

> *Which is exactly what happened with the GI Bill's requirement that government-guaranteed home loans only go to <u>new</u> construction, or the Eisenhower administration's decision to build forty thousand miles of heavily subsidized highways. The relative advantage of car-dependent suburban living didn't come from impersonal forces of the market in action, but from a sequence of decisions made by fallible human beings, decisions that could very easily have gone in an entirely different direction. ... Fifty years of sprawl in America then does, in fact, look a lot like a fifty-year mistake – one that didn't need to happen.*

Of course, this all followed the conspiracy that was a central plot point in the movie *Who Framed Roger Rabbit?* – buying streetcar lines simply to shut them down in favor of car transport.

> *For more than a decade beginning in 1936, two shell companies – National City Lines and Pacific City Lines, owned by General Motors, Firestone Tires, Standard Oil of California, Phillips Petroleum, and other huge companies with what you might call a strong bias in favor of gasoline-powered transportation – bought more than a hundred electric train and trolley systems in at least forty-five American cities ...*

Notably, the same did *not* happen in Europe and other parts of the world, with trolley and similar transit options being a key part of the cities' transportation mix on through the present. Schwartz looks at both various European examples, and the rather remarkable recent history of public transit in Bogotá, Columbia where the city has narrowed streets (by expanding sidewalks) and has even banned cars on particular days.

Street Smart[5] goes into a lot more stuff than I've been able to touch on here ... including looking at various transit systems in U.S. cities, self-driving cars (and other futurist concepts), and more historical details (as well as the author's "war stories" from his days in the NYC DOT) ... but I think you get the idea. Again, for a subject that could be expected to be fairly dry, it's coverage here is breezy and engaging – quite a bonus to the information that's presented. This is quite new (just out a couple of months at this writing), so should be easy enough to find at bookstores (when you can find book stores), and the on-line big boys have it more than a third off of cover price. If you're interested in the whole matrix of cars and cities and transportation (and Brooklyn sport teams), you'll find this quite an agreeable read.

Notes:
1. http://btripp-books.livejournal.com/175940.html
2. http://sharedusemobilitycenter.org/2015-summit/
3. http://btripp-books.livejournal.com/175716.html
4-5. http://amzn.to/1jprgX6

Saturday, November 14, 2015[1]

Have you ever wondered ...

This is another of those books that I'm pretty sure wouldn't have found its way into my library if not for the dollar store ... rah, rah, rah for serendipity, I suppose. However, poking through the books at my most-frequented Dollar Tree (of the five in town that I know how to get on public transportation), I saw Shirley McLaine's What If . . . : A Lifetime of Questions, Speculations, Reasonable Guesses, and a Few Things I Know for Sure[2], and I just couldn't find a good argument for passing it up for a buck. Not that I'm a *fan* in particular of Ms. McLaine ... although her years of media ubiquity are long past, she's still a bit of a punch-line first and an actress/dancer second when searching through my mental files.

In some sense this is a "gimmick" book, it's a collection of "what it?" musings on a variety of subjects, running from one or two sentences (there are a lot of pages with just that much text – quick read!), such as:

> *What if our subconscious controls out destiny?*
>
> or
>
> *What if evolution itself is speeding up?*
>
> or
>
> *What if there really is reincarnation?*

... etc., etc., etc. ... on to longer biographical pieces (like 24 pages inspired by her getting a Lifetime Achievement Award from the American Film Institute in 2012), with most (well, most might be the 1-2 sentence ones) clocking in at 2-4 pages. One thing I found quite odd was that there were two or three sections that *didn't* start off with "what if" ... but somehow these didn't feel like they were there in some 4th-way "look for what seems out of place" state of significance, but more like they were somehow stuff that she just couldn't figure out how to phrase in a "what if" structure.

The subject matter is all over the place, from reminiscences of "the old days" in Hollywood, to the expected "space aliens" and assorted woo-woo spirituality, to quasi-political ramblings (for having come out in 2013, she still sure has a bug up her butt about Dick Cheney). Interestingly, one of the more "things that make you go *hmmmm*" entries here starts off with a "what if" about Cheney ... it's talking about "cellular memory" and the effects observed in transplant patients:

> *Medical reports say that heart transplant patients often undergo a change of philosophy, personality, and values once they recover from surgery. The heart is a special organ, not to mention one that has tremendous cultural, symbolic, and psychological meaning. ... Transplant transference has occurred in many heart recipients. ... {One} transplant*

> recipient, a health-conscious choreographer, found herself inexplicably attracted to all kinds of junk food, ... She also began behaving in an aggressive and impetuous manner that was uncharacteristic of her, but was like the personality of her organ donor.

Another interesting section here deals with the "usual suspects" among the Founding Fathers leaving behind writings indicating that they believed in a "plurality of worlds", and claims that

> Franklin ... wondered if there was a God for every inhabited planet.

She even uses that ever-convincing *"Ancient astronaut theorists claim ..."* phrase several times (of course – <u>ALIENS!</u>[3]). On the plus side, she mentions a character I'd not previously heard of ... a free black man by the name of Benjamin Banneker, who was a surveyor who participated in laying out the various "mystical patterns" incorporated into Washington D.C.'s <u>design</u>[4]. What is notable here is that he was supposedly from the Dogon tribe, the same group that is purported to have had a great deal of advanced scientific knowledge maintained in their myths, included detailed information on the Pleiades ... which she claims the Washington Monument is sited to align with on particular days. Oh, she also lets us know which revolutionary era figure she believes she's a reincarnation of ... but you'd be disappointed if she didn't, wouldn't you?

Again, this book is all over the map ... but every once in a while it lands squarely in the "preaching to the choir" (in terms of my beliefs), and that's always refreshing. I especially liked the following, from a piece where she's bitching about the TSA (where she notes that, over the years of radiating us, has discovered via the x-ray scans 0 terrorist threats, 1,485 hernias, and 3 natural blondes):

> More important than any of the aforementioned, what if the "security" measure have never been predominantly about security, but more about the purposeful dumbing-down of Americans, making us subservient to control and authority? What if the point of amplifying fear is to render the population cooperative with its own individual captivity? Fear breed handing over control, and handing over control breeds cooperative dumbing-down. In the name of protecting freedom and democracy, we've become prisoners of our own induced obedience.

Preach that libertarian philosophy, girl!

Needless to say, the book is "uneven", with a lot of goofy open-ended "what ifs" (what are we supposed to do with *"What if we could experience psychic liberation?"*?), but these are ephemeral enough that they don't really effect the over-all tone of the book. There are moments of actual "deep thinking" here about significant topics, and the autobiographical bits are often quite fascinating. I doubt many people would find McClaine's <u>What If ...</u>[5] a life-changing read, but it's light, informative, and entertaining, so is a good "treat" if one's been delving into too many "heavy" books.

This is still in print in both hardcover and paperback (and various other formats), so it must have its audience out there. Like many books that have found their way into the dollar store channel, the hardcover can be had for a penny (four bucks with shipping) in "very good" condition. Obviously, if you stumble across this at a Dollar Tree, do pick it up – for a buck you can't go wrong ... but you might even consider it in the retail channels, if the above sounds appealing enough.

Notes:

1. http://btripp-books.livejournal.com/176281.html
2. http://amzn.to/1G3n7C8
3. http://cdn.meme.am/instances/500x/28178966.jpg
4. http://btripp-books.livejournal.com/84056.html
5. http://amzn.to/1G3n7C8

Sunday, November 15, 2015[1]

What we are becoming ...

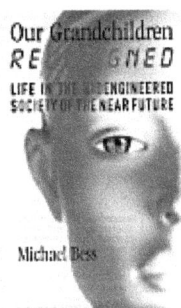

I got this book via the LibraryThing.com "Early Reviewers" program, and like most (if not all) of the books featured there, it was a bit of a "pig in a poke", as the information one is provided to make one's request decisions is typically a scant few sentences about each featured book. Fortunately, Michael Bess' Our Grandchildren Redesigned: Life in the Bioengineered Society of the Near Future[2] is pretty good ... a bit "more than I really wanted to know" on the topic, but certainly interesting and informative. I have some friends who are *very* into the thought of "posthuman" existence (especially into living forever), and this book would be *ideal* for them ... for everybody else, well, it might be a bit speculative. However, in this case, the speculation is backed up by a metric s-load of research ... the book itself is only 216 pages, which is followed with another 70 (one-third more) pages of bibliography and notes (and in this case you have to follow along in the end notes, as there are frequent major chunks of text back there supporting arguments or adding context for things in main part).

The book is structured in four sections, "Humans Redesigned", "Justice", "Identity", and "Choices". With four to six chapters each, looking at specific topics. Part of me wants to rattle these off, but there are a LOT of them. One of the admirable elements to the book is how it's integrated with a companion web site. Now, I've had bad luck with companion sites in the past (they have a bad habit of being neglected, if not ending up 404'd), but this one looks like it's a *very* well designed web site (well, with the glaring exception that the "Dialog Page", featuring what would no doubt be a fascinating forum for the various topics, is empty, and requiring one to be "logged in" - despite what appears to be the fact that one can neither register to log in, nor log in if one were registered – to start a discussion), which notably features 16 appendices of follow-up information for various parts of the book, plus "update" sections, featuring recent articles in the Science/Technology area (the first section of the book, featuring Artificial Intelligence, Bioelectronics, Genetics, Nanotechnology, Pharmaceuticals, Robotics, and Synthetic Biology) as well as the Social/Cultural arena (the three other sections, Choices, Identity, Justice). This is at the unwieldy, albeit unmistakable http://www.ourgrandchildrenredesigned.org/[3].

One of the interesting format elements here is that most chapters start with a "brief fictional vignette" which, while (naturally enough) somewhat sci-fi, allow the author to paint a rather vibrant picture of how some of these enhancements/developments might play out. There was one snippet of one of these that I found particularly engaging – part of a story about a sort of rescue shelter for bio-engineered "mistakes", this being an encounter with a orangutan which had been engineered with *"twenty percent human cognition-related genes"*:

> *She led him towards a side door. "There's one more guy I'd like you to meet before lunch. Over in*

> that small red barn over there. His name's Jeremy.
>
> He followed her into the barn. Same musky smell, only more pungent. A dappled light coming through the skylight. Steel bars, the whole place a cage. A thatched hut over in the far corner of the cage, woven from sheaves of grass and leaves.
>
> "Jeremy," she called out, "You have a visitor."
>
> Silence.
>
> David peered into the darkness, his eyes adjusting. A holo screen on the wall lit up. Letters began appearing, forming words.
>
> GO WAY.
>
> David looked at her, but she ignored him.
>
> "Come on, Jeremy. Just a few minutes so you can meet your new friend David."
>
> He noticed she was speaking more slowly and clearly than usual.
>
> Silence. Then letters.
>
> SLEPING.
>
> "No, you're not. You're just being unfriendly."
>
> THRO POOP.
>
> "You better not! If you want dinner today."
>
> Rustling, the grass parted, and he came out. An orangutan. About one-and-a-half meters tall, a huge round face, round brown eyes. He stood leaning forward, holding a large wireless keyboard in his left hand.
>
> ...
>
> "So ... why's he here? Why wasn't he considered a success?"
>
> "Because he's miserable, that's why. He's tried three times to commit suicide."

I have quite a few little bookmarks though this, flagging things that I felt were particularly notable. There is *so much stuff* covered in Our Grandchildren Redesigned[4] that I won't try to walk you through it all, but will hopefully be able to give you a sense of what's in here by dropping in on the bits I felt were worth a slip of paper …

In the Envisioning The Future chapter, the author lays down some cognitive grids to consider these developments, a chronological division into Long Structural Processes (50 years or more), Short Structural Processes (20-50 years), and Conjunctural Processes (1-20 years), which get further elaborated with:

> But here, another aspect of our three-tiered list comes into play. Novel technologies tend to change more quickly, radically, and unpredictably than human social, economic, and cultural institu-

> tion. The rise of the Internet, for example, became a major historical phenomenon in less than twenty years, but phenomena like racial prejudice, class conflict, gender bias, and similar social and cultural factors tend to evolve much more slowly. The implication is clear: we are likely to do better at predicting general patterns of the coming century, we should not try to foresee too precisely which technologies will exist in different decades. If we insist on doing so, we are likely to end up pulling a Rutherford.

Of course, one has to *love* that phrase "pulling a Rutherford", which refers to the great physicist Lord Ernest Rutherford, known as the "father of nuclear physics", who came up with the concept of radioactive half-life, among many other discoveries, yet totally dismissed the possibility of harnessing atomic energy just a scant dozen years before Hiroshima and Nagasaki were introduced to it.

In the Pharmaceuticals chapter, in a discussion of the development of memory-enhancing drugs (some of which are in clinical trials), Bess notes:

> The notion of boosting memory in humans sounds at first like a terrific development. I would be able to learn foreign languages faster, recall more accurately the names of people and places I have known, find my car keys without a lot of cursing and fuss. But what about forgetting? When we examine the functioning of memory as a practical component in a person's daily life, we find that it is just as important to be able to selectively lose information as to retain it. Without this ability we would rapidly find ourselves drowning in a sea of trivial details, impressions, emotions, and images.

He takes a look at various pills that are currently on the market (interestingly, most of these were not *developed* to be brain or mood enhancers), and how new sorts of research are able to push the envelope as researchers learn more about the underlying biology/chemistry of consciousness.

One term that I notably had not previously encountered was "epigenetics", which is dealt with (duh) in the chapter Genetics and Epigenetics. Here is how the author frames this:

> The new scientific field that studies these patterns of genetic activation and transcription is known as epigenetics. Though definitions vary, an epigenetic process can best be describe as any molecular mechanism that changes the expression of genetic information without altering the underlying DNA sequence itself. The DNA code stays the same, but certain portions of it are selectively silenced, while others are spurred to action, resulting in dramatically different phenotypic outcomes. ... In recent

> years, scientists have discovered a variety of epigenetic mechanisms that allow the DNA script to be read differently by the body's cells under distinct circumstances; the two most common of these are known as DNA methylation and histone acetylation. These two molecular mechanisms act like volume knobs on particular segments of DNA: one mechanism (methylation) turns down the potency of expression for a given section of code, all the way down to a whisper; the other (acetylation) cranks it up to a shout.

He notes that this approach is likely to allow *temporary* changes, as it alters how individual genes are expressed, without messing with the underlying code ... an important factor if genetic research speeds up, and you don't want to get stuck with "outmoded" enhancements.

Moving out of the tech section and into the "Justice" section, Bess puts forth what he refers to as a "meta-list" of "Ten Key Factors in Human Flourishing" to provide a moral framework for addressing these extremely disruptive trends. These fall under two categories, the *Individual Dimension* which includes Security, Dignity, Autonomy, Personal Fulfillment, Authenticity, and Pursuit of Practical Wisdom, and the *Societal Dimension* which includes Fairness, Interpersonal Connection, Civic Engagement, and Transcendence. He adds:

> Here, therefore, lies and excellent framework for evaluating enhancement technologies. For each of the enhancements described in this book, we can hold up an ethical yardstick by asking, "Does this device or modification contribute to human flourishing, or does it not?"

In the chapter "A Fragmenting Species?", he returns to the concept of epigenetics:

> As I described earlier, two kinds of human genetic engineering may become available over the coming decades. One form, germline reengineering, would require making changes to the DNA of individuals soon after the moment of conception. The other method, epigenetic modification, would target the molecular mechanisms that regulate DNA expression (while leaving the underlying DNA unchanged). In principle, both methods could generate powerful modifications to the body and mind of the individuals, but the epigenetic pathway would possess two major advantages. Whereas germline engineering would be a one-shot deal, fixed and irreversible, epigenetic modifications would be flexible, reversible, and upgradeable over time. Furthermore, while alterations to the germline would have to be made by parents on behalf of their just-

> *conceived offspring, epigenetic modifications would be available throughout a person's lifetime and will therefore result (in most cases) from choices that individuals will be making for themselves as the years go by.*

He goes on to look at some of the ethical issues of the germline modifications, how a child, although "engineered" to be a tennis or cello prodigy might not have the attitude necessary to excel in the path his or her parents chose. This is one of the places that I felt the author could have "enhanced" the telling by including some popular culture reference, in this case *The Boys From Brazil*, which featured a number of clones of Adolf Hitler, most of which had no interest in anything like world conquest (although there was that one right at the end...). Obviously, this was a minor quibble, but one that came up in my reading when I'd hit passages where I'd be thinking "wow, that's just like X", and wondering why he'd missed that (he does refer to the Star Wars clone armies at one point, and uses Vonnegut's "ice nine" as an example of unintended results of technological developments).

In the chapter "Why Extreme Modifications Should Be Postponed", the author sets out *"three levels of possible human enhancement"* ...

> ■ *Low-level modifications: Capabilities at the high end of today's human range.*
> ■ *Mid-level modifications: Capabilities well beyond today's human range, but still recognizably human.*
> ■ *High-level modifications: Capabilities utterly beyond human parameters.*

He further notes that *"This latter form of high-level metamorphosis appears to be what many transhumanists eagerly envision for themselves."*, and later adds:

> *... the act of undergoing extreme transmogrification inevitably entails serious risks, not just for the person doing it, but for the rest of humankind as well. Such acts of creation would bring into being new kinds of "posthuman" entities that have the potential of being extremely powerful and uncontrollable. We have no way of knowing how they would behave toward the rest of the biosphere – including all other sentient beings on our planet.*

This was another place where I felt a pop-culture reference would help frame the concept – in this case bringing up the character of Doctor Manhattan[5] the "posthuman god" of the Watchmen comics (and movie), which is, I believe, *exactly* the sort of being that Bess is worried about unleashing here.

In the chapter "What You and I Can Do Today" he outlines *"five tangible goals people can work for as they mobilize to influence the development of human biotechnologies"*:

> 1. Mandate basic education in science, technology, and society (STS).
>
> 2. Build "bioethics coalitions" across the left-right divide.
>
> 3. Create a strong governmental agency for technology assessment.
>
> 4. Adopt the precautionary principle[6] in crafting bioenhancement legislation.
>
> 5. Strengthen international cooperation in governing technology.

Obviously, the assumption here is that without a strong, stable, and wide-reaching "ethic" for channeling these developments along approved lines, the "genie will be out of the bottle" soon enough, with the possibilities of rogue states creating armies of super soldiers, or wealthy individuals trying to get to that "god" level. One of the things I've not touched on here, and which the author spends a lot of time with, is the economic concern ... how a "baseline" of enhancements will likely have to be funded globally, to ensure that less-developed parts of the world (or poorer parts of individual countries) don't devolve into a Morlock-like subservient sub-species, while the well-to-do evolve into the Eloi (another pop-culture citation – that of H.G. Wells' *The Time Machine* that could have well be used here).

In the "Enhancing Humility" chapter Bess posits an interesting cultural generalization:

> <u>Reform works better than revolution.</u> Strategies of slow, incremental change have succeeded far better at achieving the aims of historical actors than strategies of sudden, drastic change. ... it leaps out at me from the mass of historical events with such intuitive force that I feel compelled to take it seriously. I bring it up here because it has major implications for how our society chooses to pursue the bioenhancement enterprise over the coming century.

I would love to just stick in the next page or so here, where he contrasts the French revolution ending up in "the iron rule of Napoleon", the Marxist revolution ending up as "a bizarre Orwellian nightmare under Stalin", and the Maoist revolution ending up "in the famine of 1958-1962 and vicious factional strife of the Cultural Revolution", with the slow achievement of Women's rights "over a dozen generations", the growth of rights and power in Western democracies (with working conditions starkly in contrast to those detailed in the works of Charles Dickens), and the evolving status of Black rights over the past century, but that would be way too long. However, he goes on to say:

> ... Gradual reform, in short is not just morally superior because of its generally nonviolent character; it is also more <u>effective</u> in the long run, engendering forms of enduring change that penetrate deeply

into the fabric of society, altering hearts and minds as well as institutions.

When it comes to the pursuit of the enhancement enterprise, therefore, our society would do well to take the comparative history of reform and revolution into account. We should choose the long, slow, plodding road rather than the shining superhighway of radical change. Technological innovation may indeed be accelerating, but we should not allow it to transform our lives more rapidly than our social, cultural, and moral frameworks can absorb. If we permit enhancement technologies to advance too quickly, the resultant stresses could end up massively destabilizing our civilization, perhaps even tearing it apart.

Our Grandchildren Redesigned[7] has only been out for a month at this writing, so should be available in bookstores that have futurist stock. The online big boys, of course, have it at a substantial discount (currently 36% off of cover), but oddly, quite reasonable *new* copies are in the new/used channel, that even *with* shipping come in at about a 60% discount. Frankly, this book was quite the firehose of information, but if you're into the things under discussion in it, I'm sure it will be quite a gripping read ... it's certainly one of those topics that is *not* going away, and having read this will put you in a place of at least not being categorically surprised when these strange new worlds start manifesting around you!

Notes:
1. http://btripp-books.livejournal.com/176509.html
2. http://amzn.to/1ONqAGq
3. http://www.ourgrandchildrenredesigned.org/
4. http://amzn.to/1ONqAGq
5. http://farm4.static.flickr.com/3122/2679729870_9b93856ec7_o.jpg
6. http://unesdoc.unesco.org/images/0013/001395/139578e.pdf
7. http://amzn.to/1ONqAGq

Saturday, November 21, 2015[1]

A really good autobiographical book ...

This was one of those delightful dollar store finds ... something I picked up pretty much because it wasn't a novel, and was in an interesting enough subject (a memoir from somebody with whom I was at least vaguely familiar), and was, of course, *just a buck*. Of course, part of the reason I picked this up is that my younger daughter is in a performing arts program in school, and is also taking classes at Second City, so it was as "paternally focused" as the "women in engineering" books I've read largely because my elder daughter is studying to be an engineer.

Needless to say, the name Alan Arkin rang a bell, so his An Improvised Life: a Memoir[2] came with a certain degree of familiarity, however, I was rather surprised at how few of his roles I remembered from his IMDB profile[3] ... admittedly, I'm hardly a movie buff, and I think I've seen only a handful of the dozens of films he's been in (including not seeing stuff like *Argo* or *Gattaca* that were pretty big). I guess a lot of that is because my "mental image" of him is his later-years manifestation, such as The Chief in the 2008 *Get Smart* movie, and not in his younger roles in things like 1970's *Catch-22*, or (a movie that I *very* much enjoyed as a 9-year-old) 1966's *The Russians Are Coming The Russians Are Coming* ... an image not much shifted by the pic on the cover, which is him at about age 75.

One of the issues/problems I have with stuff that's not straight non-fiction, is that there tends to be a lot less "essential factoids" that will be screaming out for me to flag for future reference. In fact, it appears that I only stuck *one* of my little torn-paper bookmarks in this (which I'll quote from later), so I'm probably going to be doing more summarizing and paraphrasing in this review than usual. It was, frankly, a bit frustrating, as in numerous places he'd start with a couple of strong sentences towards a particular "bullet point" of a concept, but then take the text on a somewhat circuitous route (no doubt "the scenic route", lending a lot more interest to the telling than what would have been convenient for *my* purposes) to get where he was going with it.

Arkin appears to be one of those rare people that knew what he wanted to do from his earliest years. He notes that, from about age 5, he had decided that he wanted to act, and was *obsessed* with playing roles from pretty much anything he encountered (spending months dancing to a record of a Stravinsky opera his aunt had taken him to – recreating every part). He focused on Charlie Chaplin for a while, and Danny Kaye after that. By age 8 he was even *analyzing* film, citing perceptions such as *"The scene had instantly turned false, and I had the distinct feeling that the performances of the two people in the scene were no longer directed at each other but toward some anonymous audience."*. His growth in this area is one of the most *useful* parts of this book ... as he walks the reader though his engagement with the acting arts as his skills grew, and I'm looking forward to putting it into my actor daughter's hands as soon as I get done with posting the review of this. What is presented as a *memoir* might as well have been marketed as a workshop, as the practical advice given here (if in a narrative rather than a presentation) is well worth the price of admission (in this case, the *cover price*, since, hey, I got it for a buck!).

At the end of World War II, his family packed up and moved from Brooklyn to Los Angeles (preceding the Dodgers by a decade), his dad hoping to get work as a scenery painter in the film industry. Arkin was thrilled to be in Hollywood, and ended up in schools that had acting curriculums. Unfortunately, outside of the acting (which seems to have gone very well for him), the rest of his school experience was pretty horrible. In his senior year he began studying with a Benjamin Zemach (who had worked with Stanislavski), whose theories, at least as they were imparted to Arkin, are illustrated here. Again, where, in other contexts, the amount of reflecting on his inner reactions to stimuli and processing of events/instruction might have seemed fairly self-indulgent, here they provide a level of immersion in the art that I suspect would be useful to any aspiring actor.

In 1954 he got a call from a friend who had stumbled over a pretty amazing situation ... a total free ride at the Bennington College, a girl's school which brought on a handful of guys to act in theater productions. He put together a bag of salami, cheese, and bread, and started to hitch-hike from L.A. to Vermont, just taking a (rather reasonable) week to get cross-country. His contact had disappeared, but the school still had his appointment on the schedule, and he was soon sent to interview with the head of the English department, future poet laureate consultant to the Library of Congress, Howard Nemerov. The two, according to Arkin, hit it off from the start, giving him a fairly secure base at the university. He credits the acting professors there with developing his art, one positively, one via conflict ... unfortunately, his other school work was disastrous, and after a couple of years he parted ways with the college ... partially due to his having recently married a dance student. At that point, Arkin and his new (pregnant) wife headed to New York, with no particular plan.

Being constitutionally unsuited for "jobs", he ended up as part of a folk group called The Tarriers, which began to find some success, a recording contract (their albums[4] are, remarkably, still obtainable), and a European tour. However, mid-way through the tour he had a *"What the hell is this? Who am I?"* moment, realized that he really wanted to *act* and informed the rest of the band that he'd be moving on after the end of the tour. He parlayed his folk guitar chops into a role in an off-Broadway play that needed a lute player (a small part for which he got paid more than anybody else in the production, due to the relative strength of the musicians union contract) ... that ran for over a year, but Arkin determined to drop music afterward.

A few months later, a contact from Bennington got a hold of him and offered him a spot that with an improvisational group that was being set up for a summer run in St. Louis. During that summer, Paul Sills came down from Chicago and liked Arkin's work well enough that he told him if he ever wanted a job in Chicago, to look him up. Arkin, however, returned to New York (and unemployment) after the St. Louis run, and had another kid. This (and the uncertainty of their existence) was too much for his wife, who took the kids and left him. He hung on for a year in New York, hoping for some break, but there was nothing, so in desperation (Chicago was a black hole for theater/movies/etc. back then) he called up Sills and got a job with a hole-in-the-wall theater called Second City.

Second City very quickly got national attention, and in the year Arkin worked there he says he *"gained ten years worth of experience"*. Part of Sills' plan was to open up an extension in New York, and Arkin was one of the main elements of that ... they lasted on Broadway for only 3 months, but a restaurateur fan of theirs set up a club for the troop a block away from New York University, which was quite successful. One of the more charming stories in the book is of an evening when Groucho Marx came to the show, pretty much took it over (via audience suggestion elements), and hung out with the cast long into the night. The New York club was successful for a long time, and actors from it started to get offers for other work, and with their leaving (most of the original group were from Chicago) new blood came in, beginning the upward spiral as an "institution". The one quote that I actually marked in here (largely as it parallels my own educational experience), is from his reflections on this (from a 40th reunion event):

> *We had started out in Second City, all of us, because there was nowhere else to go. We were mavericks, misfits, almost unemployable. Most of the original members of the group had come out of the University of Chicago, where the dean had said publicly, "Get a general education. Don't specialize. You're all smart people; you'll end up on your feet." They took him at his word and as a result the University of Chicago produced a generation of brilliant people who wandered and floundered without finding specific work to do, all of them prospective Second City cast members. I fit right in.*

In New York, Arkin bounced back and forth between Second City and Broadway productions, then he got his first break in film, and built a fairly substantial career in it. In this same time he discovered both therapy and meditation, and discusses what he learned from these ... including a concept of chakras – which his meditation teacher congratulated him on when what he had thought was a heat attack was "actually" "his heart opening". From this, he discovered the work of Michael Checkhov, an acting teacher who had a theory of psychic vortexes, which Arkin incorporated in his work. He also discusses working with other teachers, such as Uta Hagen, and how their theories influenced him.

At this point (about half-way through the book), the narrative becomes somewhat less "life story" and moves more into "acting philosophy", as Arkin shifts into directing, more high-profile projects, running workshops, etc. ... and in each case looking deeply into his motivations, reactions, and experiments with the craft of acting. While this material is *fascinating*, it's also not particularly linear, and would be awfully involved to detail here.

Needless to say, there is a lot to like in An Improvised Life[5] for anybody interested in the performing arts ... plus it's a quite engaging tale in and of itself. This is a reasonably recent book, having come out in 2011, and it is still in print, available from the on-line big boys for about a third off of retail. However, as I noted at the start, this is kicking around in the dollar stores, so if you stumble across it in that setting, do add it to your cart ... as a usual side effect of being in that channel, the new/used guys do have this (in "very good" condition) for as little as a penny (plus shipping, of course). I liked this a lot, felt that I learned quite a bit from reading it, and can't wait to get it to my daughter who's in this world. If you enjoy any of the component parts of this, I'm pretty sure you'll really like this, and recommend the heck out of it!

Notes:

1. http://btripp-books.livejournal.com/176682.html
2. http://amzn.to/1kMsJH6
3. http://www.imdb.com/name/nm0000273/
4. http://amzn.to/1QBfoPl
5. http://amzn.to/1kMsJH6

Sunday, November 22, 2015[1]

Building wealth, starting from zero ...

I have been "sitting" on this one for quite a while. As those of you out there "stalking" me across my social media platforms no doubt know, I have recently started a new project with a division of Transamerica which is set up to provide "financial education"[2], and I had gotten into studying the assorted materials related to *that* just before I ran across this book at the dollar store. Because of that sequence of events, I was *thrilled* to find that Bernard Kelly's Flipping Burgers to Flipping Millions: A Guide to Financial Freedom Whether You Have Your Dream Job, Own Your Own Business, or Just Started Your First Job[3] was focused very much on the same sorts of approaches. As a matter of fact, I was *so* enthused that I spent a day trekking off to five of the six Dollar Tree locations that I can get to via public transportation in Chicago, hoping to stock up on a bunch of copies of this to give out to folks (frustratingly, the only one which had any copies was my regular one where I'd found this in the first place, and they only had another 5 copies in stock).

I'm somewhat surprised that this book hasn't become an instant classic, as it's a combination of an inspirational personal story, and a step-by-step process for creating wealth – especially in the hands of a young person. The author himself is pretty young ... 30 years old at the time of writing in 2011 ... but he had built a net worth of around a half a million dollars by *working at McDonald's*. He didn't (like my girlfriend from college) start as a manager – he came out of high school (where he found himself "failing class after class", in fact he claimed that he graduated not being able to read) at 17 and got a job at McDonald's making fries ... then doing the titular flipping burgers.

Needless to say, this is about a low on the wealth ladder as one can start, but if there was one thing that sets the author apart from others in his position, is that he *"became fascinated with all things McDonald's"*, and after encountering a group of McDonald's executives who came through on a store tour he decided:

> *"I could do what they do. I could be good at what they do. This is something I can really succeed at."*

Which he follows up with the observation:

> *The day you can say to yourself, "This is my thing," is a great day.*

Again, the author stands out by his willingness to apply himself to the opportunities presenting themselves to him (in contrast to the mobs demanding a $15/hr wage for flipping burgers), and taught himself to read (!) and immersed himself in the *"people, systems, and processes that make up the McDonald's world"*. Further:

> *It wasn't long before my passion was recognized.*

> *Passion stands out in any environment, but the more mundane the environment or job, the more passion stands out. I worked hard and produced measurable results. I was promoted over and over again. By the time I was twenty-five, I was a store manager, and throughout the process the McDonald's Corporation was educating me. I attended every course that was offered. I was hungry to learn everything I could about this business, and to grow as a person.*

Obviously, Bernard Kelly, despite having been a massive failure in school (to the extent of coming out unable to read), was able to see something in his situation that the semi-sentient slugs so often in the same positions were either incapable or unwilling to consider. He has a fascinating list of prominent people whose first jobs were at McDonald's, including Amazon's zillionaire founder Jeff Bezos. However, Flipping Burgers to Flipping Millions[4] isn't really *about* McDonald's (although it is an obvious anchor of the author's story), but a look at how anybody (especially somebody just getting started) can build wealth, even if starting from nothing. Kelly notes:

> *Money and the creation of wealth are not that difficult to understand. You save some money, invest it, and it multiplies. Save a little bit, often enough, for long enough, and it will become an enormous fortune. The problem is that most people cannot think beyond today and what they want to spend their money on right now. They do not have a vision for their life ten years from now, or twenty years from now, and nobody saves money for a future that they have not yet imagined.*

Aside from the cultural factors, generally speaking we don't teach kids about money management (the level of "financial illiteracy" is stunning), the author points out (regarding "the unchanging laws of money"):

> *We don't teach it in high school, we don't teach it in college, and we don't teach it in the business world. … In the corporate world I am amazed at how often we put people in charge of million-dollar budgets who cannot manage their own personal budget.*

Again, this book is full of really awesome quotes, here's one that I found particularly notable (comparing regular investment with a dripping faucet eventually wearing a hole in a rock slab):

> *A little bit of pressure – saving and investing – consistently applied over time can create an incredible fortune. … For example, if a person saved $1 a day for her entire life and invested it with a return of 10 percent, she would retire at sixty-five years of age with $2,404,853. One dollar a day is just like that dripping faucet. … It is difficult, but it is not impossi-*

> ble. What makes it difficult is not that it requires some extraordinary set of skills, but that it requires the discipline of consistency in a world dominated by erratic impulse.

Kelly defines four stages of one's financial life: Right Now – Quality of Life – Retirement – Legacy ... and devotes a chapter each to these, walking the reader through strategies to maximize one's wealth building in each, including multiple options ("good, better, and best") for achieving different levels.

For a relatively slim book (a mere 160 pages) this is remarkably comprehensive in terms of scope. Before it moves into the four stages of life, the author presents a chapter which has a central section of "How To Be A Great Employee", with seven steps which pretty much *anybody* would benefit from if enacted in their own lives. He then has a chapter on "the basics of wealth creation". Unfortunately for most, these basics require things like discipline, the willingness to delay gratification, and the capability to set goals, and maintain the desire to achieve them (with the quote from Henry David Thoreau that *"In the long run, men only hit what they aim at."*). For most people, much of this is *very* uncomfortable, with the realities of what one needs to have by retirement to produce a comfortable income being especially daunting. One of the exercises he offers here is looking at what that purchase you're considering today will have "cost" by retirement age. A fancy big TV system that costs $4,280 today, would represent a value of $68,480 in 30 years (again, the figures in the book to tend towards those starting out their financial lives), and that opting for a $1,500 TV (still a pretty fancy unit!) would "save" you $34,240 over that period of time. Obviously, this is sort of "modified gratification", where you're making deals with yourself between what you might *want* vs. what you actually *need*, in regards to how it would effect your future finances.

One thing he brings up as "almost legendary" is something that *I* hadn't heard about previously, the "Latte Factor" ... this counts up small regular *indulgences* that build up over time – the author says that instead of Lattes, for him it was cigarettes in his youth – figuring a $5/day habit. If instead of consuming $5/day of fancy coffees or smokes, one were to *invest* the equivalent $150.00/month, at the end of 40 years that would have built up to just shy of a million dollars! It's amazing how most people don't think they can find $150/mo to invest, yet they'll blithely spend on trivial expenses like high-priced coffees, fast food lunches (as opposed to bringing one's own), and the like.

Another "factoid" which I found disturbing was that *"The average American spends 106 percent of his or her annual income annually."* Needless to say, there's *no way* that one can "build wealth" doing that. He also notes that *"Less than 10 percent of Americans have and use a budget."*, and that a budget is essential to, well, *budgeting* money for investing.

Again, the issue of what one *needs* vs. what one might want comes into play here. I must admit that the author was rather extreme in his willingness to "go without" ... he challenged himself to not buy any clothes for an entire year, and he did not "indulge" in buying a car until he was 30, using public transportation to get around. He goes on an interesting side piece on the self-storage industry in the U.S. – using it as an example of how much "extra stuff" most of us have ... to the extent that *"In the United States today, the self-storage business is larger than the motion picture business."*(!).

He recommends way to make some of this self-denying fun, with things like "Zero Dollar Days" where one strives to not spend *anything* for the day. The flip side of this is what he calls "Guilt-Free Money", an amount that one sets aside to spend on anything one wants once a month.

In the first phase of the 4-stage program, he looks at what one could expect to be making starting out at age 18 working for McDonald's, and how that would likely increase over 8 years. Now, here again I think the author is a bit of an outlier ... in his good-better-best figures it goes saving 10% of one's income to saving 30%, the latter being what *he* did from ages 18 to 25. The total paychecks for those 8 years come to $245,567 and he was able to save $135,326 (with interest) over that period, which invested through age 65 would be over six million dollars. Now, he is aware that the assumptions for returns on investment sound pretty extreme, but he also notes that if one had bought McDonald's shares, the return would have been in excess of 10%.

Now, if one has been diligent in one's early years, it sets one up to be able to spend pretty much what one makes in the next phase, but continued saving/investing would be better, especially in terms of putting money away for one's kids. He has some other eye-opening figures about houses, etc., and how making a choice to live a bit more simply (and invest the difference) can make huge returns down the line.

Obviously, the last two parts, on retirement and "legacy" really depend on the previous phases, as it's mighty hard to *start* planning once one gets to retirement, let alone considering any sort of (positive) financial legacy. Interestingly, part of what Kelly considers *his* legacy is the lessons imparted in this book. I know that I was eager to get copies of this into the hands of my daughters (and I *really* hope they'll read it – but "you can take a horse to water" and all, and one of the hardest things for a parent to do is to *force* a kid to read something they're not inclined to).

The final chapter in Flipping Burgers to Flipping Millions[5] is something of a rah-rah session about McDonald's, which I found somewhat irritating at the time of reading it, but in reflection, it's pretty much all the author knows firsthand, and the points he raises are certainly good illustrations of the principles in the book in practice. There is, however, one *glaring* fault with the book ... in several places the author points the reader to a web site, http://www.MoneyClassroom.com[6] ...which, four years after the book's release, is "under construction" with a field to put in one's email to get notified when it goes live. The "whois" listing doesn't seem to have anything to do with the author or his publisher, so I wonder if somehow over the past four years the domain got lost and is being "squatted" by another group. It's a pity, as the references in the book to the site sound like there was supposed to be some interesting material there.

Anyway, this is one of those that I would recommend to "all and sundry", especially as the recommendation in it hone so closely to my own "financial literacy" project[7]. It appears to not currently be in print (expect via the publisher), except for in the e-book format, however the new/used guys have it with "very good" copies for as little as a penny, and new copies for under a buck (plus shipping). If you can find it in the dollar stores, pick it up ... I wish I'd been able to get more copies via that channel myself!

Notes:

1. http://btripp-books.livejournal.com/176974.html
2. http://xcurvewealth.com/
3-5. http://amzn.to/1MCB75e
6. http://www.moneyclassroom.com/
7. http://xcurvewealth.com/

Tuesday, December 1, 2015[1]

Freak Think ...

I'm not exactly sure what I was thinking I was getting into when I ordered Steven D. Levitt & Stephen J. Dubner's Think Like a Freak: The Authors of Freakonomics Offer to Retrain Your Brain[2], sure, I'd read the authors' Freakonomics[3] and Super Freakonomics[4], but this was supposedly something different, something offering to "retrain" my brain ... how fun would that be? I was even thinking this might be in the same territory as Chris Brogan's The Freaks Shall Inherit the Earth[5], if, perhaps, not so much focused on the entrepreneurial crowd. However, although it was an entertaining, interesting read, it really didn't significantly engage me ... I ended up with a paltry 3 little slips of paper pointing me to "the good parts" in this, and all those in the first half ... a good indication that I'd "given up" trying to extract info and just opted to enjoy the book. Not a bad thing, but it sucks as the basis of a useful review.

One thing that did stand out a bit, and that this was a bit self-referential. I don't recall from their earlier books if they wrote as much about *themselves*, but there are significant stories here based on their own experiences, at least a couple catching my attention. Since I flagged so few things to mention, I'm just going to wing it, *and* fall back on the crutch of listing the chapter headings to give you a sense of whatever arc the book has:

1. What Does It Mean to Think Like a Freak?
2. The Three Hardest Words in the English Language
3. What's Your Problem?
4. Like a Bad Dye Job, the Truth is in the Roots
5. Think Like a Child
6. Like Giving Candy to a Baby
7. What Do King Solomon and David Lee Roth Have in Common?
8. How to Persuade People Who Don't Want to Be Persuaded
9. The Upside of Quitting

The book starts off with a little bit of snark, which I think is one of most telling points they cover ... it's a follow-up question to a previous subject (they get a lot of mail, it seems): *"Whatever happened to the carpal tunnel syndrome epidemic?"* – their answer was *"Once journalists stopped getting it, they stopped writing about it"* – which is something to keep in mind whenever you see a "talking head" yakking about something ... odds are very good that they're trying to score points with their particular "in group" and *aren't* "reporting" anything close to the "truth"! They point out that they can't possibly answer all the questions they get, so they opted to *"write a book that can teach anyone to think like a Freak"* (although, as suggested above, I'm not sure that this achieves that goal).

The first extensive "story" in here deals with soccer ... which I know and appreciate slightly less than paint drying. The particular focus of this is something called a "penalty kick" (no, I don't care enough to Google that, really I don't) which I guess is a major factor in soccer. They note that roughly 75% of these are successful in scoring a goal (which I take it needs a few dozen extra "o"s in it to express the excitement of there actually being a score in the match). They also note that the strategy is generally to kick towards one of the upper corners of the goal, causing the "keeper" to have to decide where to make the big leap – left or right – with leaping to the kicker's left 57% of the time, and to the right 41% of the time. Given that 57+41=98, it suggests that soccer "keeper" vacates the center of the goal in all but 2% of penalty kicks. No doubt due to this math, a full 17% of kicks *are* aimed at the center, but one would expect that *more* would (at least initially), as it would be increasing a 75% rate of scoring to 98% ... however, if your kick ended up as one of the 2%, you'd be in big trouble with the soccer-crazed fans/countries that watch this stuff (the authors suggest that you'd have to *"move your family abroad to avoid assassination"* ... lovely people, these soccer fans). This is where the subject of incentives – the main theme here, and in the other books – comes up. If the kicker does the expected – aiming towards a corner – and is blocked, it's a great play by the keeper, but no shame (assuming the kick isn't wide of the goal) for the kicker. However, if the kicker opts for the higher odds of actually *scoring* – the "greater good", he's risking a lot ... and in 83% of the cases the kicker will go with the *private benefit* instead of the interest of team and/or country.

This is followed by a summation of the key concepts of the previous books:

- Incentives are the cornerstone of modern life.
- Knowing what to measure, and how to measure it, can make a complicated world less so.
- The conventional wisdom is often wrong.
- Correlation does not equal causality.

They point out that the biggest blocks to "thinking like a Freak" is not questioning one's own assorted biases, and "running with the herd" (see my comment about the MSM above). They draw on George Bernard Shaw when suggesting that most people really *don't think* much at all, so never get around to thinking about their and/or their associates' biases and reality assumptions. He's quoted as saying: *"Few people think more than two or three times a year ... I have made an international reputation for myself by thinking once or twice a week."* The implication (given that the authors claim to try to think once or twice a week), is that most of the fascinating stuff in the previous books was simply due to having *thought* about it .. be it the data showing that children's car seats are a waste of time and money or that violent crime was reduced by making abortion easily available to inner-city women.

One of the personal stories here deals with a meeting of the cabinet of U.K. Prime Minister David Cameron (following the release of *SuperFreakonomics*). A cabinet minister made an announcement that he classified as *"a matter of the highest moral obligation"*:

> *This made our ears prick up. One thing we've learned is that when people, especially politicians, start making decisions based on a reading of their moral compass, facts tend to be among the first casualties.*

In a later chapter they expand on this:

> *When you are consumed with the rightness or wrongness of a given issue ... it's easy to lose track of what the issue actually is. A moral compass can convince you that all the answers are obvious (even when they're not); that there is a bright line between right and wrong (when often there isn't); and, worst, that you are certain you already know everything you need to know about a subject so you stop trying to learn more.*

There are some "tasty" stories here too ... like the advertising one about a company that was *certain* that they knew that their TV ads produced sales at 4x the rate of print ads – but the only *ran* the ads on days like "black friday", so the sales boost could well have been coming from "ambient" sales. This was compared to another story, about a company that buys newspaper ads in Sunday supplements every week in every market for the past 20 years, except for one market over one summer, when an intern screwed up placing the ads. What happened in that market, with no ads over those months? Well, first, nobody had ever bothered to *check*, and when they ran the numbers, it turned out that there had been *no change*, that the sales that came through came through equally when there were no ads as when the company was spending large sums on advertising. Did the company change? Nope. The corporate "common knowledge" trumped the actual numbers, and they're still throwing away that money today. This leads into "the three hardest words in the English language", which are *I don't know*. If you think you know the answer, you're unlikely to bother to try an experiment ... since you're sure you know.

Another "tasty" story here is based on wine snobbery. First a young member of an academic group set up an experiment to see how the expensive wines fared without them being in the context of being the expensive wines. He threw in a ringer, as he put one expensive wine in *twice* – same wine, just different decanters – and it came in *both* first and fourth, bracketing another expensive wine and a cheap wine. This, when revealed, created quite a stir. Inspired by this, one wine critic decided to run a series of experiments, culminating on a test with a *major* wine publication, for which he created a fake restaurant (with a very convincing web site), and a "reserve" wine list which featured bottles specifically chosen from the publication's own ratings – but only wines earning a "not recommended" rating. The result – the magazine presented him (or his fake restaurant) with an Award of Excellence ... prompting him to opine: *"My hypothesis was that the $250 fee was really the functional part of the application."*

There are lots of interesting tales told here, from looking at "competitive eating" to how a $15 pair of glasses could increase the learning ability of kids by as much as 50%, to how a scientist self-experimented to prove that bacteria cause ulcers, to a comparison of David Lee Roth's notorious "no brown M&Ms" rider to King Solomon's baby-splitting solution.

Speaking of M&Ms, one of the other "personal" stories here hinges on them. The daughter of one of the authors was having potty-training issues, and her father decided to make an offer, that if she went to the toilet, he'd give her a bag of M&Ms (I'm assuming that's one of the Halloween hand-out mini bags and not a full-size bag!). Here's how that ended up playing out, with a summation:

> How powerful are the right incentives? Within four days, a little girl went from potty-challenged to having the most finely tuned bladder in history. She simply figured out what it made sense to do given the incentives she faced. There was no fine print, no two-bag limit, not time-interval caveat. There was just a girl, a bag of candy, and a toilet.
>
> If there is one mantra a Freak lives by, it is this: <u>people respond to incentives</u>. As utterly obvious as this point may seem, we are amazed at how frequently people forget it, and it often leads to their undoing. Understanding the incentives of all the players in a given scenario is a fundamental step in solving any problem.

The last chapter is about "quitting" (which made me feel less guilty about trying to find stuff in the book as I went along), although they eventually fudge a bit on the definition to frame it as "letting go" ... but with it still being "at the very core of thinking like a Freak":

> Letting go of the conventional wisdoms that torment us. Letting go of the artificial limits that hold us back – and of the fear of admitting that we don't know. Letting go of the habits of mind that tell us to kick into the corner of the goal even though we stand a better chance by going up the middle.

<u>Think Like A Freak</u>[6] has only been out a year and a half at this point, but has moved into the used channels (I got an ex-library copy of the deckle-edge hardcover). Given the popularity of the authors' "Freak" books, I'd expect that this would be available in the real-world bookstores, and it appears to still be in print in both hardcover and paperback (and e- and audio-editions). The online big boys have these at over a third off of cover, if you want to go with "new" (the used guys have "very good" copies – which I believe is what I got – for just over a buck, before shipping). I enjoyed the read, found the info of interest, but never quite synced with the book ... again, I'm not sure what sort of brain retraining I was expecting, but this – as useful as its various points might be – wasn't it. I would, nonetheless recommend it for being a "fun read".

Notes:

1. http://btripp-books.livejournal.com/177402.html
2. http://amzn.to/1S3jFZp
3. http://btripp-books.livejournal.com/84471.html
4. http://btripp-books.livejournal.com/89019.html
5. http://btripp-books.livejournal.com/155126.html
6. http://amzn.to/1S3jFZp

Wednesday, December 2, 2015[1]

Around and around and around we go ...

I'm not sure where I ran across a mention of Dr. Alex Korb's The Upward Spiral: Using Neuroscience to Reverse the Course of Depression, One Small Change at a Time[2], but as it is a very recent release (and I don't recall contacting the publisher for a review copy), I'm having to guess that it was mentioned in a recent LTER[3] book, possibly The Upside of Stress[4], and I picked up a copy via Amazon.

Needless to say, I'm open to reading about pretty much anything that promises to *"reverse the course of depression"*, as my on-going financial difficulties (looking for work for over 6½ *years* will do horrible things to your life) have had me living on the edge of depression for a *very* long time, and this book sounded pretty on-target. After all, how "fluffy" could a book based on neuroscience be?

Well ...

One would think a book involving both neuroscience and fighting off depression would be a home run for me, but somehow most of the stuff didn't ring true for me ... or, at least, seem applicable as he presents it here. While the science stuff is *fascinating*, achieving most of the suggestions here would *at least* involve a coach, if not partial hospitalization. How am I supposed to arrange a "long hug" to release oxytocin and lower amygdala reactivity, if I'm lucky to score a random hug (from my daughters) 2-3 times a year? How can one *"play Frisbee with friends in the park"*, when it's been over a decade since one has had "friends" who weren't exclusively on the other side of a computer screen? Frankly, much of what Dr. Korb recommends as action points in here sound (to me) like he's saying "get your life together, and leverage that, then you can get out of being depressed" ... with no suggestion how one can arrange to have people around (and note the economic element above – I'm not in a position to *buy* these) who want to hug or play with you. Anyway, that's *me* and the particular existential hell that I live in, I'm assuming that "your mileage may vary" and some of the stuff in here will be more actionable for others.

The book is divided in two parts with various chapters walking the reader through the underlying systems that either cause or are effected by depression ... I hadn't wanted to fall back on a chapter listing in this, but it looks like I'm going to be less "summarizing the arc" of the book here, and more "cherry-picking choice bits", so here's how the book is laid out ...

> Part 1 – Stuck in a Downward Spiral
>   1 – A Brain Map of Depression
>   2 – Trapped with Anxiety and Worry
>   3 – Always Noticing the Negative
>   4 – Caught in Bad Habits
> Part 2 – Creating an Upward Spiral

> 5 – Exercise Your Brain
> 6 – Set Goals, Make Decisions
> 7 – Give Your Brain a Rest
> 8 – Develop Positive Habits
> 9 – Take Advantage of Biofeedback
> 10 – Activate a Gratitude Circuit
> 11 – Rely on the Power of Others
> 12 – Your brain in Therapy

One piece that I thought was pretty "defining" on how slippery the whole subject can be was: *"Whereas most diseases are defined by their cause … the disorder of depression is currently defined by a collection of symptoms."* for which *"There's no lab test, no MRI scan, it's just the symptoms."* and that *"… there's nothing fundamentally wrong with the brain. It's simply that the particular tuning of the neural circuits creates the tendency towards a pattern of depression."*

Sounds like a pretty raw deal, eh? The brain's functioning *fine*, it's just mistuned without a nice adjustment knob to fiddle with. He does go into the chemistry of neurotransmitter systems, which includes a basic listing/defining of each:

- Serotonin – improves willpower, motivation, and mood
- Norepinephrine – enhances thinking, focus, and dealing with stress
- Dopamine – increases enjoyment and is necessary for changing bad habits
- Oxytocin – promotes feelings of trust, love, and connection, and reduces anxiety
- GABA – increases feelings of relaxation and reduces anxiety
- Melatonin – enhances the quality of sleep
- Endorphins – provide pain relief and feelings of elation
- Endocannabinoids – improve your appetite and increase feelings of peacefulness and well-being

These keep coming up in various settings and combinations … one example of a "doable" suggestion is *"go out in sunlight"* which will help boost serotonin production, and the release of melatonin.

The author also goes through the basic parts of the brain, the Prefrontal Cortex, with the various regions: Dorsomedial, Ventromedial, Dorsolateral, Ventrolateral, and Orbitofrontal … and the Limbic System, with the assorted parts: Anterior Cingulate, Hypotalamus, Hippocampus, and Amygdala ... along with a couple of other bits, the Striatum, with the Dorsal Striatum and the Nuclear Accumbens, and the Insula. He goes through the known functions of these in relation to depression (but, obviously, it's too much to get into detail on here) an example is:

> *Dopamine is released in the nucleus accumbens whenever you do anything fun and exciting – or at least it's supposed to. In depression, reduced dopamine activity in the nuclear accumbens explains why nothing seems enjoyable.*

In advocating for attempting to move into an "upward spiral", he notes:

> *... depression comes from problems with frontal-limbic communication, and that it happens because of the specific tuning of your neural circuits ... it turns out that just a little change can be enough to push you away from depression ... that's because in complex systems like the brain, even a little shift can change the resonance of the whole system.*

And, while that last statement sounds a bit *woo-woo* Korb got his neuroscience undergraduate at Brown and his PhD at UCLA, and is a post-doctoral researcher in the UCLA department of psychiatry, so ought to have a pretty good fix on this (although part of me thinks that the phrase *"resonance of the whole system"* evokes images of Tibetan Singing Bowl "therapies" more than anything).

Throughout the book he has grey boxes that feature "suggestions" for things to do. Frankly, a lot of these came across (to me) as "nagging" (OK, *especially* all those having to do with exercise), but some are pretty perceptive, direct, and *doable*, here's one (fairly lengthy – sorry about that) that I found particularly useful:

> **Make a good decision, not the best decision.**
> *When trying to make a decision, we tend to focus on the relative drawbacks of each option, which often makes every decision seem less appealing. Nor do we usually have enough information to feel confident in the decision – the world's just too complex. But remember, it's better to do something only partly right than do nothing at all. Trying for the best, instead of good enough, brings too much emotional ventromedial prefrontal activity into the decision-making process. In contrast, recognizing that good enough is good enough activates more dorsolateral prefrontal areas, which helps you feel more in control.*

As is evident from that "to-do item", there's a lot of stuff in here that is brain-area specific, targeted to either enhancing or inhibiting levels of the neurotransmitters listed above. He elaborates on the suggestion for *making decisions* by noting:

> *Your brain, like your muscles, operates on a use-it-or-lose-it basis. Using a particular brain region will strengthen it, while disuse will weaken it. One problem with depression is that it makes you use a lot of the brain circuits that keep you stuck and less of the brain circuits that help you get better.*

An interesting chapter (that I also found somewhat "naggy") is the "Give Your Brain a Rest" one, which deals with what he refers to as "sleep hygiene". One factoid I found fascinating was the "sleep architecture" piece where Korb walks the reader through a phase-by-phase look at what happens in a "sleep cycle" – which typically takes 90 minutes. I guess I glommed onto this because for *years* I was pretty much a 3-hour-of-sleep guy, which means that I was making do with 2 sleep cycles (instead of the 5-6 an 8-hour rest would entail) … which has grown to 4 as I've gotten older. One of the more "naggy" things here is when he gets into syncing one's sleep schedule with one's Circadian Rhythms … and some of his suggestions there are just *extreme* if one lives with a lot of electronics (or, in my case, an environment with a lot of ambient light).

In the "Developing Positive Habits" chapter, he starts off highlighting the underlying problem:

> *Habits are created by repetition. Interestingly, some habits require less repetition than others, because some actions inherently release more dopamine. Unfortunately, bad habits are the ones that often release lots of dopamine, so you don't need to do them very often to get hooked. Smoking releases a lot of dopamine in the nucleus accumbens, so you don't have to smoke very many cigarettes to start a habit. In contrast, flossing doesn't release very much dopamine, so you have to floss every day for a long time to make it a habit. … The good news is that the dorsal striatum responds to repetition. It doesn't matter if you want to do something – every single time you do it, it gets further wired into the dorsal striatum … if you can power through, things will feel easier as the burden of the action shifts from the consciously effortful prefrontal cortex to the unconsciously effortless dorsal striatum.*

Bizarrely, he also says that (to me, a bit newagey, touchy-feely) self affirmations help break bad habits … he reports on a study that had participants complete a questionnaire which highlighted their positive qualities before being exposed to negative information about a bad habit (in this case smoking) … *"smokers in the self-affirmation group developed a greater intention to quit smoking … {and} the effect of self-affirmation was strongest on the heaviest smokers"*. Who knew that Stewart Smalley[5] was that clued in?

The "biofeedback" chapter isn't about getting your head wired up to a machine (or Yoga, which the author starts off discussing), but is more generically about how *"the brain changes its activity based on what the body is doing"*. One amusing sidebar discusses how a stress sensation in the gut is very likely to be interpreted by the brain as hunger – hence the familiar phenomenon of "nervous eating" – he suggests that *"These types of signals are like your car's check-engine light – alerting you that something is happening, but not being very helpful in telling you what."*! He has a number of suggestions to use to make those physical messages work on your brain, from splashing cold water on your face to break a cycle of *"feeling overwhelmed, stressed, or anxious"*, to using music to *"help regulate your emotions"*, to even forcing yourself to smile[6]. He further suggests to laugh even if nothing is funny ... noting: *"The brain doesn't distinguish much between genuine laughter and fake laughter."*, which he further elaborates with:

> Facial feedback works because the brain senses the flexing of certain facial muscles (like the zygomatic major muscle at the corners of your mouth), to which the brain thinks, I must be happy about something. Similarly, if that muscle isn't flexed, you brain thinks, Oh, ... I must not be happy.

He also suggests (along with your mother and/or drill sergeant) standing up straight. And, to avoid things (like squinting) that would mimic stress patterns in the facial muscles (to the extent of recommending wearing sunglasses to avoid one's *corrugator supercilii* contracting and messaging the brain that one is upset or worried). There are more tips about breathing and various muscle cues to either avoid or to mimic. Stupid brain ... what a sucker!

I was probably most "reactive" against the "Gratitude" chapter, because, hey, those "Laws of Attraction" folks are *real* irritating. Fortunately, it's only 10 pages and not insufferably newagey. He hits about a dozen key points here, and while he *footnotes* studies for these he doesn't go into much detail other than glossing the results with statements like *"activates the brain stem region that produces dopamine"*, or *"increases serotonin production in the anterior cingulate cortex"*. I was similarly fighting against the "other people" chapter, given my general isolation over the past few decades (the author does not at the start of the chapter: *"Depression is an isolating disease. It makes you feel separate and alone, even around other people ..."* and later follows with *"Humans are a social species ... that means that when we feel disconnected, the consequences can be devastating."*. None of this is helped by the "downward spiral" effects – noting that depressed people *"have even greater anterior cingulate activation, suggesting their brains are more sensitive to social rejection ... generating a stronger stress response"*), which makes much of the info here, well ... *depressing*. However, there was one fascinating bit here that came out of a study of 8-12-year-old girls who were subjected to a stressful event (having to *"solve difficult SAT questions in front of an audience"*), there were four groups, differentiated by what they did after the stressful experience – one set got to visit with their mothers, one set got to talk to their mothers on the phone, one set got to "text" with their mothers, and one set got no follow-up contact at all. The first two groups had "improved" cortisol-oxytocin levels, while the no-contact group had a bad mix (high cortisol, low oxytocin) of the neurotransmitters. What was especially notable in this study was that the girls who were just able to text with their mothers had very similar levels to the no-contact group ... indicating that something (emotion?) wasn't coming across via the text messages. I found this especially illuminating as I always prefer email to the phone – primarily to avoid any emotional "Jedi mind tricks" that people tend to use in spoken communications! One of the other things he recommends is rooting for sports teams – with others – so I wouldn't be surprised to find him doing promos for sports bars.

The last chapter is about getting therapy, from standard talk therapy to massively invasive things involving brain surgery or ECT, with a discussion of assorted drugs being used (or developed) for various issues. All nice stuff if you can afford it, I suppose.

The key element that he ends with is urging the reader to at least try to do *something* to break the brain out of its depressive cycles. This might be (for the deeply depressed) as basic as *getting out of bed* even if one can't come up with a reason to do so ... sort of like Nike's "just do it" – it will help break the cycle (somewhat like splashing cold water creates a neural shock and can interrupt a state of mind). He closes by pointing out the act of *finishing* the book is likely to create a puff of dopamine ... which may be why I'm so fond of reading books.

Anyway, The Upward Spiral[7] has only been out since March, so you have a reasonable chance of finding it in the still extant brick-and-mortar book vendors with "self help" sections (and which of those *don't*?). The on-line big boys have it, of course, presently at about 25% off of cover price. Interestingly, this hasn't gotten deeply into the new/used channels, so you'd not be saving much (with shipping) going there at this point. As is evident in all the preceding, I'm pretty torn on this, I found the science parts quite educational, but had a "dark/sarcastic/reactive" response to most of the touchy-feely stuff, although I'm likely to add several bits and pieces to my on-going activity when nothing else is working. If you're fighting depression (or are close to somebody who is), and aren't as cantankerous as I am, you'll likely get a lot of this and be quite enthusiastic about it. I guess *I'm* going to have to wait for "Fighting Depression for Cranky Cynics" to come out.

Notes:
1. http://btripp-books.livejournal.com/177533.html
2. http://amzn.to/1MflIda
3. https://www.librarything.com/wiki/index.php/HelpThing:Er_list
4. http://btripp-books.livejournal.com/168938.html.html
5. https://youtu.be/-DIETIxquzY?rel=0
6. https://youtu.be/buZZyUBwymA?rel=0
7. http://amzn.to/1MflIda

Wednesday, December 16, 2015[1]

Once upon a time, in a corporation not so far away ...

One of the less frequent pathways for books to get into my to-be-read piles is via "coaching", or the "highly recommended" route. As I *am* coachable, I will often heed these sorts of "suggestions", and I recently picked up a couple of books that one of the head guys at my recent "financial education" project[2] was singing the praises of.

Of course, one guy's "must read" book can be another guy's "meh" read, and this one was, unfortunately, sort of in that category. As regular readers of this space may recall, I don't synch particularly well with "parable" sorts of things ... if you're going to tell me something, *tell* me it outright, don't make me have to tease it out of some cute story! Needless to say, Leadership and Self-Deception: Getting Out of the Box[3] *is* one of those "teaching stories" that I can never seem to get the point of. What's also irritating about this book (which has sold over a million copies and has a 4.5 star rating on Amazon – so it certainly has its fans, and I'm an obvious "outlier" when it come to this style of writing) is that it's not credited to a *person* but to something called The Arbinger Institute. One would think a "cute story" book would be coming out from some touchy-feely individual trying to mess with your mind by doing an end-around on your rational faculties, and not an *organization*, so I was constantly having to filter for what they were trying to sneak into my head!

That said, this was a much *less* aggravating "parable" than most things I've read in that format. It was flirting with actually being *useful* in that parts of the book involve stuff written on a whiteboard, which ebbed and flowed over the course of the story (stuff getting erased, replaced, updated, etc.) ... which, while never quite getting to an actual bullet list, at least has a certain periodic linearity to it that allows for a less-arcane method of extraction of the main points. I suspect that if one stripped away all the *story* elements here, you could distill what they were trying to convey in a dozen or so pages ... and I *really* wish they had included an appendix for the "parable-averse" reader along those lines. Again, as regular readers of these reviews know, I've read nearly *zero* fiction over the past dozen years, so I *really* am not a "story person" ... I suspect that this was set up the way it was because there are LOTS more fiction readers out there than ~~serious~~ non-fiction book readers, and most of *those people* wouldn't ever think of picking up the sort of psychological study that this book could have been, so it's a way of sugar-coating the material for the masses.

Anyway, this is a tale about an executive who is finally hired by this company that he's been admiring (and competing against) for a long time. Early on in his new job, he is put into a one-on-one training situation with a senior executive to get him up to speed with how the company culture works. They have a theory called "the box" (confusingly, *not* like the popular concept of "thinking outside the box"), and insist on having all their people on board with this. Of course, as is the endlessly frustrating habit of "parable" books, they never really get out a *definition* of "the box", just examples of when one is in or out of it (and in this context, being *in* the box is bad, and being *out* of the box is good). About the most direct thing I could find was that it's described at one point as *"seeing others as people or seeing them as objects"*. Yes, that sounds like "newage sewage", but at least they point out that *everybody* is "in the box" to a certain extent, and the difference (at that company) was that they were systematically trying to *not* be in the box, and attributed their success to the times when they managed to get out of the box.

The second concept here is "self-betrayal", which, essentially, is when you have a gut feeling about what you *should* do but don't, and suddenly spin out all sorts of justifications for not doing it. They have this largely set up in interpersonal and home-life examples from the main characters, all of which is just plain unpleasant to read. In a side-bar to one of the "whiteboard" sections they have probably the most straight-forward description of this process (with the added bonus of working in the title concept):

> *When I betray myself, I enter the box – I become self-deceived*
> ↓
> 1. *Inflate others' faults*
> 2. *Inflate own virtue*
> 3. *Inflate the value of things that justify my self-betrayal*
> 4. *Blame*

And, there are different boxes for different situations/relationships, some being momentary, and others being ingrained. Plus, over time certain boxes become characteristic, and one carries them around as regular features of one's personality.

A related concept is "collusion", where multiple people's "in the box" behavior and attitudes encourage others to be "in the box" as well and *"the same pattern of mutual provocation and justification always emerges"*. A lot of families (I'd hazard to guess that *most*) fall into this model, and to a similar extent work relationships. The way they define this is that if one is "out of the box" at work, one's "what-focus" is on achieving results, while when "in the box", one's "what-focus" is on *justification* of one's behaviors and attitudes.

While they do discuss how one gets "out of the box", this is sort of murky and convoluted, with lots of info on what *won't* work, and only vague stuff about what will ... the one thing I was able to identify that directly addressed this was: *"You get out of the box as you cease resisting other people."* ... but that "resisting" concept was not particularly fleshed out. I guess that was to create something of a cliff-hanger to get you to buy the sequel, of which an 18-page excerpt is included.

As noted, I generally *hate* having to slog through these sorts of things to try to sift out what the author (or, in this case, *organization*) is trying to actually say. The concepts here are certainly interesting, and, I think (as much as I was able to dig same out of the damn story) quite important, I just wish it wasn't in a freak'n "parable". Of course, that's me ... *you* might find this the bestest thing in the whole world.

Since Leadership and Self-Deception[4] is such a popular title, I'm pretty sure that you'd be able to find it in the bigger surviving bookstores, but the online big boys currently have the paperback of the 2010 second edition at 40% off of a very reasonable cover price. Despite all my bitching above, I *do* think this is a very worthwhile read (I just wish it was in a plain presentation – but I guess they wanted to offer up all sorts of "interpersonal" stories and didn't want to be shifting in and out of styles), and would be useful to pretty much anybody.

Notes:

1. http://btripp-books.livejournal.com/177850.html
2. http://xcurvewealth.com/
3-4. http://amzn.to/1YhCtrD

Thursday, December 17, 2015[1]

Exponential endeavors ...

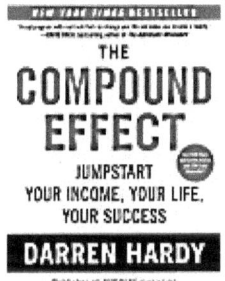

This is the second of those books that a mentor in the company that I'm currently developing a business[2] with had suggested that folks in his group read. I found it odd that, sitting down to write this review, I could (unaided) recall *nothing* about this book ... which is hardly the usual case. Fortunately, I had quite a few of my little bookmarks tucked into this (and so was able to re-familiarize myself with it a few weeks past the initial read). The Compound Effect: Jumpstart Your Income, Your Life, Your Success[3] is by Darren Hardy, the publisher of *Success* magazine, and is, as one might expect, something in that rah-rah self-development niche, but not obnoxiously so.

To cut to the chase (and I appreciate the author being willing to define his terms up front), *"The Compound Effect is the principle of reaping huge rewards from a series of small, smart choices."* ... where *"small, seemingly insignificant steps completed consistently over time"* end up producing radical differences in long-term results. A classic example of this is the grain-on-the-chessboard tale that the author updates to a calendar, asking if you'd prefer to get three million dollars or a penny that doubled every day for 31 days (while starting slowly, the penny approach pulls ahead on day 30, and ends up with nearly eleven million dollars at the end of the month).

The book has a fairly straight-forward arc, with chapters on "Choices", "Habits", "Momentum", "Influences", and "Acceleration", following the initial introductory chapter. One of the things that I think works well here is that each chapter ends with a "Summary Action Steps" section that plays off of the examples in each chapter to chart out suggestions for moving forward with the ideas. There are also a number of assessment tools, which appear in the book in very compressed form, but have printable (and expanded) versions available free at the book's companion website[4].

The book is hardly a "textbook", however, presenting a mélange of "self-development" stuff (like the "formula" for luck), stories from the author's life (like discovering, to his shock, early in his real estate career that he owed over a hundred grand in taxes that he'd not put away money for – his accountant insisted that he start to carry around a little notebook and begin to keep track of every cent he spent), and lot of random examples of how things escalate (like a $4/day coffee habit costing $50k over 20 years).

The little notebook concept is something that he especially encourages:

> To help you become aware of your choices, I want you to track every action that relates to the area of your life you want to improve. If you've decided you want to get out of debt, you're going to track every penny you pull from your pocket. If you've decided you want to lose weight, you're going to track everything you put into your mouth.

> *If you've decided to train for an athletic event, you're going to track every step you take, every workout you do. Simply carry around a small notebook, something you'll keep in your pocket or purse at all times, and a writing instrument. You're going to write it all down. Every day. Without fail. No excuses, no exceptions. As if Big Brother's watching you.*

He further suggests that you do this for a minimum of three weeks ... the first week will shock you, the second week will find you modifying your behaviors to either avoid writing stuff in the book or wanting to write stuff in the book, and hopefully by week three keeping track of things will have established itself as a habit.

Oh, that coffee example, he suggests that you look at the cost of something that you're considering buying and multiplying it by *five*, to give you a ballpark on what the same amount of money invested for 20 years would produce ... so he wants you to ask yourself if that $50 item is worth $250 to you ... if so, then buy it, if not *"chances are you'll put down that fifty-dollar crepe maker"*. Most of the changes described here are very slight, yet he illustrates how big a difference they can make with numerous examples, such as the difference between the No.1 ranked golfer and the No.10 ranked golfer is only 1.9 strokes – about 2.7% better – but resulting in a 5x difference in prize money.

A concept that shows up in the Habits chapter is finding your "why-power" as opposed on relying in on your willpower. The illustration he makes is of a 10" wide 30ft long plank ... anybody would be happy to walk that for a small reward ... but put that plank across the gap between two tall buildings and nobody would try it ... *unless* ... if your kid was on top of the other building, which was on fire, almost everybody would venture across to attempt a rescue (although I'd not like to figure the odds on how many make it across both ways). When the "why" is big enough *"you will be willing to perform almost any<u>how</u>".*

This leads into "core motivation" and "find your fight" ... one needs to find something that makes you "fully motivated" – even if that something is "less-than-noble", even hate ... using *"a powerfully negative emotion or experience to create an even more powerful and successful end"*.

In the section on Goals, Hardy gives the most lucid explanation of the Law of Attraction that I've seen:

> *You only see, experience, and get what you look for. If you don't know what to look for, you certainly won't get it. By our very nature, we are goal-seeking creatures. Our brain is always trying to align our outer world with what we're seeing and expecting in our inner world. So, when you instruct your brain to look for the things you want, you will begin to see them. In fact, the object of your desire has probably always existed around you, but your mind and eyes weren't open to*

> "seeing" it.

One of the more extensive things on the companion website is an 8-page .pdf file on setting and working with goals. There is also a "Habits" form on the site, which relates directly to the identified Goals. In the book there is a long section which talks about "Five Strategies for Eliminating Bad Habits" and "Six Techniques for Installing Good Habits" which bookend a small, but fascinating, piece called "Run a Vice Check" ...

> About every three months, I pick one vice and abstain for thirty days ... I love proving to myself that I'm still in charge. Try this yourself. Pick a vice – something you do in moderation, but you know doesn't contribute to your higher good – and take yourself on a thirty-day wagon run. If you find it seriously difficult to abstain for those thirty days, you may have found a habit worth cutting out of your life.

He goes into "momentum" which really is about routine and consistency building towards self-driving habits ... including setting up rituals for the morning and evening to "bookend" the day:

> All hell can break loose throughout the day, but because I control the bookends, I know I'm always going to start and finish strong.

The "Influences" chapter goes into ideas like going on a "media diet" ... the media always works on a "if it bleeds, it leads" play on our hard-wired instincts, and it takes shutting that out to keep this negativity at bay. Similarly, there's a look at one's "associations", and even a worksheet to evaluate the ones you want to keep and the ones you need to avoid.

There *is* quite a lot of "shilling" in this book for other products from *Success* (like several pages of ads surrounding the "resource" forms in the back – but since the ones on the website are more comprehensive, it's safe to ignore the back matter), including the Conclusion which devolves into a guilt play to buy at least 5 extra copies to give to friends/family/associates, complete with a place to write down the names. Blech! Nice way to create a *"why* did I just read this?" final impression.

All in all, The Compound Effect[5] is a pretty decent book ... interesting perspectives, fascinating data tidbits, some useful materials ... if occasionally a bit heavy-handed on the rah-rah, "you must do what I'm saying or your life will be a horrid pit of despair", standard self-help vibe. It's reasonably priced, and the on-line guys have it at a discount that drops it under ten bucks. I'm guessing it's also easy to find in the brick-and-mortars (and airport kiosks, etc.) as it has a 4.8 star rating on Amazon and is a NYT bestseller. As usual, my take on this is probably way off on the cranky cynical curmudgeon extreme of the scale, and most folks wouldn't mind the parts that I found irritating. While I wouldn't necessarily say this is an "all and sundry" recommendation, it's one of those that most people would benefit from reading.

Notes:
1. http://btripp-books.livejournal.com/177965.html
2. http://xcurvewealth.com/
3. http://amzn.to/1SqhaQy
4. http://thecompoundeffect.com/resources.php
5. http://amzn.to/1SqhaQy

Monday, December 28, 2015

As Seen On TV ...

OK, so this one is *obviously* a dollar store find (it's not exactly the sort of thing that I'd go looking for, either in a bookstore or online!) ... but *Dog the Bounty Hunter* is one of the things that are typically playing when I'm getting my coffee and breakfast, so I'm familiar with the characters, and, frankly, I had enough curiosity about the "back story" of the show to be willing to read an autobiographical book by The Dog. It turns out that Where Mercy Is Shown, Mercy Is Given by Duane "Dog" Chapman is a fairly fascinating read ... covering lots of stuff that I'd not gotten from my occasional watching of the show. I suspect that co-author Laura Morton has a *lot* to do with this book being as high-quality as it is ... as Dog himself notes that he's lacking in a lot of the stuff that would keep something like this from being embarrassing to both the author and the reader.

One thing that's hard to miss in the show is what a train wreck the Chapman family is (I've frequently thought when hearing of the legal troubles of various folks on the show "these folks are in law enforcement, how do they keep getting in trouble like that???") ... and that is certainly a key theme here. As folks familiar with the show will know, Dog has had at least a couple of families, as he has grown kids working with him, and little kids living with him. He goes into some of his own background, including the events (as a member of the Disciples motorcycle gang) that landed him in prison in his youth. His prison experience has a lot to do with him becoming the sort of bounty hunter one sees on TV, both in terms of relating to pretty much everybody, and the whole "counseling" thing he does with the skips he catches.

I had been vaguely aware (via the internet) that he'd gotten in trouble chasing a guy down to Mexico, but hadn't had much details on that. This was one of the main story lines in the book ... his pursuit of "wealthy playboy" (heir to the Max Factor fortune) Andrew Luster – connected to *eighty-seven* counts of rape – into Mexico, while successful in capturing the suspect, resulted in him and his team being thrown into jail for a charge similar to kidnapping. Due to the corruption of the Mexican legal system, this dragged on and on, with Luster's "people" trying to make things as difficult as possible for him. When he did get out, he wasn't able to get paid because of the legal entanglements, and he was spending tons of money on what turned out to be less-than-efficient legal counsel. Eventually he got new lawyers who got things straightened out, but it was financially devastating.

There's a lot of material about various "family" issues. One of his previous wives (he seems to have had several prior to Beth) was rather vindictive and not exactly an ideal "role model" for his kids, several of which got totally messed up on drugs. He ended up losing one daughter up in Alaska, and having a son turn completely against him ... which produced the other ongoing issue in the book. This son was hanging out with a "bad crowd", including a black girlfriend who was controlling the kid – pushing him to "get that TV money" out of Dog ... leading to them recording their phone, and eventually catching Dog using the "N-word" (which he was totally comfortable using from his prison time), and selling the tape to one of the tabloids. The media frenzy was predictable, with the "usual suspects" spewing outrage and insisting that A&E cancel the show. Dog seemed to be genuinely blind-sided by this, and really had to scramble to get things back on track. He was fortunate to have some ministers who were in his corner who were able to smooth some of the rougher patches, and eventually the reality of him being "clueless" rather than "racist" eventually won out.

Honestly, given the number of "nightmare" stories in here it makes one wonder how he was able to keep in business. He had problems with insurance companies (which resulted in him having to give up his license in Hawaii for a while), former employees making fraudulent charges against the company, and near-disasters with assorted law enforcement groups.

There are a lot of other behind-the-scenes stories as well, featuring characters from the show, his on-going relationship with the network (one wonders if much of this would have gone quite differently if the show wasn't their top program), plus a couple of "hunt stories" sprinkled in. Needless to say, Where Mercy Is Shown, Mercy Is Given[3] is going to appeal mainly to fans of the *Dog the Bounty Hunter* program ... while the stories in it play out without necessarily *needing* to know the show, I'm not sure that it would be as *interesting* if one didn't have the familiarity with the context and characters that folks who *do* watch Dog would have going in.

I'm surprised that this doesn't have any 1¢ copies out in the new/used channels, but you can get a "very good" copy of the hardcover for just over buck (before shipping) ... it's still in print, and the on-line big boys currently have it at a 60% discount. Of course, if you can find it at Dollar Tree, you'll only be spending a buck ... but that's an iffy thing once the books hit those shelves. Did I *need* to read this? No. Was it an interesting read? Yeah, sure. Would I have read this if I didn't occasionally watch the show? Don't think so. If you're a fan, you'll probably want to check this out ... if not, well ... it's not a bad book.

Notes:

1. http://btripp-books.livejournal.com/178206.html

2-3. http://amzn.to/1OsPwSc

Tuesday, December 29, 2015

When is enlightenment not enlightenment?

I'm sort of surprised that I didn't get around to reading this back in high school or college ... I certainly remember the more "hippie-ish" folks in high school being big fans of the book. Honestly, had I read Hermann Hesse's Siddhartha in those days I'd probably have been more enthusiastic about it than I am encountering it now. I ordered the Dover Thrift Edition of this (and a few other titles), in order to have some "quick reads" to counter a couple of big thick things I'm currently reading (and will be for months), and I figured that this was one of the notable gaps in my literature background.

The problem I had with this probably starts with the title ... *why* would Hesse name the protagonist the same name as the historical Buddha – while including the Buddha in the story? It's like naming a character Arjuna and not having Krsna involved! Plus, the general story arc ... at least through the first part of the book ... sounds quite like a re-telling of the Buddha's story, albeit differing in the particulars. Having had 40 years since high school to study Buddhist material, I found the parallels being confusing rather than enticing, with the noted "WTF?" element of *this* Siddhartha being a *different* character than the Buddha.

Of course, I'm the wrong person to ask about fiction or parables, and I take it (from some of the info in the Introduction) that Hesse habitually has his characters *"undergo the arduous process of self-discovery to reconcile {their} warring halves and find harmony and peace"* via some process which combines *"psychoanalysis and Eastern religion"*. This is a relatively new translation, by Stanley Applebaum in 1999 (a fairly rare thing for these Dover books), and his commentary and notes raise some interesting issues. It turns out that Hesse, despite his intents to do so, never actually visited *India*, but was on a steamer trip through other parts of southeast Asia ... leading to his using Pali words for things, and making some major misstatements (such as including Chimpanzees and Jaguars in the north Indian fauna, although those are native to Africa and the Americas, respectively).

The cynic in me wants to say this was popular with the "drug culture" because you'd have to be *stoned* to take it at face value, but that would be unkind. Perhaps the main character's constantly changing his path was the key element in the book's appeal.

Anyway, like the Buddha, *this* Siddhartha was a child of wealth (son of a prominent Brahman, rather than a king), who rejected that life. In this case, his rejection comes from looking at the results of the priests, scholars, and others in his life ... that they have, even into old age, not achieved enlightenment – leading him to assume that their methods are wanting. Like the Buddha he leaves to join a group of wandering ascetics (here called *Samanas*, a Pali term) and learns the basics of what he later claims as "what he knows" – to think, to wait, and to fast. His childhood friend Govinda (confusingly, a name related to Krsna) comes with him and they travel together.

Govinda has heard of the teachings of the Buddha (here Gotama) and wants to see this teacher ... Siddhartha has already bored of the teachings of the Samanas, and agrees that they'll go see Gotama. There is a passage there which shows Siddhartha to be somewhat sarcastic ... mocking Govinda and saying that they already have the "finest fruits" of Gotama's teaching – his calling them away from the Samanas. He specifically notes:

> But please also recollect that other thing you heard me say, that I have become distrustful and weary of teaching and learning, and that I have little faith in words that come to us from teachers.

... not exactly the best frame of mind to be looking at a whole new philosophy. He also, in taking leave of the ascetic elder, has a major confrontation, and basically tells Govinda "watch this!" and puts an advanced enchantment spell on the old man to give them his blessing.

It is, perhaps, not surprising that Siddhartha does *not* join Govinda in "taking refuge" with Gotama, but tells him that he's leaving. On his way out, he encounters Gotama, and has the audacity to engage him in discussion ... which the Buddha brushes off as "quarreling over mere words", adding:

> But the doctrine you have heard from me is not an opinion of mine; its goal is not to explain the world to thirsters after knowledge. Its goal is different; its goal is deliverance from suffering.

This does not suit Siddhartha, and he goes into something of a tantrum, including:

> O Sublime One – no one will achieve salvation through teachings! O Venerable One, you will not be able to inform and tell a single person in words and by means of teachings what happened to you in the hour of your enlightenment! The doctrine of the enlightened Buddha contains a great deal, it teaches many to live righteously, to shun evil. But one thing this doctrine, so clear, so venerable, does not contain: it does not contain the secrets of what the Sublime One himself experienced, he alone among the hundreds of thousands.

... basically saying he's leaving because he isn't being handed enlightenment on a silver platter! He leaves the Buddha and heads back into the world (as it were), and has his own sort of illumination, although this is largely just rejecting everything he's studied.

The book shifts dramatically here, as Siddhartha goes very much back to the world, he falls in love with a courtesan who promises (if he "cleans up" and gets fine clothes and money) to teach him the arts of love, she introduces him to a merchant who can use his skills (in reading, writing, and analytic thought) and apprentices him ... over a few years he becomes rich, comfortable, and addicted to gambling. He eventually gets disgusted with himself, and goes off to a pleasure garden he owns, and (like the Buddha story, again), sits under a tree and reviews his life. He eventually "dies to" all those things and simply leaves ... wandering to the same river crossing where a kindly ferryman had brought him across years before. Here he contemplates suicide, but falls asleep. He awakes to find a monk sitting with him – which is his old companion Govinda (who does not recognize him). The two chat for a while, and Govinda leaves. Eventually Siddhartha convinces the Ferryman to take him on as an apprentice, and he spends years "learning from the river".

The courtesan had had a son by him, and they come by ... but she's killed by a snake, and the boy stays with Siddhartha and the Ferryman. The kid's a spoiled brat, and eventually steals their money and the boat and heads back to the city. Much psychological processing ensues. Eventually, the Ferryman leaves to be a *vanaprastha* (forest hermit), and Siddhartha is the new Ferryman-slash-sage at the river crossing. At the end of the story, Govinda shows up again, they discuss their differing views of reality (at this point Siddhartha has developed his own version of enlightenment) and, after a long visionary description, he bows and leaves and the book ends (and, frankly, I thought it really needed a coda to sort of wrap things up somewhat, but it just *stops*).

Again, this book is a *classic*, but it really is a jumble of things, not particularly well paced, and leading to an ending all too similar to *The Sopranos* notorious cut-to-black final scene. Of course, if one was young, impressionable, stoned, and encountering Eastern Mysticism for the first time in reading Siddhartha[3], none of the caveats I've brought up would likely matter. Heck, the main character's moving away from everything that he gets bored/dissatisfied with would probably be a *draw*, as would his immersion in the erotic arts in the penultimate phase of his existence. One must wonder what was Hesse's *intent* here ... was he trying to forge some syncretic form of western psychological theory with his understanding of Indian teachings?

While I enjoyed the book, it was hard for me to disengage my "critical" mind that was constantly cross-referencing what was in the book with what I knew about the supposed source material. If you've read less about Buddhism (and other Indian religions) you're likely to have less resistance to the story as it's presented. And while this is nowhere near as abstruse as most of those "teaching stories" that I find so irritating, it's still something of a "parable", so I'm likely fighting with it in ways that others wouldn't be.

Being a Dover Thrift book, it's cheap ... with a cover price of a whopping $3.50 ... so even a penny copy used (which there are several available) would be more than that with shipping – so your best bet might be to request your local brick-and-mortar to order in a copy for you (although a free ebook version – in a different translation – is available via Project Gutenberg[4]).Text

Notes:

1. http://btripp-books.livejournal.com/178438.html

2-3. http://amzn.to/1O6BDdX

4. https://www.gutenberg.org/files/2500/2500-h/2500-h.htm

Wednesday, December 30, 2015[1]

They don't make leaders like this anymore ...

Here's one that I missed in my schooling ... although it's understandable as I really didn't do much in the Roman stuff (it's not like I went to a Catholic school or a seminary). However, the emperor Marcus Aurelius (who lived from 121 - 180 ce and reigned from 161 - 180 ce) was about as ideal a ruler as one might wish for ... not only did he have all the requisite military and organizational skills you'd want, he was also a significant Stoic philosopher.

Marcus Aurelius had been hand-picked by Hadrian to be his successor (being adopted by Pius Antonius, who was adopted by Hadrian – as a sort of two generation succession plan), and was made Consul (leader of the Senate) at the young age of 19. He was a student of the Stoic philosophers, very little of whose actual writings have survived ... meaning that his Meditations[2], which are basically notes to himself (in fact, the original title of these was "To Himself" – which he wrote in his 50's while in Germany), is one of the most coherent expressions of that philosophy.

The Meditations[3] are twelve "books" with varying subject matter. The first of these is a listing of people who had an influence on his thought, and parts of this are remarkably modern in their approach ... I especially noted section 14:

> *From my brother Severus, to love my kin, and to love truth, and to love justice ... and from him I received the idea of a polity I which there is the same law for all, a polity administered with regard to equal rights and equal freedom of speech, and the idea of a kingly government that respects most of all the freedom of the governed ...*

I was a bit frustrated sitting down to write this review, as (except for the preceding) I wasn't able to immediately suss out what specific passages I'd meant to be flagging with my little book marks, several of which were in the various parts of this book. So, I guess I'm going to have to dig a bit to find stuff to give you a feel of this. Again, this is a bunch of "notes", really, most of the 10-page-or-shorter "books" here have 40-60 numbered sections with individual thoughts, so it's *not* a "philosophical *system*" so much that would have a logical arc to it ... making it a bit of a challenge to summarize.

Here's one from Book IV, section 40:

> *Constantly regard the universe as one living being, having one substance and one soul; and observe how all things have reference to one perception of this one living being; and how all things act with one movement; and how all things are cooperating causes of all things that exist; observe, too, the*

> *continuous spinning of the thread and the contexture of the web.*

Marcus Aurelius was writing these in his 50's, and he spends a lot of text returning to a concept of how fleeting human life is (*"All ephemeral, dead long ago."* VIII:25) ... there are many sections here which rattle off a list of names (no doubt famous in his time) who are gone, the courts, the kings, etc. This next bit is a more concise example of this, from Book VII, section 21:

> *In a little while you will have forgotten everything; in a little while everything will have forgotten you.*

One of the interesting bits of info from the introductory material here was the source of the term "Stoic", which has come to mean having the ability to *endure pain or hardship without showing feelings or complaining*, but it actually comes from the Greek "Stoa", a covered colonnaded walkway around a building, which is where the philosopher Zeno held gatherings ... which fits in to the idea that Stoicism *"is not so much a single systematic doctrine as a winding intellectual current"* – so it got named for where its adherents hung out!

While he writes about various more "mystical" things (how substances move from state to state over time, all a part of keeping *"the whole universe ever youthful and in its prime"* – XII:23), and how one can best make one's way through society, much of the Meditations[4] are focused on what one has to assume to be his own contemplation of death, which I think is well summed up in this bit from Book XII, section 21:

> *Consider that before long you will be nobody and nowhere, nor will any of the things exist that you now see, nor any of those who are now living. For all things are formed by nature to change and be turned and perish in order that other things in continuous success may exist.*

This is not to say that the entire book is a downer contemplation on dissolution and death, but – given the biographical context in which this was created – it is an over-riding theme which puts in context all the *other* material about how to conduct oneself, how to manage one's internal states, and the contemplations about how the universe operates (including what could well have been somewhat blasphemous at the time – his occasional questioning about the existence of the Gods).

The version of Meditations[5] that I have is one of those trusty Dover Thrift books, with a $3.00 cover price. Needless to say, these can be thrown in on another order from the on-line guys (I've recently gotten Amazon Prime, so no longer have to navigate orders to the free-shipping promised land, but these were always handy for pushing things over that line), but you should be able to talk your local brick-and-mortar book vendor into ordering in a copy (I doubt they're on the shelves, given the very slim profit margin on a book that inexpensive). This is a classic of Western thought, and I'm glad to have "caught up with it" (especially as I'm currently at the age which the author wrote this, and am dealing with some of the same things *my* life). It's one of those things that everybody *should* read, but in our currently degraded society, there are few that would actually make the effort ... but for three bucks and a few hours of reading, why not?

Notes:

1. http://btripp-books.livejournal.com/178849.html

2-5. http://amzn.to/1P88OPf

Thursday, December 31, 2015[1]

More like "when stuff went wrong" with America ...

This is a really awesome book, one of the best scores from the Dollar Store in quite a while (although, admittedly, I *bought* it almost two years prior to getting around to *reading* it). Larry Schweikart's Seven Events That Made America America: And Proved That the Founding Fathers Were Right All Along[2] is a great read, and *way* more engaging than what I'd assumed when letting it linger in my to-be-read piles for as long as I did.

I suppose I should, perhaps, offer up one caveat here: it you're of the left/liberal persuasion, you'll probably not be happy with this, because the author is working from the other side of the fence, and a lot of stuff that you might think is "progress (ive)", is what he (and I) consider the destruction of America. This is not, however, a political rant, but an vivid and informative look at various historical "events" (a term that's sort of broadly used here) that changed the course of our country's history to assorted extents (some of this is more about tone or tenor of the culture, or directions on policy, etc.).

The book starts with fairly "old news", looking back to the time of Martin Van Buren ... and a cast of characters that include such currency-enshrined folks as Thomas Jefferson and Alexander Hamilton ... in an era when the entire Federal budget was a mere $10,000,000.00! The initial chapter is nominally about the birth of "big government", but some of the more fascinating bits are about electoral politics, starting with:

> At the time, it wasn't necessary for individual politicians to resist "big government" because the system the Founders had established fought against it in myriad ways on its own. One important restriction came in the requirement that most voters still had to own property, hence they were reluctant to suffer high taxes or accept burdensome regulations. Property requirements also ensured high voter turnout because voters had a stake in the system.

While it's hard to advocate for a return to suffrage being limited to "landed white males" (despite how appealing that might be to those of us who *are* "landed white males"), one has to admit the system was originally set up to make sure there was a level of "ownership" (and responsibility) amongst the electorate that has not been seen in a *long* time.

One of the most intriguing parts here is, in the wake of Van Buren's establishment of the "Jacksonian Democrats" party, and the counter-establishment of the Whigs (both, arguably, established to avoid an outright national debate on slavery—*"on the assumption that principles were for sale"*), the creation of a matrix of political corruption still with us today (hellllooo Chicago):

> The structure of the new party ... employed a division of national, state, county, district, ward, and precinct division of the electorate, assigning to each level a partisan director charged with getting out the vote. Electoral success was then rewarded with promotion, in which ward captains became district directors, and so on, until all possible job holders in the party organization were appointed to paid government positions ... the across-the-board process of handing out positions to custom collectors, sheriffs, county clerks, and hundreds of other plum political jobs. Since the total number of government jobs remained small, however, the bureaucracy grew slowly – a few thousand new jobs per every state and general election – concealing the corrosive dynamic at work.

I was further surprised to find how long-standing the corruption of the news media has been. I thought the current monolithic Leftist slant of the MSM was a poison of recent vintage, however:

> ... at the time "newspapers" emerged as a driving force in American political life, they had almost nothing to do with objective news. To the contrary, they deliberately slanted every report and openly advertised their partisan purposes through their names. Partisanship was their primary raison d'etre. Editors viewed readers as voters who needed to be guided to appropriate views, then mobilized to vote. {One paper} flatly condemned neutrality as an absence of principles, and overall, editors increasing discarded news in favor of propaganda.

Sounds like they're talking about CNBC! Anyway, the effort to keep slavery out of debate failed, and this moves into the second chapter, dealing with the Dred Scott decision by the Supreme Court, which helped to push the new (anti-slavery) Republican party to the forefront (quickly replacing the Whigs), and resulting in the Civil War. This chapter is fascinating in its legal analysis (and "following the money"), but without much to directly quote, aside from the comment *"What is clear is that the Founders did not favor a supremely powerful, activist judiciary."*, and goes on to describe *numerous* instances where the courts have created massively bad results from their decisions.

The next chapter deals with the devastating flood that hit Johnstown, PA in 1899, killing 2,200 people and displacing 27,000 ... and focuses on the differences of how local, non-governmental, help is vastly more efficient than when government gets involved. In the case of the Johnstown flood, the chairman of the local NCR – National Cash Register – company almost single-handedly took control of the situation in the initial hours and early days, and threw all the resources at his disposal at helping remediate the situation well in advance of when the government (the local government proved useless) could respond. This goes on to look at how government involvement kept (over-) reaching into more and more areas, from the New Deal programs and on into the nightmares of FEMA inadequacies on up through the response to Hurricane Katrina and the total debacle of New Orleans.

The fourth event is covered in the chapter *"Ike Has A Heart Attack, Triggering Dietary Nannyism"* which looks at governmental meddling into what we eat, and other health issues ... frequently based more on *political* concerns (like the vile stuff being pushed by the current FLOTUS), and not so much on anywhere near solid science. Eisenhower's supposed heart attack (there seems to be some doubt even about that) launched a spiral of *"we must do something"* lunacy among the political and media classes ... and resulted in the on-going war on meat consumption and cholesterol – which is looking more and more like a misguided crusade.

> *It is true that coronary cases seemed to increase dramatically between 1940 and 1970 – but this was entirely because other diseases were being conquered and thus were not as rampant. A quarter of all men died of coronary disease in 1910, for example, and another quarter died from infections, parasites, flu, pneumonia, bronchitis, or tuberculosis, virtually all of which were eliminated or greatly suppressed by 1970. Cancer, meanwhile, went from eighth on the list to number two, and the rate of heart disease "doubled". Simply put, modern medicine had conquered so many diseases over the previous century that people lived long enough to encounter (and die from) new or rare diseases. Cancer and heart disease, which took longer to manifest themselves than, say, smallpox, became the leading killers. ... Even the World Health Organization acknowledged that "much of the apparent increase in [heart disease] mortality may simply be due to improvements in the quality of certification and more accurate diagnoses ...*

Heart disease was only the first salvo, as nearly every political faction has its own "food fetish" (remember when Chicago banned *foie gras*?) and year after year more and more *idiotic* regulations are put in place to salve some social activist's personal pet peeve in the area of food ... devolving into the current politics-trumping-reality morass of the climate crusaders (a topic the author gets into a good bit in here as well).

> *Tom Paine once said, "He that would make his own liberty secure, must guard even his enemy from oppression." In the decades after Eisenhower's heart attack, intrusions on economic liberty were common ... but perhaps the most insidious threat of all was the erosion of freedom in the name of "a person's own good." At the very time that some*

> well-meaning, but myopic, Americans sought to limit everyone's freedoms – to choose what to eat, what to drink, even what to drive – under the auspices of "helping" them become "healthier," Paine would have screamed "Someone guard them from oppression!" Edmund Burke seemed to have the government's diet police and global warming in mind when he wrote in 1784, "The people never give up their liberties but under some delusion."

Chapter 5 is primarily about rock and roll and the fall of Communism in Europe. The author is a former rock drummer (his band Rampage was an opening act for Steppenwolf and numerous other groups back in the day), and his enthusiasm for the subject is evident in this (aided by his access to many rock luminaries for background interviews). However, it is *also* about how big government has muscled into arenas that the Founders never intended:

> Rock and roll's contribution to the collapse of communism provides one more piece of evidence that the human soul longs for freedom in all areas. It was a principle the Founders understood when they limited government's ability to intrude on arts, speech, and business. ... Overall, though, the Founders were cautious in their support for government aid to any sort of art or entertainment, aware that with money came strings, and with strings, political agendas. With a few exceptions, they favored keeping government out of human affairs wherever possible.

The sixth chapter deals with an "event" in as much as it pivots on the bombing of the Marines barracks in Beirut in 1983, but it's a much more convoluted look at the descent of the Middle East into a destabilized mess in the wake of WW2 (and the colonial powers ceding control to local factions), how Reagan got coerced into getting the U.S. involved in the region, and how the current wave of radicalized Islam arose, spread, and performed terrorist attacks that the mainstream media for decades insistently whitewashed as "criminal acts" and not "acts of war" and/or terrorism. This is dense, though informative, and ends with a question:

> What would George Washington, John Adams, and Thomas Jefferson make of militant Islam ...? It's difficult to say ... In the case of the Barbary pirates, however, whose actions did constitute the terrorism of the day, Jefferson's response was quick, substantial, and sharp. He sent the entire U.S. Navy to crush all the Barbary States, not just Tripoli (the only one to declare war on the United States).

Finally, the book looks at the media, with the "event" being the election of the current POTUS (and associated "thrills up the leg"), who benefited from nearly start-to-finish support from the MSM. Here Schweikart returns to his previous looks at the historical context of the American press. This is fascinating, but it largely serves to provide context for a look at how one-sided "news" has become:

> When those influencing others' political choices were members of the media, a significant inbreeding started to develop. Contrary to the notion that the elites were always "conservative," in journalism the predominance of the peer group ensured that primarily liberal views would triumph. ... Journalism's homogeneity went beyond a commonly shared view among reporters about gaining, and extending, the authority of the news media. Rather than diversifying, media elites homogenized even further. From 1964 to 1976, the percentage voting for the Democratic candidate in national elections <u>never fell below 81 percent</u>.

The author goes into a lot of research into how the Left/liberal candidate or story regularly received 5x or so "positive" stories.

> Increasingly, all "news" credibility disappeared. Major newspapers and especially television "news" programs had become entirely propagandistic ... Nor did the news organizations seem concerned about losing their audience and readers, because ... "the mainstream media's audience is the mainstream media." Reporters {write} for each other, to impress each other, to generate prestige points at cocktail parties and social affairs, and, of course, for access to the levers of government when that government was in Democratic hands.

Further ...

> The protections that the Founders put in the Constitution for freedom of speech were meant to specifically ensure freedom of political dissent by the press – but what happens if the press, for its own purposes, refuses to serve as a check on government? In their well-deserved focus on protecting political speech, the Founders never addressed the possibility that the Fourth Estate would find itself in bed with government itself.

Needless to say, <u>Seven Events That Made America America</u>[3] is wide ranging in its subject matter, but is presented in a very readable style, and is extensively supported by significant end notes. This is definitely one of those books that I wish *everybody* would read.

As noted, I got this at the dollar store almost two years ago (so it's pretty much certainly off of those shelves by now), but it *is* still in print (in a paperback edition), so should be easy enough to find or order. You can also get copies from the new/used guys for as little as 1¢ (plus shipping) for a "like new" copy of the hardcover or a new copy of the paperback. Again, this is an "all and sundry" recommendation from me ... it's a great read and throws a cold hard light on some of horrible things that have been trying to make America *less like* the America we deserve.

Notes:

1. http://btripp-books.livejournal.com/179156.html
2-3. http://amzn.to/1OsPo5m

QR code links to the on-line reviews:

Do More, Spend Less:
The New Secrets of Living the Good Life for Less
by
Brad Wilson

Will the Real You Please Stand Up:
Show Up, Be Authentic, and Prosper in Social Media
by
Kim Garst

The Wizard of Ads: Turning
Words into Magic and Dreamers into Millionaires
by
Roy H. Williams

Secret Formulas of the Wizard of Ads:
Turning Paupers into Princes and Lead into Gold
by
Roy H. Williams

Magical Worlds of the Wizard of Ads: Tools and
Techniques for Profitable Persuasion
by
Roy H. Williams

The Fran Lebowitz Reader
by
Fran Lebowitz

Conquering the Electron: The Geniuses,
Visionaries, Egomaniacs, and Scoundrels
Who Built Our Electronic Age
by
Derek Cheung & Eric Brach

Age of Conversation 3: It's Time to Get Busy!
by
Drew McLellan & Gavin Heaton

The Moral Arc: How Science and Reason
Lead Humanity toward Truth, Justice, and Freedom
by
Michael Shermer

Bold: How to Go Big, Create Wealth
and Impact the World
by
Peter Diamandis

Manifesto for the Noosphere: The Next Stage
in the Evolution of Human Consciousness
by
José Argüelles

Trust Me, I'm Lying:
Confessions of a Media Manipulator
by
Ryan Holiday

Mugged: Racial Demagoguery
from the Seventies to Obama
by
Ann Coulter

Win the Game of Googleopoly:
Unlocking the Secret Strategy of Search Engines
by
Sean V. Bradley

A God That Could Be Real:
Spirituality, Science, and the Future of Our Planet
by
Nancy Ellen Abrams

A Death on Diamond Mountain: A True Story of
Obsession, Madness, and the Path to Enlightenment
by
Scott Carney

Everybody Writes: Your Go-To Guide
to Creating Ridiculously Good Content
by
Ann Handley

Waking Up: A Guide to Spirituality Without Religion
by
Sam Harris

The Art of Work: A Proven Path
to Discovering What You Were Meant to Do
by
Jeff Goins

Stand Out: How to Find Your Breakthrough Idea
and Build a Following Around It
by
Dorie Clark

Mind Wars: Brain Science
and the Military in the 21st Century
by
Jonathan D. Moreno

Headstrong: 52 Women
Who Changed Science – and the World
by
Rachel Swaby

The Divine Spark: A Graham Hancock Reader:
Psychedelics, Consciousness,
and the Birth of Civilization
by
Graham Hancock

The Only Woman in the Room:
Why Science Is Still a Boys' Club
by
Eileen Pollack

The Upside of Stress: Why Stress Is Good
for You, and How to Get Good at It
by
Kelly McGonigal

Twitter Power 3.0: How to Dominate
Your Market One Tweet at a Time
by
Joel Comm & Dave Taylor

Highly Effective Networking:
Meet the Right People and Get a Great Job
by
Orville Pierson

The Picture of Dorian Gray
by
Oscar Wilde

One Spirit Medicine:
Ancient Ways to Ultimate Wellness
by
Alberto Villoldo

ALL THINGS GO: How I Became A Shaman
by
Eric Durchholz

Motivation Manifesto:
9 Declarations to Claim Your Personal Power
by
Brendon Burchard

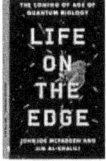

Life on the Edge:
The Coming of Age of Quantum Biology
by
Johnjoe McFadden & Jim Al-Khalili

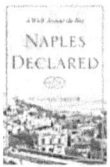

Naples Declared: A Walk Around the Bay
by
Benjamin Taylor

Our Last Best Chance:
The Pursuit of Peace in a Time of Peril
by
King Abdullah II of Jordan

The Zero Marginal Cost Society:
The Internet of Things, the Collaborative
Commons, and the Eclipse of Capitalism
by
Jeremy Rifkin

Forgotten Civilization:
The Role of Solar Outbursts in Our Past and Future
by
Robert M. Schoch

Real Skills, Real Income: A Proven Marketing System
to Land Well-Paid Freelance and Consulting Work
in 30 Days or Less
by
Diana Schneidman

The Optimism Bias:
A Tour of the Irrationally Positive Brain
by
Tali Sharot

Godless Grace: How Nonbelievers
Are Making the World Safer, Richer and Kinder
by
David Orenstein, Ph.D. & Linda Ford Blaikie, LC.S.W.

The Power of Relentless: 7 Secrets to Achieving
Mega-Success, Financial Freedom,
and the Life of Your Dreams
by
Wayne Allyn Root

Spreading the Wealth: How Obama is
Robbing the Suburbs to Pay for the Cities
by
Stanley Kurtz

The Legend of Sigurd and Gudrún
by
J.R.R. Tolkien

Dataclysm: Love, Sex, Race, and Identity – What
Our Online Lives Tell Us about Our Offline Selves
by
Christian Rudder

The Happiness Project: Or, Why I Spent a Year
Trying to Sing in the Morning, Clean My Closets, Fight
Right, Read Aristotle, and Generally Have More Fun
by
Gretchen Rubin

A Simple Government: Twelve Things We Really Need
from Washington (and a Trillion That We Don't!)
by
Mike Huckabee

Now, Discover Your Strengths
by
Marcus Buckingham & Donald O. Clifton

Harness the Sun:
America's Quest for a Solar-Powered Future
by
Philip Warburg

Free for All: Defending Liberty in America Today
by
Wendy Kaminer

Questions & Answers About Sleep Apnea
by
Sudhansu Chokroverty

The War of Art: Break Through the Blocks
and Win Your Inner Creative Battles
by
Steven Pressfield

Public Apology: In Which a Man Grapples With
a Lifetime of Regret, One Incident at a Time
by
Dave Bry

Start-Up City:
nspiring Private and Public Entrepreneurship,
Getting Projects Done, and Having Fun
by
Gabe Klein

Street Smart:
The Rise of Cities and the Fall of Cars
by
Samuel I. Schwartz

What If . . .: A Lifetime of Questions,
Speculations, Reasonable Guesses,
and a Few Things I Know for Sure
by
Shirley McLaine

Our Grandchildren Redesigned: Life in the
Bioengineered Society of the Near Future
by
Michael Bess

An Improvised Life: a Memoir
by
Alan Arkin

Flipping Burgers to Flipping Millions: A Guide to Financial Freedom Whether You Have Your Dream Job, Own Your Own Business, or Just Started Your First Job
by
Bernard Kelly

Think Like a Freak: The Authors of Freakonomics Offer to Retrain Your Brain
by
Steven D. Levitt & Stephen J. Dubner

The Upward Spiral: Using Neuroscience to Reverse the Course of Depression, One Small Change at a Time
by
Dr. Alex Korb

Leadership and Self-Deception: Getting Out of the Box
by
The Arbinger Institute

The Compound Effect:
Jumpstart Your Income, Your Life, Your Success
by
Darren Hardy

Where Mercy Is Shown, Mercy Is Given
by
Duane "Dog" Chapman

Siddhartha
by
Hermann Hesse

Meditations
by
Marcus Aurelius

Seven Events That Made America America:
And Proved That the Founding Fathers
Were Right All Along
by
Larry Schweikart

CONTENTS - ALPHABETICAL BY AUTHOR

King Abdullah II of Jordan	page	131
Our Last Best Chance		
Nancy Ellen Abrams	page	57
A God That Could Be Real		
José Argüelles	page	41
Manifesto for the Noosphere		
Alan Arkin	page	220
An Improvised Life		
Marcus Aurelius	page	253
Meditations		
Michael Bess	page	213
Our Grandchildren Redesigned		
Sean V. Bradley	page	53
Win the Game of Googleopoly		
Dave Bry	page	201
Public Apology		
Marcus Buckingham & Donald O. Clifton	page	187
Now, Discover Your Strengths		
Brendon Burchard	page	121
The Motivation Manifesto		
Scott Carney	page	61
A Death on Diamond Mountain		
Duane "Dog" Chapman	page	247
Where Mercy Is Shown, Mercy Is Given		
Derek Cheung & Eric Brach	page	22
Conquering the Electron		
Sudhansu Chokroverty	page	196
Questions & Answers About Sleep Apnea		
Dorie Clark	page	76
Stand Out		
Joel Comm & Dave Taylor	page	99
Twitter Power 3.0		
Ann Coulter	page	50
Mugged		

Author	Title	Page
Peter H. Diamandis	*Bold*	37
Eric Durchholz & Patrick John Coleman	*ALL THINGS GO*	117
Kim Garst	*Will the Real You Please Stand Up*	4
Jeff Goins	*The Art of Work*	72
Graham Hancock	*The Divine Spark*	88
Ann Handley	*Everybody Writes*	64
Darren Hardy	*The Compound Effect*	243
Sam Harris	*Waking Up*	67
Hermann Hesse	*Siddhartha*	249
Ryan Holiday	*Trust Me, I'm Lying*	45
Mike Huckabee	*A Simple Government*	184
Arbinger Institute	*Leadership and Self-Deception*	240
Wendy Kaminer	*Free for All*	192
Bernard Kelly	*Flipping Burgers to Flipping Millions*	224
Gabe Klein	*Start-Up City*	203
Alex Korb PhD	*The Upward Spiral*	234
Stanley Kurtz	*Spreading the Wealth*	164
Fran Lebowitz	*The Fran Lebowitz Reader*	18

Author	Title	Page
Steven D. Levitt & Stephen J. Dubner	Think Like a Freak	229
Shirley MacLaine	What If . . .	210
Johnjoe McFadden & Jim Al-Khalili	Life on the Edge	124
Kelly McGonigal	The Upside of Stress	94
Drew McLellan & Gavin Heaton	Age of Conversation 3	26
Jonathan D. Moreno	Mind Wars	80
David Orenstein, Ph.D. & Linda Ford Blaikie, L.C.S.W.	Godless Grace	155
Orville Pierson	Highly Effective Networking	102
Eileen Pollack	The Only Woman in the Room	91
Steven Pressfield	The War of Art	198
Jeremy Rifkin	The Zero Marginal Cost Society	134
Wayne Allyn Root	The Power of Relentless	159
Gretchen Rubin	The Happiness Project	180
Christian Rudder	Dataclysm	175
Diana Schneidman	Real Skills, Real Income	145
Robert M. Schoch	Forgotten Civilization	139
Samuel I. Schwartz	Street Smart	206
Larry Schweikart	Seven Events That Made America America	256

Author	Title	Page
Tali Sharot	*The Optimism Bias*	150
Michael Shermer	*The Moral Arc*	31
Rachel Swaby	*Headstrong*	85
Benjamin Taylor	*Naples Declared*	128
J.R.R. Tolkien	*The Legend of Sigurd and Gudrún*	169
Alberto Villoldo	*One Spirit Medicine*	110
Philip Warburg	*Harness the Sun*	190
Oscar Wilde	*The Picture of Dorian Gray*	106
Roy H. Williams	*Magical Worlds of the Wizard of Ads*	15
Roy H. Williams	*Secret Formulas of the Wizard of Ads*	11
Roy H. Williams	*The Wizard of Ads*	8
Brad Wilson	*Do More, Spend Less*	1

CONTENTS - ALPHABETICAL BY TITLE

Age of Conversation 3
Drew McLellan & Gavin Heaton — page 26

ALL THINGS GO
Eric Durchholz & Patrick John Coleman — page 117

The Art of Work
Jeff Goins — page 72

Bold
Peter H. Diamandis — page 37

The Compound Effect
Darren Hardy — page 243

Conquering the Electron
Derek Cheung & Eric Brach — page 22

Dataclysm
Christian Rudder — page 175

A Death on Diamond Mountain
Scott Carney — page 61

The Divine Spark
Graham Hancock — page 88

Do More, Spend Less
Brad Wilson — page 1

Everybody Writes
Ann Handley — page 64

Flipping Burgers to Flipping Millions
Bernard Kelly — page 224

Forgotten Civilization
Robert M. Schoch — page 139

The Fran Lebowitz Reader
Fran Lebowitz — page 18

Free for All
Wendy Kaminer — page 192

A God That Could Be Real
Nancy Ellen Abrams — page 57

Godless Grace
David Orenstein, Ph.D. & Linda Ford Blaikie, L.C.S.W. — page 155

Gretchen Rubin	The Happiness Project	page 180
Philip Warburg	Harness the Sun	page 190
Rachel Swaby	Headstrong	page 85
Orville Pierson	Highly Effective Networking	page 102
Alan Arkin	An Improvised Life	page 220
Arbinger Institute	Leadership and Self-Deception	page 240
J.R.R. Tolkien	The Legend of Sigurd and Gudrún	page 169
Johnjoe McFadden & Jim Al-Khalili	Life on the Edge	page 124
Roy H. Williams	Magical Worlds of the Wizard of Ads	page 15
José Argüelles	Manifesto for the Noosphere	page 41
Marcus Aurelius	Meditations	page 253
Jonathan D. Moreno	Mind Wars	page 80
Michael Shermer	The Moral Arc	page 31
Brendon Burchard	The Motivation Manifesto	page 121
Ann Coulter	Mugged	page 50
Benjamin Taylor	Naples Declared	page 128
Marcus Buckingham & Donald O. Clifton	Now, Discover Your Strengths	page 187
Alberto Villoldo	One Spirit Medicine	page 110

The Only Woman in the Room	Eileen Pollack	page 91
The Optimism Bias	Tali Sharot	page 150
Our Grandchildren Redesigned	Michael Bess	page 213
Our Last Best Chance	King Abdullah II of Jordan	page 131
The Picture of Dorian Gray	Oscar Wilde	page 106
The Power of Relentless	Wayne Allyn Root	page 159
Public Apology	Dave Bry	page 201
Questions & Answers About Sleep Apnea	Sudhansu Chokroverty	page 196
Real Skills, Real Income	Diana Schneidman	page 145
Secret Formulas of the Wizard of Ads	Roy H. Williams	page 11
Seven Events That Made America America	Larry Schweikart	page 256
Siddhartha	Hermann Hesse	page 249
A Simple Government	Mike Huckabee	page 184
Spreading the Wealth	Stanley Kurtz	page 164
Stand Out	Dorie Clark	page 76
Start-Up City	Gabe Klein	page 203
Street Smart	Samuel I. Schwartz	page 206
Think Like a Freak	Steven D. Levitt & Stephen J. Dubner	page 229

Trust Me, I'm Lying		
Ryan Holiday	page	45
Twitter Power 3.0		
Joel Comm & Dave Taylor	page	99
The Upside of Stress		
Kelly McGonigal	page	94
The Upward Spiral		
Alex Korb PhD	page	234
Waking Up		
Sam Harris	page	67
The War of Art		
Steven Pressfield	page	198
What If . . .		
Shirley MacLaine	page	210
Where Mercy Is Shown, Mercy Is Given		
Duane "Dog" Chapman	page	247
Will the Real You Please Stand Up		
Kim Garst	page	4
Win the Game of Googleopoly		
Sean V. Bradley	page	53
The Wizard of Ads		
Roy H. Williams	page	8
The Zero Marginal Cost Society		
Jeremy Rifkin	page	134

www.ingramcontent.com/pod-product-compliance
Lightning Source LLC
Chambersburg PA
CBHW071302110426
42743CB00042B/1145